This broad ambitious study deals
nature conceived in a way quite d
oriented account of it that domii
Drawing on the thought of Martin ᴴᴱⁱᵈᵉgger, the author presents
an alternative to both dualism and materialism in the philosophy
of mind and forces a reappraisal of commonsense notions of mind
as our "inner" reality as well. We are not, Olafson argues, compound entities – body and mind – but unitary entities that are
distinguished by "having a world." The central constructive concept of the book is that of "presence" – the being there for us of
the entities that make up the world, without any special mental
intermediation. Successive chapters explore how this concept applies to the major areas of what we usually think of as our mental
life. The final chapter offers a sustained critique of physicalism, the
currently popular version of a unitary theory of human nature.

This book is both an original application of Heidegger's thought
to the themes of contemporary philosophical discussion and a vig-
orous argument for a humanistic account of what it is to be a human
being as a presupposition of any other account we give.

WHAT IS A HUMAN BEING?

MODERN EUROPEAN PHILOSOPHY

This series comprises a range of high-quality books on philosophers, topics, and schools of thought prominent in the Kantian and post-Kantian European tradition. The series is nonsectarian in approach and methodology and includes both introductory and more specialized treatments of these thinkers and topics. Authors are encouraged to interpret the boundaries of the modern European tradition in a broad way and to engage with it in primarily philosophical rather than historical terms.

David Bakhurst, *Consciousness and Revolution in Soviet Philosophy*
Wolfgang Carl, *Frege's Theory of Sense and Reference*
R. M. Chisholm, *Brentano and Intrinsic Value*
Maudemarie Clark, *Nietzsche on Truth and Philosophy*
Raymond Geuss, *The Idea of a Critical Theory: Habermas and the Frankfurt School*
Gary Gutting, *Michel Foucault's Archaeology of Scientific Reason*
Michael O. Hardimon, *Hegel's Social Philosophy: The Project of Reconciliation*
David Holdcroft, *Saussure: Signs, System, and Arbitrariness*
Karel Lambert, *Meinong and the Principle of Independence*
Frederick Neuhouser, *Fichte's Theory of Subjectivity*
Charles Taylor, *Hegel and Modern Society*
Mary Tiles, *Bachelard: Science and Objectivity*
Robert S. Tragesser, *Husserl and Realism in Logic and Mathematics*
Stephen K. White, *Political Theory and Postmodernism*
Peter Winch, *Simone Weil: The Just Balance*

WHAT IS
A HUMAN BEING?

A HEIDEGGERIAN VIEW

FREDERICK A. OLAFSON

University of California, San Diego

CAMBRIDGE
UNIVERSITY PRESS

Published by the Press Syndicate of the University of Cambridge
The Pitt Building, Trumpington Street, Cambridge CB2 1RP
40 West 20th Street, New York, NY 10011-4211, USA
10 Stamford Road, Oakleigh, Melbourne 3166, Australia

First published 1995

Printed in the United States of America

Library of Congress Cataloging-in-Publication Data
Olafson, Frederick A.
What is a human being? : a Heideggerian view / Frederick A.
Olafson.
p.   cm. – (Modern European philosophy)
Includes index.
ISBN 0-521-47395-0
1. Philosophy of mind.   2. Heidegger, Martin, 1889–1976.
3. Humanism – 20th century.   I. Title.
BD418.3.O42   1995
128–dc20   94-34854
                                                 CIP

A catalog record for this book is available from the British Library.

ISBN   0-521-47395-0 hardback
ISBN   0-521-47937-1 paperback

For
Sigrun and Robert MacDonald
and the late Hannah Lewis
with love and gratitude

CONTENTS

vii

INTRODUCTION

I

An interest in human nature has long been a motive driving philosophical inquiry. In the ancient world it was associated most closely with the name of Socrates and with his claim that the most valuable knowledge is self-knowledge. In the modern period a distinctive kind of philosophical thought got under way with Descartes's attempt to show that rigorous scientific knowledge must be grounded in a new kind of self-knowledge. In the following century, David Hume published *A Treatise of Human Nature*, in which he dealt with all the major issues of philosophical inquiry as facets of that most general topic. Most notably, perhaps, Immanuel Kant argued that the domain of philosophy was defined by three questions – What can I know?, What ought I to do?, and What may I hope? – and that these questions are facets of the more general question, What is man?[1]

An interest in human nature can take many forms, and the questions in which it finds expression can range from such matters as the character of human motivation (Is altruistic conduct really possible?) to the prospects for human happiness (Can a man really be called happy before his life is complete?). Philosophers have asked questions like these, but they have been more interested in what differentiates human beings from other living things and generally from the natural world in which they live. The answer

1. *Immanuel Kant's Werke*, edited by E. Cassirer (Berlin: Bruno Cassirer, 1923), vol. VIII, *Vorlesungen Kants uber Logik*, p. 343. Another statement of this view of the "interest of reason," but without the fourth question about "man," can be found in *Immanuel Kant's Critique of Pure Reason*, translated by N. Kemp-Smith (London: Macmillan, 1958), p. 635.

they have most often given to such questions is that the distinctive features of human nature have to do with the mental functioning of human beings – more specifically, with their intellectual and moral powers. It has been widely agreed that if there is some respect in which human beings differ from even the higher animals, it must be their capacity for rational thought that makes the difference. Because it has not been clear to many philosophers how intellectual functions *could* be carried out by any of the organs of the body, these most distinctive capabilities of human beings, together with others, like perception, that are shared with animals, have typically been assigned to a part of a human being that is not part of the body. This part has been variously conceived as the soul and the mind; and the part of philosophy that addresses questions about the human essence, if there is one, is now usually called the "philosophy of mind."

This book is an essay in the philosophy of mind, although, paradoxically, it will turn out that the concept of mind itself has to be abandoned; and it will proceed under the auspices of the broadly humanistic conception of the business of philosophy suggested by the names I have cited. Hence, it stands in a somewhat skewed relation to the main tendencies in the practice of philosophy at the present time. If the philosophers I have mentioned and many others have understood the central business of philosophy as having to do with human nature, their views have certainly not gone uncontested. Socrates himself found his way to his view of philosophy only after the disillusionment he suffered as a student of those philosophers who were primarily interested in the explanation of natural processes and were, in his view, indifferent to the reasons why people live and act as they do. In our own time as well, there has been a good deal of skepticism about the special association between philosophy and human nature. To many, such an association is reminiscent of outmoded ideas of man as the center of the universe, and of the self-importance and complacency that such ideas are thought to inspire in those who hold them. Philosophies imbued with a sense of the special importance of things human are more likely, it is thought, to flatter than to expose human illusions, and to engage in edification rather than rigorous inquiry. At a time when the natural sciences are the accepted paradigms of knowledge and have achieved this status, at least in part, because they refuse to be edifying, philosophy can, on this view, ill afford to go on espousing such a conception of itself.

To these perennial objections to a conception of philosophy as human self-knowledge, there is often added another that appears to have a special appeal in our own time. It takes the form of a challenge to the assumption that there is something so remarkable about human nature that it deserves the special attention the Socratic conception of philosophy claims for it. In the background of this challenge, there is often a principled refusal to be impressed by the standard versions of the doctrine of human uniqueness that have been current since the Renaissance. It is argued that whatever attributes are supposed to constitute a special human excellence, they can all be employed for evil purposes as well as for good and all too often have been so used. In a century of genocide, it is hardly surprising that the terrible negative possibilities of human nature should have almost replaced the traditional positive images of the being that is ultimately responsible for the horrors we have witnessed in our time. There is, it is true, often something polemical and tendentious in this antihumanistic temper of mind, and the conclusions it draws from the events of our time deserve closer critical scrutiny than they typically receive. However that may be, the result is an intellectual and moral atmosphere in which any attempt to revive a conception of philosophy that centers on the concept of human being has little plausibility or appeal.

Nevertheless, just such an undertaking is attempted in this study. The reasons why I believe it makes sense to embark on such an effort at this time are complex and can be fully set forth only by the argument of the book itself. In general, however, the considerations that favor such an enterprise may be said to stem from a reading of the history of modern, and especially twentieth-century, philosophy that is quite different from those that are most widely influential at the present time, especially in the English-speaking world. A brief account of these differences will, therefore, provide an introduction to my wider theme.

II

The great positive fact in the evolution of philosophy in the last few decades is commonly held to be the "linguistic turn" in the course of which philosophers have increasingly come to conceive their own inquiries as being concerned not with the nature of things in the old comprehensive sense but with language as the medium in which whatever we claim to know must be expressed. There have been many different accounts of the way this linguistic turn is to be understood; but in all of them, a line is drawn between language and its "logic," on the one hand, and "the world," on the other; and philosophy is regularly assigned to the language side of this distinction. This means that it cannot be any part of the proper business of philosophy to propound theses of its own about the nature of the world. If all philosophical questions are questions about language, then the contribution the philosopher can make to knowledge must take the form of an analysis from a logicolinguistic point of view of the concepts deployed in some area of inquiry. More specifically, when these concepts turn out to have logical peculiarities that raise questions about the coherence and intelligibility of any form of discourse in which they figure, it becomes the responsibility of the philosopher to propose an appropriate reform or reconstruction of the language we use. If follows that although such a contribution to the progress of knowledge may be highly significant, it is almost certain to be indirect and to have a critical rather than a constructive character.

The disqualification of philosophy as a source of independent pronouncements about the world might have been expected to leave all areas of language use equally free to pursue their own distinctive business without undue fear of philosophical censorship as long as they did not fall into any gross incoherence. This was not, however, the way things went. The first sponsors of the thesis that identified philosophy with the logic of concepts were also committed to the view that only one form of thought – natural science – was largely free of the logical defects that philosophy made it its business to detect; and the language of science was accordingly assigned a privileged status *ab initio*. Other modes of thought that claimed to have something distinctive to say about the world but did not use the conceptual idiom of the natural sciences were sharply devaluated. Admittedly, over time, it gradually became apparent that there were serious difficulties in the way of any such postulation of a unique harmony between the logical criteria that philosophy brings to bear on the products of human thought and natural science as an exemplary theory of the world. Most notably, the attempt to define criteria of meaningfulness that would consign everything except the propositions of science to the status of the noncognitive and the emotive bogged down. It also became increasingly evident that there are many "languages" that elude classification in terms of such alternatives and that there is no simple test that can be used to judge the ontological claims of any language – any "conceptual system" – to represent the world as it "really" is. Considerations of this kind have raised doubts about the possibility of simply identifying the program and purposes of linguistic philosophy with those of natural science; and in some subsequent phases of this movement, a relativistic view of the competing claims of different languages to represent the world has found defenders. Nevertheless, a strong sense that the language and, with it, the ontology of natural science are somehow privileged has persisted among most adherents of linguistic philosophy.

One index of the continuing authority of science in ontological matters is the fact that the vicissitudes through which the relationship between linguistic philosophy and science has passed have not led to any significant reassessment of the mode of being of language itself. This issue is the more pressing since in the more science-oriented or naturalistic versions of linguistic philosophy, it is taken for granted that language use is an overt and observable function of the human organism and thus takes its place unproblematically within the same natural milieu as all the other processes with which the sciences are concerned. Indeed, one great attraction of the replacement of "thought" and "consciousness" by "language" in recent decades has been the sense that these supposedly private and mysterious functions have finally been assigned their proper places in a public domain where claims of privileged access are disallowed. On the strength of such advantages as these, it tends to be simply assumed that language, particularly its distinctive semantic and referential functions, presents no special problem for a naturalistic account of human nature.[2]

If an inquiry were to be mounted into the mode of being of language, however, it is clear that it would have to question this assumption. It should also try to determine whether the place of language in human life does not have to be more deeply conceived than it is when we refer to ourselves simply as "language users." But instead of such an inquiry, there has been a pronounced tendency to treat language use conceived in this rather perfunctory way as the paradigm instance of mental activity generally, without troubling oneself further about such matters. In part, this is a result of a rule of method adopted by philosophers that says that, consistently with their abstention from first-order pronouncements about the world, they must confine what they say about perception or memory or imagination or any other mental function that might be supposed to be a necessary condition for language use to the language in which these functions would themselves be described or expressed. When this rule of method is rigorously adhered to, the utterances in question themselves can appear to constitute the domain of the mental, at least for all legitimate philosophical purposes. Equally important, on this view only the relevant natural science – in this case, psychology – is supposed to have the authority to talk about perception or memory as such. Accordingly, philosophy must not meddle in such matters, in which it has no special competence even though the psychological account that is given may be visibly guided by philosophical premises. Together, these procedural constraints under which linguistic philosophy conducts its business can harden into what amounts to a foreclosure of inquiry in areas of primary importance to philosophy. And through the refusal of philosophy to enter the lists against physicalistic theories of perception or thought, a substantive thesis about the nature of the mental may be tacitly ratified.

All of this is highly relevant to the question of what becomes of the concept of a human being in linguistic philosophy. Human beings have

---

2. As I try to show in some detail in later chapters, this is an excellent example of what Alfred Whitehead called "the fallacy of misplaced concreteness." It plays on the ambiguity between language as speech (or writing) – this is what is conceived of as "concrete" – and language as a modality of having a world, and thereby makes it appear that, for ontological purposes, all the "abstract" matters that fall under the latter heading can be subsumed under the former. The agenda implicit in this assimilation is naturalistic; and its great advantage is that it enables naturalistically inclined philosophers to deal with the issues of first philosophy and yet assure themselves that they have remained faithful to their ontology by treating these matters as being entirely "logical" or "conceptual" (and thus implicitly linguistic) in nature.

sometimes been called "language animals," and so it might have been reasonable to expect that in this new linguistic orientation of philosophy there would be a more positive attitude toward an interest in the concept of a human being. At the very least, the fact that by reason of their being "language users" the location of human beings on the map drawn in terms of the language–world distinction is ambiguous might have provoked more thought than it appears to have done. After all, language, if it is to be used, requires a speaker; and intuitively, at least, it is hard to see how that speaker, however conceived, could fail to be on the same side of the language–world distinction as the language he uses. In that event, however, since human beings are also in the world as one kind of entity among the many empirically determinable kinds that make up the world, they would have a dual status for which no provision is made by philosophies that build on the original distinction. Nevertheless, the special character of this status has not stimulated any renewal of philosophical interest in the concept of a human being. It is true that there has been a good deal of interest lately in the concept of the person; but the sources of this interest appear to lie mainly in moral philosophy, and even when that is not so, the ontological status of the person is left largely indeterminate.

There has been at least one significant dissent from the view that language, as the aspect of human nature that is of unique interest to the philosopher, can be abstracted from the wider context of human life without detriment to the inquiries initiated in this way. I am referring to the effort that has been made, especially on the part of those influenced by the later Wittgenstein, to show that there is a deeper connection between various modes of language use and some of the most general conditions of human life than is recognized in the standard view of these matters. Most notably, there has been an interest in the pragmatic dimension of language use – those features of it that have to be understood in terms of its relationship to its user – and this interest has led to the elaboration of a theory of speech acts. It seems fair to say, however, that for all its interest, the work done under this rubric has remained intralogical in the sense that it explores what is implicit in, and presupposed by, speech acts performed in certain contexts. These explorations do not contribute much, if anything, to a philosophical understanding of the kind of context that is presupposed by language use as such. Nor does it appear that those who work in the pragmatics of language have a stronger interest in the kind of entity that a human being is than their colleagues who devote themselves to the syntactic and semantic aspects of language.

This condensed account of what has been happening in philosophy during this century would benefit considerably from a longer historical perspective. Linguistic philosophy itself, especially in its earlier phases, was disinclined to take such a view, because it was full of a sense of having broken with the philosophical tradition and of constituting what was, in effect, to be a new discipline free of the obsessive and sterile preoccupations of the past. As so often happens, however, those who think they have freed themselves from the influence of some tradition are the ones most likely to continue in it. In the case of linguistic philosophy, its short way with issues concerning the ontological status of language and its broader lack of interest in the concept of a human being can be shown to be continuous with a line of thought Western philosophy has followed throughout the modern period.

That line is the steady movement of modern philosophy since Descartes toward a transcendental conception of the human mind or, as it came increasingly to be called, the "subject." In that conception, the mind is understood no longer as a mental substance that is one of the entities that together make up the world but, rather, as the act of thought itself. This act is transcendental in the sense that it is a prior and necessary condition for any knowledge of objects at all, including what is referred to in this tradition as the "empirical self" – the self that has a particular identity and a locus in space and time. There has also been a strong tendency to conceive this transcendental condition more and more in logical rather than in psychological terms; and even Kant refers to the "I" that expresses the unity of thought and experience that is a condition of the possibility of empirical knowledge as a "logical act." It seems clear that in the contrast between a transcendental self so conceived and the domain of empirical objects, and in the disjunction between the transcendental and the empirical selves, we have the essential elements of the contrast that linguistic philosophy makes between language and the world. In both cases, the ultimate subject of experience and of knowledge is conceived in terms of a logical function that has become largely autonomous even though it is still nominally assigned to a person or self whose act it is supposed to be. There is, to be sure, this difference between the two conceptions that Kant evidently still thinks of this ultimate subject of experience as plural in a way that corresponds to the plurality of empirical selves. In the language–world contrast, however, language is singular and there is nothing at that (transcendental) level that corresponds to the plurality of the "users" of language. One could therefore say that the language–world distinction of linguistic philosophy takes the transcendental subject a step beyond either Kant or Husserl inasmuch as it abstracts from the fact of the plurality of subjects that those philosophers recognized at even the highest transcendental level. It does so, moreover, in favor of a unitary impersonal subject – language as such – to which it seems incongruous to attribute an action of any kind in the way one does to a subject that refers to itself as an "I."[3]

3. This aspiration has not been confined to the English-speaking philosophical world but has been shared by many philosophers on the European continent. On this topic, see Vincent Descombes, *Modern French Philosophy*, translated by L. Scott-Fox and J. M. Harding (Cambridge: Cambridge University Press, 1980), and K. O. Apel, *Toward A Transformation of*

This evolution in the concept of the subject is carried to a paradoxical conclusion in the physicalistic treatment of language use. What is thereby effected may be described as a final divorce of language as a semantic function that is the a priori constitutive condition for an experience of the world and the human beings whose "act" this condition has been supposed to be or, at least, to require. The result is that human beings come to be understood as subsystems within the comprehensive physical system that is the world; and language in its semantic and constitutive aspects no longer has any essential conceptual linkage with human beings as so conceived. No longer is there any entity that is qualified by a distinctive ontological character to be the "bearer" of language as a semantic and referential function; and so language may be said to have floated free of any ground it may have been supposed to have *in* the world. It does not, of course, simply pass off into the empyrean as a consequence of having been thus dispossessed; and one can hardly deny that its distinctive semantic function remains perfectly familiar to the very human beings – linguistic philosophers among them – from whom it has been conceptually detached. It is equally evident that, like everyone else, these philosophers must continue to count on this understanding of language in their own use of it. It is hard to see how they could do this if they were only engaging in verbal behavior or how, in these circumstances, they could refuse language in its strong constitutive aspect a place within their own natures.

The conclusion to which this brief historical excursion points is that, in its treatment of human beings, linguistic philosophy uses a concept of language as verbal behavior that is quite different from (and dubiously consistent with) the understanding of language as a semantic and referential function that is implicit in its own enterprise. As long as this peculiar duality remains unaddressed, there will be something inherently unstable about this conception of philosophy. That is not likely to happen, however, until it is recognized that the two components in the original inspiration of linguistic philosophy are, at the very least, independent of one another. On the one hand, this new kind of philosophy was supposed to confine itself to logical-conceptual matters in a way that does not require (and perhaps does not even permit) any real commitment about what kinds of entities there are in the world. On the other hand, there was a strong conviction that the natural sciences had an exclusive right to determine what the world is like. It is as though, on the strength of this second component of their creed, these philosophers had assigned a power of attorney to their scientific colleagues and were, as a result, committed to a view of their own nature as human beings (and more specifically as language users) that

Philosophy, translated by Glynn Adey and David Frisby (London: Routledge and Kegan Paul, 1980).

excludes much of their own implicit self-understanding from their official concept of human nature. The result is a philosophy that moves on two levels and associates an explicit physicalistic ontology with an implicit log-icolinguistic transcendentalism.

Not only is it clear that this situation is extremely unstable, but there have also been signs recently that the working consensus on which the unity of linguistic philosophy depends may be breaking up. Significant defections from this consensus have been occurring in the direction of positions that in one way or another break the linkage between the two essential elements of linguistic philosophy. Some philosophers, for example, would associate philosophy much more closely with the actual work of the natural sciences and, in effect, abandon all pretensions to a transcendental, language-based independence of philosophy from these inquiries. It scarcely needs to be said that, under these auspices, the concept of a human being is interpreted in unambiguously physicalistic terms and that language use in all its cul-turally significant forms is absorbed into a more general theory of the func-tioning of organisms. Others, however, would resolve the tension between these dual commitments of philosophy to language and to the ontology of science in the opposite way, that is, in favor of language. They espouse a position that, in effect, repudiates the assumption that language requires either a world that it is to be about or a speaker who, as it were, sets it in motion. At any rate, there are now philosophers in this country who, under mainly French influences, are prepared to conceive language in a wholly autonomous manner that dispenses with references beyond language and with any "world" – physical or otherwise – that is not itself a creature of language. At the same time, these philosophers are even more hostile to the idea of a subject, however conceived, than are their scientistic col-leagues; and this animus against the subject has, in association with certain political and cultural attitudes, become a virulent antihumanism.

III

If one is not prepared to accept either one of these positions or the unstable synthesis of the two from which they broke away, there is no alternative to a new inquiry into the status of this human subject that is now being slight-ingly treated by the major schools of thought. Such an inquiry would come under the heading of "philosophical anthropology" – a term much more familiar to European philosophers than to those in this country, where "anthropology" is the name of a social-scientific discipline that has no special philosophical character. To speak of philosophical anthropology is to claim that philosophy still has something to say about what it is to be a human being, and that at least this domain of "fact" has not been ceded to a corresponding empirical science. More specifically, in the tradition of

thought that I have in mind, the issues posed by a transcendental conception of the mind – the conception that in the hands of Descartes and Kant
and Husserl dominates the modern period – are directly engaged instead
of becoming the unspoken and unquestioned presupposition of both philosophical and scientific thought in the manner just described. It may be
that because the transcendental status of thought had been so emphatically
asserted and so widely accepted in European philosophy, the question
about the existence – the locus in the world – of the subject that exercises
these transcendental functions had to be explicitly dealt with and not simply finessed by identifying mind with language use. Certainly this is suggested by the fact that European philosophy has thus far remained largely
immune to the attractions of physicalism as a philosophy of mind and more
sensitive to the obligation to replace a transcendental concept of the mind
with one that does not simply disallow every "'mental' fact that might prove
unincorporable into physicalism.

Two philosophers who made major contributions to this critique of transcendentalism, and to the effort to replace it with a more nearly adequate
theory of human being, are Martin Heidegger and Maurice Merleau-
Ponty.[4] Their thought, and the broader phenomenological tradition on
which they draw, will inform the argument of this book at many points; but
my intention is not to offer a defense or even an interpretation of what
they or others have said about the matters with which I deal. It is rather to
carry forward the line of thought they so powerfully initiated, and to do so
in a way that brings their theses into closer contact with a variety of contemporary philosophical concerns and challenges. The major element of
continuity between their thought and the position I present in this book
will be the ontological approach to questions in the philosophy of mind.
Since that description by itself conveys little even to a reader with a background in the relevant literature, it may be helpful to make one or two
preliminary points designed to anticipate objections to the use of the concept of ontology in this context.

In the philosophical tradition, ontology has been understood as the
study of being qua being; and the way it studies being may be either "regional," to use a Husserlian term, or general. In the first case, the ontologist

---

4. I have already given an account of Heidegger's thought in my *Heidegger and the Philosophy
of Mind* (New Haven, Conn.: Yale University Press, 1989), and this book builds on the
interpretation set forth there. With regard to the contrast between Heidegger's earlier and
later thought and the affinities of this study with the one or the other, I hold, as I did in
that book, to the thesis of the essential unity of Heidegger's thought in both periods and
to the complementarity of the concepts of being and *Dasein* – in my terminology, which is
itself borrowed from Heidegger, of presence and ek-sistence. See my essay *The Unity of
Heidegger's Thought* in *The Cambridge Companion to Heidegger* (Cambridge: Cambridge University Press, 1993), pp. 97–121. To this I would add that in the present stage of our relation
to his thought, Heidegger greatly needs to be understood once again as a philosopher
rather than as a mystagogue or a prophet.

addresses himself to entities of a certain kind – material objects, say – and attempts to characterize the "being" of those entities. Descartes, for example, explicated the being of nature in terms of the concept of extended substance. As a concept belonging to regional ontology, "human being" – the term I have used in the title of this book – would accordingly denote whatever turns out to be distinctive about this kind of entity. The question that arises for regional ontology in this sense is whether it presupposes a theory of natural kinds – some conception, that is, of things as having identities that are not simply stipulated by convention and that make them, as we say, the kinds of things they are. But if things do not have essences or sets of properties that make them what they are in this privileged sense, there will be no way of determining which one of the indefinitely numerous and various kinds to which an entity belongs constitutes its *being* in the strong sense that is required. In that event, the kind of ontological analysis that is supposed to define that being would inevitably take on a problematic aspect. Of course, one or another of these kinds may be conventionally designated as taking precedence over others for practical purposes of classification and description, but that fact alone does not confer any special ontological priority on the kind so designated.

General ontology, by contrast, is not primarily concerned with this or that kind of entity but rather with the import of the concept of being as such, wherever and however it is used. Traditionally, being in this sense has been conceived as a *summum genus* – the most general kind under which the regional concepts of the various classes of entities would be subsumed. But if the subkinds so subsumed have not been shown to express the being of the entities that fall under them in any special or privileged way, the status of the most general kind must be equally dubious. Heidegger argues, however, that this whole conception of being as such is profoundly mistaken, and that it goes wrong by associating the concept of being as such much too closely with that of entities and the kinds to which they belong, so that it finally becomes itself the concept of a superentity, that is, of God. A proper understanding of being as such can be achieved. Heidegger thinks, only through a radical contrast with entities that turns on the difference between a thing and a thing's *being* something – being something, that is, in the sense that gives rise to the notion of truth.

This contrast will be explained in much greater detail in the body of the book; it is introduced now only for the purpose of clarifying my use of the term "human being." The relevant point for this purpose is that, at least in the case of human beings, the notion of being as the kind of entity something is can be construed in a new way that links it with the conception of being as such that has just been briefly characterized. This is because human beings are, in fact, the entities for which entities generally are what they are and in fact are *überhaupt;* and human beings are thus the entities that are familiar with being as such. The ontological approach to issues in the philosophy of mind is best characterized as the disposition to replace the concepts of "mind" and "consciousness" with this familiarity with being in all its modes as the defining character of human being. To speak about the being of human beings in this sense is not, therefore, just to light on one of their properties rather than another in order to dignify it, arbitrarily, as their essence in some honorific sense. It is rather to single out this familiarity with being as such (and thus with an order of truth as well) as a necessary preliminary to the exploration of its role in a variety of functions that are held to be distinctively human and that are usually described in psychological language. Accordingly, although I claim that this familiarity with being is indeed constitutive for human being, this claim is not based on a priori or intuitive grounds. It is based instead on the centrality this familiarity with being can be shown to have in the full range of human functions considered in this book.

What has just been said also makes it possible to respond to those who may be surprised to see ontology of the Heideggerian type associated with any project that is well disposed toward humanism. Heidegger was the author of a famous *Letter on Humanism* in which he strongly condemned a kind of philosophical thought about human beings that might appear to have marked affinities with what I have just been proposing.[5] It would not be appropriate to give the details of Heidegger's argument at this point, but it can be noted that what he censures in the philosophical anthropology of the past is a failure to raise the right kinds of questions about the ontological character of the entity – man – that is at issue, and a resultant tendency to assimilate its mode of being to that of other kinds of entities in a way that misses what is distinctive about human beings. What is missed is precisely the implication of human beings in being as such that was touched on previously. Because, in Heidegger's view, the term "humanism" has been so closely associated with this tendency and with the uncritical ontological assumptions that go with it, he no longer has a positive use for it. At the same time, it is clear that he does not repudiate the idea itself of an inquiry into what he is still willing to call in a positive sense the "*humanitas* of the *homo humanus.*" What emerges as the principal implication of this critique of philosophical anthropology is not so much a rejection in principle of every such undertaking as it is a thesis about the way it must be conducted. Heidegger insists on the requirement that the level at which this inquiry is pitched must differ from that of the usual definitions of a human being as an *animal rationale*. This is not because man is not a

5. Martin Heidegger, "Brief über den 'Humanismus,' " in *Wegmarken* (Frankfurt am Main: V. Klostermann, 1967). Those who still harbor doubts about Heidegger's interest in human beings will find it much in evidence in the talks he gave to Swiss medical students in the 1960s. These were published in *Zollikoner Seminare*, edited by Medard Boss (Frankfurt am Main: V. Klostermann, 1987).

rational animal but because, in its standard versions, the concept of rationality captures too little of what is presupposed by it, especially its rapport with being as such.

The task this book sets itself is thus to raise into the right kind of visibility matters that are typically passed over in silence by prevailing concepts of human nature. One reason for this is that these features of our being are so familiar that it is all too easy to rely on them without ever noticing them explicitly even though they are presupposed in everything we say and do. Such exploration of the familiar and the implicit is, I would argue, as central a task for philosophy as the opening up of new domains of knowledge is for the natural sciences. A philosophical effort of this kind would have the further advantage of providing an element of ballast that might help to keep the winds of scientific doctrine from sweeping everything before them as though there were no prior understanding of human nature and human life that could offer any serious resistance to them.

This last point has special importance in my eyes; and although I will argue that our understanding of ourselves as human beings has been distorted at many points by both science and philosophy, I also claim that there remains, under the many layers of technical and pseudotechnical language that have been applied to our nature as human beings, another sound, though largely inarticulate, understanding on which I hope to draw as best I can. There is also a great corpus of thought, formulated in the major cultural traditions, that expresses an understanding of what it is to be a human being that was well established before the scientific worldview took shape and eventually claimed that it could deal with human fact across the board in its own terms. I am not suggesting, of course, that these classic texts of the humanistic tradition can simply be stirred together so as to yield, after enough boiling, a common residue of universal truths about man. It would be equally misguided, however, to assume, as is commonly done at present, that discontinuity and incommensurability are the only common features that characterize the efforts at self-understanding that human beings have made in the course of their history. Doubtless there are points at which theory must contravene the understandings about human fact that are already in place, but this does not mean that these understandings are to be disqualified a priori on grounds that merely invoke theoretical commitments made elsewhere. This happens all too often, and so it is important to emphasize the importance of the kind of humane literacy that can serve as protection against the excesses of theory that has been formed in a high degree of abstraction from any personal or culturally mediated experience of life.

IV

A word about the way I propose to go about the task I have set myself is in order here. Since that task amounts to a critique and reconstruction of the

central concepts in the philosophy of mind, it will begin with a review of
the conceptual vocabulary employed by philosophers of mind, especially
the assumptions implicit in this terminology about the kind of entity that
a mind is. It will then be shown that for all the naturalness and apparent
inevitability of these ways of conceiving and describing ourselves and our
mental lives, a number of them – most notably, the famous contrast between the inner and the outer – are egregiously inappropriate to that task.
The following chapters then move through the major topics in the philosophy of mind and make the case for a replacement of the traditional psychological apparatus by a concept of presence. This is the central concept
of the book, and it names what I take to be the principal notion in terms
of which an ontological understanding of human being must be formulated. I introduce it first in the context of an account of perception; I then
attempt to show how the different modalities of presence (and absence)
are involved in the several departments of what we usually think of as mental activity. These include not only memory and thought and imagination
but also feeling and desire and agency. The question of the individuation
– the particularity – of human being is also taken up, as are the distinctive
kinds of unity and reflexivity that characterize an entity that "ek-sists."[6]
This is the term that, in spite of a strong distaste for such fiddling with
words, I have decided to use for the purpose of designating the mode of
being of the kind of entity to which other entities are present. In Chapter
6 an attempt is made to show that the mode of being of the human body
is that of ek-sistence in this sense. The pairing of ek-sistence with presence
is central to the unitary concept of human being that I am proposing, and
this concept emerges fully in the final chapter, entitled "The Entity Each
of Us Is."

To this condensed outline of what I hope to accomplish, I should add
that I have given this inquiry a wide scope in order to show what a theory
of this kind might look like across the board. Clearly there are hazards in
such an ambitious undertaking, and I have no doubt that my account of
various aspects of my topic stands in need of emendation at many points.
Given the constructive character of my task, however, it seemed appropriate
to devote the whole text to the development of the theory I am proposing,
and not to discuss the views of other philosophers in any detail except
where they can help to clarify the import of some aspect of the position I

6. Heidegger makes extensive use of the Greek word *ekstasis* to express the idea of the going
   beyond or transcendence that is a constitutive feature of human being. *Ecstasis* is itself a
   nominalization of the Greek verb *existemi*, which normally means something like "to move
   away from." Occasionally he also uses the corresponding Latin verb *existere* and spells it
   "ek-sistere," presumably in order to bring out more perspicuously the root idea of "standing out from." I have adopted this usage because I want to continue to use "existence" in
   its normal non-Heideggerian sense, and I hope the difference in spelling will prevent confusion.

am working out. Such a procedure has drawbacks as well as advantages, and there are many discussions of the topics with which I deal that I should have liked to note and to comment on. Because of the vastness of the literature dealing with each of these topics, that was simply not feasible, and so I have decided not to take on a task I cannot properly execute. My overriding goal has been to give a recognizable and interesting shape to a kind of theory that is, at the very least, not familiar to most of those who discuss these matters in the United States. If I have succeeded in that effort, I shall willingly accept blame for my failure to explore more fully the affinities and disaffinities of that theory with areas of current discussion on which I do not touch.

1

INSIDE AND OUTSIDE

I

The importance of the decision one makes about where an inquiry is to begin can hardly be overestimated. That decision sets the character of the questions to be addressed; and by laying down the terms in which they are formulated, it can even carry an implicit commitment to a certain kind of answer to those questions. In the philosophy of mind especially, the terminology traditionally used to describe mental phenomena is so rich in presuppositions that once it is introduced, it seems to guide the inquiry so initiated along preordained paths to familiar conclusions. Even so, it is not easy to see how a completely fresh start could be made. If new language were simply introduced at the outset for the purpose of replacing old formulations, the relationship of these new questions to the ones that were raised in the old terminology would be at best problematic. As a result, in order to show what has been achieved by this reform, it would be necessary to explain the relevance of these new kinds of questions and answers to the matters discussed in the superseded idiom. To do this, however, would be to effect a rapprochement, however provisional, between the old and the new terminology and to surrender the hope for a completely new start.

It is necessary, then, to begin with the vocabulary of "mind" and the "mental" that has traditionally been used to render the aspect of human nature with which this book is concerned. This is the terminology that is now usually referred to as "psychological"; and it may be worth noting that the latter term designates the phenomena to which it applies by reference to the science – psychology – that studies them, whereas the older term –

"mental" – attributes to them a common property that is logically prior to (and is supposed to provide the ground for) their being objects of one branch of knowledge. That property is, of course, the property of being in (or in some way having to do with) the mind (*mens*). The notion of the mind as a part of a human being, and a special and privileged part at that, no longer enjoys universal acceptance, as it once did; and it may be that "psychological" is now preferred to a word like "mental" precisely because it at least sounds more non-committal about the status accorded to mind as so conceived. This naming procedure also enables us to avoid being more explicit about something we feel a good deal less confident about than people did in the past. There is admittedly something strange about our feeling more confident about the identity of the discipline that studies these phenomena than we are about whatever it may be that justifies their being treated as the objects of a single branch of inquiry. It appears, however, that in our increasingly bureaucratized intellectual life we tend to defer to some discipline that is assumed to hold the proprietary rights to any given area of thought, even when it is one with which, in the nature of the case, we have to be closely familiar. Even philosophers who in the past would typically have spoken of the "philosophy of mind" now tend to speak of the "philosophy of psychology," as though to acknowledge the priority of another discipline's claim to the terrain on which they are entering.

However that may be, it is generally agreed that these mental or psychological phenomena comprise a variety of states or events like feeling, perception, memory, thought, imagination, and others; and all of these are understood to be states *of* human beings or processes going on *in* them. To describe them in this way may seem innocuous enough; and yet there is reason to think that some of the locutions involved in this description, and especially the notion of mental phenomena as being *in* human beings, may have far-reaching implications that need careful scrutiny at the outset. It is, of course, accepted that even though psychological states are conceived as being internal to human beings in this way, they have causal antecedents that lie outside the human being in whom they occur. When such states have a cognitive character, they may also "represent" something that is, at least in most cases, not itself a part of that human being. What *is* implied by characterizing these states as "psychological," and thus as being in some sense contained within the human being to whom they belong, is that they can be described in a way that effectively abstracts from both these sets of relationships – the causal and the referential – in which they may stand to what lies outside that human being. It would be irrelevant, for example, to a psychological account of thought to determine whether what is thought by someone on some occasion is true in the sense of correctly representing some actual state of affairs; and an explanation of how a

mousetrap works would also have no bearing on a psychological account
of the pain felt by someone whose finger has been caught in it.

This conception of psychological states as internal to human beings in
the manner described needs to be examined more closely. Obviously, in
so treating them, we are invoking a certain picture not just of these phenomena but also of the human beings to whom they are attributed. In this
picture, the latter are evidently being treated as bounded in such a way that
they can contain certain things within themselves and exclude others; and
psychological or mental states are held to be among the former. Here
again, it is likely that this way of conceiving human beings will strike most
people as wholly unproblematic and thus in no need of closer scrutiny.
Even so, it cannot hurt to get a little clearer about how we come by this
conception and what its wider import may be.

There is, I suggest, a standpoint from which it is especially natural to
think of human beings in this way. This standpoint is not the one that is
postulated by traditional doctrines of introspection; and I argue that there
is no natural or intuitive basis for the conception of an inner self on which
those doctrines rest. Instead, the standpoint I have in mind is one from
which we observe a human being other than ourselves, and that human
being appears to us as a distinct unit within a larger natural environment.
It is, in other words, the occupant of a certain three-dimensional envelope
within an encompassing physical space. When we observe another human
being in this way, we have an especially clear sense of the contours or
boundaries of his body, and thus of the demarcation of what lies within it
from what lies without. The relevant sense of "in" that applies to whatever
might be said to be in a human being that is envisaged in this way would
thus be that of spatial inclusion. What is in a human being would accordingly be something located somewhere within the spatial confines of his
body.

In suggesting that the envelope of the human body as it is presented to
an observer serves as a principal clue to the way we interpret the notion of
something's being *in* a human being, I am not attributing a scientific or a
physicalistic concept of that body to such observers. For most purposes, the
human being we observe is perceived not as a physical system but as an
agent – a being that moves and acts in ways that are intended to effect
changes in its surroundings at the same time as it is itself affected in a
variety of ways by the action of others, as well as by purely physical processes.
In all these transactions, however, there is, in the picture I am describing,
a distinction between what is taking place within the human being and
what is taking place outside him; and for this distinction the contours of
the body offer a ready line of demarcation. There must, accordingly, be a
point in time at which some process in the environment reaches and passes
that boundary line and becomes a process *in* that human being; and there

must also be a point in time at which a process within that human being passes the boundary in the other direction and becomes a process in the environment. This distinction, moreover, applies at the level of purely phys-ical and physiological transactions but also at the level of actions like turn-ing on a light or even speaking. Here, too, there is a distinction between the last movement of the hand or tongue and the first effect it produces outside the organism.[1]

It is important to note that the human being who appears in the picture I have been characterizing appears as he does *to* an observer who is himself a human being but another human being – not the one who is being en-visaged and described in the way just set forth. That observer could, of course, be observed himself and by the very human being he is observing; and if that happens, this picture would apply to him as well. It might, there-fore, be supposed that this is a picture that he could equally well apply to himself, and in a sense this too is true. We can in fact imagine how we would appear to another person who observed us. But if a human being can imagine himself as he would appear to an observer other than himself, it does not follow that the standpoint of the external observer is the only one or even the primary one in terms of which he understands himself. He is, after all, not just the one who is observed but also the one who does the observing – whether directly, as in the case of another person, or vicari-ously, as in his own case. It is, therefore, fair to ask what kind of picture we form of ourselves in this second capacity and whether it represents my body as being the container of my mental states in anything like the way the body of another human being is supposed to be according to the first picture.

There is much in our philosophical tradition that predisposes us in favor of an affirmative answer to the second of these questions, but that answer would nevertheless be almost certainly mistaken. Before that can be shown, however, there are some complexities to be reckoned with. When we are engaged in observing someone or something, our own person remains, as a rule, in the background; and precisely because we are, on these occasions, so absorbed in something outside ourselves, it may be questioned whether we form any picture of ourselves at all. It is almost as though the very idea of making the self the object of explicit attention required that the obser-vation of anything external to that self be suspended. Such, at least, is the assumption on which the traditional philosophical models of self-knowledge seem to proceed when they construe such knowledge in terms of a kind of introspection in which the self is isolated from its wider environment.

---

1. I would not want it to be thought that because I express things this way, I am thereby committing myself to the notion of basic actions in the sense developed by Arthur Danto. There is, I think, something seriously misleading in the idea that all our actions can be divided into a part that is a movement of some part of the body and another part that is the effect produced by this movement. My quite different conception of human action is stated in Chapter 5.

More will be said about that misleading conception of self-knowledge later in this chapter. For now, it is enough to point to certain facts about first-personal observation that seem clear even if our grasp of them remains implicit and inarticulate – as it tends, in the main, to do. For one thing, although what is being observed is something external to us as the observers, there does not seem to be any place in this observing activity of ours for the former distinction between what is outside and what is inside. Although in a typical case the object we observe is certainly not a part of ourselves, our perception of it, understood as an activity in which we engage, is not bisected by any such distinction. More concretely, when I see something that lies outside the boundaries of my body, I have no sense of any distinction in the process of visual perception between the last stage that is internal to my person and the first stage that lies outside it. Instead, seeing is typically unsegmented in any such way as this; and it seems likely that the same would hold for other kinds of perception as well.[2] Of course, if I imagine myself as I would appear if I could observe myself in the way I do others, that distinction once again becomes applicable, and with it the role of the physical and neural processes of transmission that perception unquestionably involves, in our own case as well as in that of other human beings. In the ordinary implicit understanding we have of ourselves, however, nothing suggests to us that our own seeing and hearing are the last stage of any process of transmission or that they are occurring *in* us in any sense that would render problematic the fact of their being perceptions *of* objects and events outside us.

It thus appears that we have at least a preliminary answer to the question that was posed about the picture or understanding we have of ourselves. It is a picture in which we figure simply as the "first person" for whom the "third person" – the one that was observed in the other picture – as well as the whole natural setting in which he appears is there in the sense of being perceptually present.[3] Two points follow from this. One is that the two pictures are much more closely linked to one another than is the case when the self is understood as the object of introspection rather than as

2. It may be questioned whether this is true of the sense of touch since the thing we touch is in immediate contact with our skin. The skin, however, certainly does not act as a barrier of any kind, nor does it divide the perception in which it is involved into an inner and an outer part, any more than do the organs of the distance senses. In Chapter 6, I propose a conception of the macrobody, and it is as a function of the body as so characterized that the sense of touch has to be understood.

3. It may be asked what becomes of the second person in this scheme. Briefly, the communicative relation in which "I" stand to a person I refer to as "you" blocks the objectification that the "it" of the third person appears to invite. In other words, an equivalence of status between "I" and "you" is already implicit in this mode of address; and that is doubtless the reason why such elaborate precautions are taken in many languages to qualify that equivalence in one way or another by differentiating our forms of address to the "second person."

the subject of observation, as it is here. The second is that despite this linkage, there is not only an intuitive difference between the two pictures; there is also a demonstrable lack of fit between them. In the first picture, human beings are the containers of their mental states and functions; and from this it seems to follow that the latter must be distinct from the objects that lie outside the boundaries of the human being in question and that are ordinarily supposed to be *what* we perceive. In the other picture, these same human beings perceive just these "external" objects, and they do so in a way that seems unaffected by the distinction between inside and outside that assigns mental functions like perception to the inside.

But if these pictures are in such marked contrast with one another, it does not appear that we can resolve the matter by simply dropping one of them in favor of the other or, more incongruously still, by resolving on an explicitly asymmetrical treatment of one's own case and that of others. (The latter option may tempt us, and at an unacknowledged and perhaps even unconscious level it may well capture the way we order our relations with other human beings, but it can do so only if it is not brought out into the light of day.) Not only do both these ways of thinking about human beings have a strong claim to acceptance by us; in spite of the discrepancy between them, the idea of observing other human beings (or, for that matter, anything at all) can hardly be separated from that of a being that is capable of such observation. Since it has already been acknowledged that this observer can, in turn, be observed and thus understood in terms of the same contrast between inside and outside, the difficulty is evidently quite general, and the question that confronts philosophers is one of reconciling two disparate elements in our understanding of ourselves and our fellow human beings.

II

To this point, I have spoken mainly of "human beings" and have avoided using terms like "body" and "mind" in a way that implies a conceptual splitting of a unitary entity into two disparate constituent parts. This is a usage in which I will try to persevere and for which a philosophical justification will eventually be offered. At the same time, it must be recognized that the anomaly deriving from the two pictures of human beings in contexts like those of perception has led many thinkers to conclude that such an analytical resolution of the concept of a human being into two parts – a body and a mind – cannot be avoided. In what follows, I want to reconstruct what I believe to be the train of thought that leads to this inference; but I will do so in a way that does not closely conform to any of the major historical defenses of mind–body dualism. The latter tend to assume that we have just the immediate apprehension of ourselves as minds, and thus as "insides" contrasted with "outsides," that I want to deny we have. In my account of dualism, this contrast itself emerges as a resolution of the conflict set forth earlier; and it is this same conflict that, in my view, constitutes the primitive datum driving the process of thought that issues in a concept of mind.

To begin with, if human beings have been understood to be the containers of their mental states, during most of our history relatively little has been known about what was actually to be found beneath the skin that is the outer boundary of this container. This ignorance made it possible to accommodate there a jumble of very different kinds of states and events, with little sense of any possible incompatibility among them. But when our knowledge of the body is progressively refined and enriched by the scientific investigation of processes like the transmission of light and sound from an object at some distance from the human being we are observing to the sense organs of the latter, as well as of the processes that take place in the nervous system and brain after such stimulation, things grow more complex. As perception generally comes to be thought of as a causal and a physical process in a new and more exact sense of these terms, the distinctness of the external object from this process of transmission and whatever events it produces in a human being is greatly reinforced. At the same time, however, and as a result of this growing knowledge of what goes on in the body, questions arise about the seeing or hearing that is supposed to be the last event in the causal chain initiated outside the body of the perceiver.

The difficulty here is that it becomes more and more obvious that no form of scientific observation is going to turn up anything within the human body that would be identifiable as the kind of perceptual event that we are all familiar with in our own case – that is, of perception as it is understood in the terms set by the second picture. This is what Leibniz had in mind when he said that if the brain were to be vastly increased in size so that we could stroll through its corridors, we would find no perceptions there.[4] It is, therefore, clear that if the notion of mental states being *in* human beings is to maintain itself in the face of this new knowledge of the kind of thing that can actually be assigned a location within our bodies, it will have to be modified in a way that takes these facts into account. After all, if something is in something, it will normally be in some part of that something; and this would lead us to expect to find processes of perception as they are described in the second picture somewhere in the observed body of the first picture. It may seem to be in keeping with this expectation that people say, for example, that a pain is in their fingers or that a thought is in their heads. It does not seem likely, however, that such locutions as

---

4. G. W. Leibniz, *The Monadology and Other Philosophical Essays*, translated by P. Schrecker and A. M. Schrecker (Indianapolis: Bobbs Merrill/LLA, 1965), p. 150.

these should be interpreted literally as implying some sort of demarcated spatial location within the body for these pains or thoughts; and in any case, the development of scientific concepts of matter and of living organisms eventually makes any such literal construal impossible.

The situation is thus one in which we want to assign a location within other human beings to perceptual and other events of a kind that their bodies, as understood by the physical sciences, cannot accommodate. The underlying thought here is that if this were not done, the relationship in which we as observers stand to the human beings we observe would be asymmetrical. We would perceive them but they would not in any identifiable way perceive us. In these circumstances, there appears to be no way out of this impasse unless a human being includes a part that is other than his body and unlike it in those respects that make it impossible to situate perceptions (and other mental states) in the body. Many other motives have, of course, played a role in the postulation of the existence of such a part – that is, of what has been known as a soul or mind. Within the dialectic of observing and being observed, however, the significance of this move is that it attempts to preserve a symmetry between the self and the other that would otherwise be endangered by the new scientific understanding of what goes on inside the human body. What is especially interesting about the way this supplementary part of human beings is conceived is the fact that it is described as "inner" even though it is now accepted that it cannot be inside the body in any literal or physical sense. Instead, it is inside a human being in the sense that it is not itself in view, as the human body is, and also that it is reached, to the extent that it can be, through the body or those of its parts that are its organs of sense. What we are dealing with is thus a nonvisible and nonspatial inside; and for an entity so conceived, there are no available analogies or comparisons that are of much use.

Perhaps the best method of describing this new way of conceiving human beings is to say that it is a compound of the two pictures with which we began – the first based on the observation of others and the second drawn from one's own case. One might even speak of an insertion of the second picture into the first in the sense that the contrast between the outside and the inside of the first picture is being adapted in such a way that everything in the second picture can be assigned to the inside of that first picture but in a way that effects a momentous modification of the notion itself of this inside. On the one hand, in place of the original inside that accommodated both "physical" and "mental" on an equal, if somewhat ambiguous, footing, there are now two insides – one physical in a new, rigorous sense and the other nonphysical but nevertheless a constituent part of the human being and still on an equal footing with the other. More remarkably still, this second inside itself has an inside, namely, the various mental states and acts of perception, thought, and so on that are now to be thought of as taking place *in* the mind and that are the counterparts in a human being that we observe of our own mental activity. In this sense, the mind is the counterpart of the perceptual functioning of the self as delineated in the second picture – a counterpart domiciled in a suitably reconstituted inside of the first picture.

Just how this elaborate apparatus is supposed to work, and how it combines the two pictures with which we began, can be clarified by a closer look at its implications for the analysis of perception. Since the object perceived is also the object at the origin of the causal process that makes that perception possible, and since it figures in the one picture in the first capacity and in the other in the second capacity, it is clear that to identify the two in a unified picture would be to confuse something that is outside with something that is inside – in this new sense – the human being in question. It follows that these pictures cannot be combined unless some way is found to get around this difficulty. The obvious way to do this is to split the object to which an act of perception is directed into two parts.[5] One of these is the object that lies outside the body *and* the mind of the perceiving human being; and the other is that object as it is *represented* within the latter's mind. In other words, as the "scene" that presents itself to my vision in the second picture, perceptual objects are transferred to the mind, where they constitute an *inner* scene. At the same time, as the stimulus objects that initiate the causal process of perception, they remain right where they are outside the body. As a result of this division of the object, the nonsegmented picture of the mental life of a human being in relation to objects outside the body is preserved; but it is now understood to render something that is internal to the mind. As a result, what appears in perception is that object as represented rather than the object itself. At the same time, an essential feature of the picture that is based on the observation of other human beings is also preserved. This is the distinction between the outside and the inside; and the introduction of the concept of the mind as a nonphysical part of a human being makes it possible to

---

5. It is of great interest that Descartes used the word "objective" to characterize the specifically mental or representational term in this contrast. This is often treated as if it were merely a confusing reversal of our use of the terms "objective" and "subjective," but a great deal more is involved. For one thing, our present use of "objective" for what is truly out there in the public world derives from Descartes's notion of the tests that have to be applied to what is "objective" in his sense in order to determine what is "objective" in ours – that is, not merely in the mind or "subjective" (our sense). There is thus a clear affinity between the two apparently disparate uses of this term. The other point is that in Latin, long before Descartes, *objectum* – literally, something that is thrown across one's path – had been used to convey the idea of being visible or in view. The use of this word thus seems to be like that of *lanthano* in Greek and *facies* in Latin in that all are cases of nonpsychological, "worldly" ways of expressing the fact of presence or absence. The use of the term *objectum* in medieval theology to denote a specifically mental dimension of a thing's reality presumably derives from this usage, but at the same time at least partially "mentalizes" it.

say that seeing, for example, in the sense that, as we would normally say, involves the presence of the object to consciousness, takes place inside the human being even though it does not in any discoverable way take place in the body.

Once this apparatus is in place, it becomes possible to reinterpret self-knowledge itself in a way that conforms to the new understanding of what is inside me that is introduced with the concept of mind. Self-knowledge now comes to be thought of as inner sense – a reflexive act of the mind in which the latter becomes aware of itself, as well as of its representational contents and of its own acts. As inner sense, such knowledge is supposed to be quite different from the kind of knowledge that we have of other human beings as well as of natural objects. The latter is held to be observational knowledge; and in the nature of the case, such observation of other human beings must always be observation of their bodies since the kind of access we have to our own mental life is excluded in the case of other people. What is effectively elided in this account is, of course, the linkage to which attention was drawn earlier between such observation of other human beings and the kind of self-knowledge that found expression in the second picture – the kind that has now been replaced by a conception of inner sense. Nevertheless, this new way of making a contrast between knowledge of others and knowledge of self became the dominant one in the modern period; and that has meant that the contrast between the two pictures with which this chapter began has been treated as merely a rather crude first approximation to this more accurate understanding. Against this view, it is an important thesis of this book that the two ways of making this contrast are *not* in fact equivalent, and that it is important to keep the first contrast, which involves human beings, not minds and bodies, clearly distinct from the second so that it is not lost amid the strong negative reactions that the new model of self-knowledge quite understandably provokes.

To this end I will try to show that there are very serious difficulties associated with the strategy of reconciling the two pictures of human beings as observed and as observing that has just been described. It has already been pointed out that this strategy, which introduces the concept of mind as a nonphysical part of a human being, also involves treating the mind as the locus of representations. This commitment to representations in fact becomes a central element in the philosophical case that supports the postulation of a mind as an inner domain of some sort. But if representation becomes in this way the tail that wags the dog, it can be shown that the introduction of this concept is attended by major difficulties, and that it is doubtful whether it can accomplish its purpose of maintaining intact the governing distinction between what is in the mind and what is not. That will be the task of the next section.

III

The notion of "re-presentation" is in much heavier use among philosophers these days than is that of "presentation, " from which it is formed by the addition of a prefix that means "again" or "back."[6] One would think that the notion of something happening for the first time must be as well established as that of its happening again, but that does not seem to be the case in this instance. Instead, in its current use, the word "representation" seems to have broken most of its links not just with "presentation" but with other still simpler derivatives, like "present" and "presence," from their common root in the Latin verb *praeesse*: "to be present, at hand, in sight, before one." In Latin, *praesentatio* means "a showing or a placing before," and so apparently does *repraesentatio*, although in this case what is itself present may be something like an image – a son, for example, who so closely resembles his father that he may be said to "represent" him. This sense seems to have been carried forward in the Middle Ages, when *repraesentatio* became a term of art in law and politics. It then applied to occasions when the person who might have been present at some earlier time was "re-presented" by someone who served as his proxy and thus, in a special sense that has become the standard meaning of the word, "re-presented" him. In this sense, the king was represented by his ambassadors; the client, by his lawyer; and so on.

There is another and still more potent sense in which something can be said to be re-presented – not by another person, but by a picture or a symbol. Pictures, especially, widen the meaning of re-presentation in a way that has played an important role in the specifically philosophical use of this notion that eventually emerged. That did not happen until early in the modern period; but when it did, re-presentations came to be understood as denizens of the mind that mediated the relation between the mind and the objects of its knowledge. Up to a point, the idea of a picture lends itself quite naturally to this greatly widened use. If something is present when we first observe it, then one way of understanding what is involved in our later thinking of it or remembering it is to think of memory as having a picture of it in our mind – a picture that represents it to us. Indeed, there is good reason to suppose that "representation" in its philosophical sense derives from the notion of an image or a picture. Such a mental picture could not, of course, be like an ordinary one that has its own properties as a picture – being an oil painting, for example, or a photograph. Neverthe-

6. The term "presentation" is as close as most philosophers are willing to come to "presence" as I understand it; and it was in common use until fairly recently, as for example in the writings of C. I. Lewis. It was used to denote the sense data or qualia that were held to be the immediate objects of consciousness – in other words, something in the mind and thus, paradoxically, the presence to the mind of what, on a wider view, would have to be described as a "representation."

less, this picture is supposed to be in the mind and to re-present to that mind something that is not present to it in the way that the picture itself is supposed to be. It is this picture-based concept of representation that was eventually generalized to become the master concept in the modern philosophy of mind, most often in the terminology of "ideas." The premise of what came to be called the "way of ideas" was that *all* mental activity must somehow involve representations; and in this way, a model designed for cases in which the object of knowledge is absent was put into service in cases in which this condition is not met as well. So fundamental did this notion of representation become that the mind itself came to be conceived mainly as the locus of the "ideas" in terms of which all forms of mental activity were to be understood. Indeed, both Hume and Kant, who were in a profound sense adherents to the way of ideas, eventually called into doubt the very possibility of our having any apprehension of the mind itself, as contrasted with the representations it was supposed to contain.

When the concept of representation is applied primarily to contexts in which, as in the original legal–political case, something is understood to be absent, one would expect that what is so absent and therefore has to be re-presented would be such that it could, at least in principle, appear in its own right, independent of any intermediary. This expectation, however, creates difficulties when the use of the concept of representation is extended to mental activity generally. More specifically, these difficulties develop when we attempt to apply the concept of representation not just to memory, thought, or imagination but to perception itself. The reason for this is simply that if perception itself is mediated by representations, it will no longer be possible to preserve the contrast between presentations and representations or to give it an empirical interpretation. Instead, the only comparisons that will be possible will be comparisons of one representation with another; and in the absence of anything that could be said to be present and with which its re-presentation could be contrasted, the ground is cut out from under the concept of representation itself as we normally understand it.

Although this objection to the generalized use of the concept of representation seems as decisive as anything it is reasonable to demand in philosophical argument, it has never been able to put representationalism out of business. In our everyday talk, we have gone on using the concept of representation (or some equivalent) in speaking about our mental lives – mostly, of course, without knowing that this is what we are doing. In these circumstances, it seems fair to conjecture that this has been possible only by virtue of tacit exceptions that limit the full generality of the representationalist thesis. For one thing, perception itself tends to be implicitly exempted from the scope of the latter; and then, when it has to be included, certain differences among the various sense modalities are exploited, again tacitly, to make it appear as though some were representational in nature and others not. It has been pointed out, for example, that for some sense modalities there are, in our ordinary prephilosophical vocabulary, words that seem to denote objects of these senses that are not identical with the external objects in question. Hence, it can be argued that what we hear is proximally a sound and what we smell is an odor; and these "internal accusatives" appear to be numerically distinct from the objects that produce these sounds or smells. In these circumstances, it can seem plausible to understand the relationship between the one and the other as the representation of an extramental object by an intramental content even though the latter may not resemble the former.

It is evident that if this kind of representation is to have an empirical interpretation in the case of the senses to which it is applied, there must be some form of access to the extramental object in question. It is at just this point that certain facts about vision or at least our ordinary ways of describing vision become relevant. Most relevantly, there are, in the case of vision, no such internal accusatives – no counterparts of "sound" or "odor" that would enable us to distinguish between what we see and the corresponding extramental object. In the absence of a word that would express this distinction in the case of vision, however, it is plausible to treat vision implicitly as though it were nonrepresentational in character. What is interesting about this is that when it is understood in this way, vision can supply a nonrepresentational context for the other senses that are being conceived in representational terms. Typically, if we smell something, we can locate visually the object from which the odor in question issues; and similarly with hearing and tasting something. Because we are able to do this, we have a sense that both terms in the representational picture are accessible to us and that the notion of the relationship we have posited between them is empirically grounded.

If this is how the application of the representational schema to perception works in practice, it is clear that it dilutes that thesis by tacitly admitting, in the case of vision, a nonrepresentational mode of access to extramental objects, which serves to supply the contrast required by the representational character of the other senses. But if it is to be consistent, the thesis of representationalism cannot, in its application to perception, tacitly exempt one sense modality from its requirements. It must apply to vision as it does to every other sense modality. But if vision is itself representational in character, then it offers no way of contrasting the representations in terms of which the other sense modalities are analyzed with something that is not itself a representation. The plain implication of all this would seem to be that the concept of representation cannot be extended to all departments of mental activity without being denatured in so fundamental a respect that its import would become thoroughly problematic.

The inescapable conclusion is thus that the continuing and considerable utility of this concept depends on its not being overextended in that way. From this it would certainly seem to follow that any conception of the mind that rests its case on the need for something in which representations can be accommodated cannot be any more coherent than that of representation itself appears to be.

IV

In the preceding discussion, I dealt with unavowed procedures that are employed in the everyday dealings with mental facts of people who are not philosophers, as well as of philosophers in their nonprofessional moments.[7] Although the objections I reviewed are well known to philosophers, representationalism has nevertheless found many defenders, perhaps because so few plausible alternatives are available; and attempts have been made to meet the difficulties pointed out here. There is, for example, a line of thought, associated with the names of Berkeley and Leibniz, that accepts the conclusion that representations or ideas can be compared only with other representations and works out a more or less idealistic theory of mind on this basis. Another alternative, which is usually attributed to Kant, is to argue that the contrast that undergirds the concept of representation is indeed a contrast between representations and something that is not a representation, but that the latter need not be given an empirical interpretation. Instead, this contrast can be construed as one between everything "empirical" – *all* the contents of experience, and this means all representations – on the one hand and a transempirical domain of objects on the other. It has been widely agreed that both of these versions of representationalism generate serious difficulties of their own; but in somewhat different guise, both are still options for those who want to make representation the master concept for the philosophy of mind. In this section I want to examine what I take to be the principal arguments in behalf of representationalism that are typically presupposed by such thinkers as these. If the case for representations can be shown to be invalid, then it will follow that the need for a mind that serves mainly as a storehouse for representations can no longer be persuasively demonstrated. At that point, it will be possible to suggest a new way in which this whole matter, which has been

7. The current wide use of the term "representation" among people working in the theory of literature also deserves notice although it appears to be motivated mainly by considerations of a different order from those guiding the present discussion. The idea seems to be that decisions about what to call something or someone – the guise in which it is allowed to figure in "discourse" about it – have a strategic character and constitute an exercise of social power. There appears to be little awareness on the part of those who make such intensive use of this term that there may be some hazards associated with treating it as the master concept for mental activity generally.

conceived in the terms made available by the language of mind, can be approached.

In what follows, I will mount two different kinds of arguments against what I will call "strong" representationalism – the kind that insists that all forms of mental activity are mediated by representations. First, I will show that the philosophical case that has been made for the representational character of mental activity, mainly on the basis of the experience of error, is itself faulty. But I also want to show that even if that argument were valid and the concept of representation were to be applied consistently to all forms and domains of perception and of mental life generally, the result would be quite different from the one expected by the philosophers who proceed in this way. Instead of our being introduced into a new realm of experience in which sense data and meanings take the place of objects, as Husserl for example thought, the result would be to reproduce, under more exotic forms of description, the familiar world of the "natural attitude" – Husserl's term for common sense – that the representational theory was designed to replace.

There are, at bottom, two arguments that can be offered for concluding that what one sees, as well as what one hears, touches, and so on, is not an independent, external object but, rather, an intermediate entity that somehow represents that object. Not surprisingly, there is a clear affinity between each of these lines of argument and one of the two pictures cited at the beginning of this chapter. The first of these is based on our observation of other human beings in their relationship to the objects they are said to perceive. Since these objects are the external point of origin of the causal process that is a necessary condition for the perceiving that takes place in the human being we observe, it follows that the relationship between that object and the perceptual event or state that occurs in that human being must be an external one. What this comes to is that the spatial (and, in certain cases, the temporal) distance of the one from the other makes it impossible for the external object and the internal state to stand in the kind of relationship to one another that would permit the content of the latter to be a property of the former. This conclusion is then applied reflexively to itself by the human being who has reached it in the course of his observations of other human beings. As a result, the contents of the perceptual field of that person, which up to this point have typically (and quite unproblematically) been identified with the objects themselves that are external to the latter's body, come to be reconceived as a set of representations.

When the representational argument travels by this route, however, there is the disadvantage that it does not seem to be motivated by anything internal to the experience of the human being to whom it is reflexively applied in this way. As a result, the substitution of the language of representations for that of natural objects for the purpose of describing that experience takes on the character of a theory-derived fiat; and it is not clear that it responds to any difficulty arising out of the application of the language of objects to one's own experience. It is, however, just such a difficulty that serves as the point of departure for the second argument in support of a representational theory of perception. Unlike the one just presented, it appeals to considerations that are available simply on the basis of one's own perceptual experience and independently of observations we make of other observers. The facts to which it points have to do with those anomalous occasions when the object as perceived changes, although there is no reason to suppose that the object itself has changed. When this happens, that object takes on features in our perception of it that we know it does not and perhaps could not really have. The straight stick that is half immersed in water looks bent, and the circular penny looks elliptical when viewed from a certain angle. In less routine cases, a limb that has been amputated is felt to be still in place and a drunken person sees snakes that are not there. If we ask ourselves what we are seeing in such cases, the answer cannot be "a bent stick" or "a snake" since *ex hypothesi* there is no bent stick or snake in the situation in question. Nevertheless, so the argument runs, the something that we *do* see and that *is* bent is not nothing; there is something that is bent, only that something is not a material object but, rather, an appearance that has no existence apart from my perception and must therefore be a mental content or representation. But it can hardly be the case that my perceptions are sometimes mediated by such representations and sometimes not, especially since such misleading appearances are internally indistinguishable from the way real objects appear to me in normal conditions. It must, therefore, be the case that what I see and hear is always in the first instance an intermediary state of mind or representation. From this I must infer that my experience as a whole is composed of such appearances that in some way represent the real objects that do not themselves appear; and to say this is to conclude that all of my perceptual experiences are really representational in character.

It is in some such way as this that the concept of experience itself is usually construed. It is arrived at by taking what is common to veridical and nonveridical appearances and treating the resulting concept – the concept, that is, of an appearance that is antecedent to the distinction between truth and falsity – as defining the unit in terms of which this primary stratum of our mental lives is to be analyzed. A notable feature of such units is their atomic character, by which is meant the fact that they are logically self-contained and enter into only external relations with other similarly self-contained sense data. One consequence of this state of affairs is that it is impossible in principle ever to identify a representation of sense – a sense datum – as being the *same* one that was present on another occasion. It also follows from this same fact that such representations cannot be identified with the properties that ordinary objects possess because such properties are not logically atomic in the relevant sense and many different observations can converge on the *same* property. It should also be noted that a sense datum cannot have any features that could be better viewed from another angle, and one cannot walk around a sense datum as one can around a house or a hill to examine its reverse side. In any case, since the kind of reidentification of which objects and properties in our ordinary understanding of them are susceptible is fundamental to empirical and scientific knowledge, those who subscribe to this concept of experience have had to exert themselves to explain how it is possible to acquire such knowledge when the materials of sense are held to be so completely lacking in the relevant logical properties.

In the Kantian way of answering this question, the various forms of logical connectedness that are constitutive of the concept of an object are held to be inherent in the human mind. They are, Kant tells us, superimposed on the material contents of sense experience in some mysterious way to which we have no access. Even when the concept of an empirical object has been accounted for in this way, however, it remains the concept of a *phenomenal* object and as such stands in a problematic relationship to the extraexperiential thing-in-itself that is supposed to have produced the original representations of sense by its action on our sensibility.

In light of the obvious difficulties attendant on this whole conception of our access to objects as being mediated by representations of sense, one cannot help wondering whether the reasoning that leads into it may not be faulty at some point. Of the two arguments that were presented, the first does indeed look vulnerable to criticism. This is because it bases its conclusion that the content of our perceptual experience is made up of representations on an account of how these representations are generated. It is evident that that conception itself presupposes that there is access to the nonrepresentational term in the causal relationship that is postulated in the case of the human beings we observe in the manner of the first picture. The only way to avoid the inconsistency this produces would be to try to translate the causal theory of perception itself into the language of representations along the lines of some forms of phenomenalism. The success of such an undertaking is highly questionable, however, and even if it were to succeed, it would have the effect of making the first argument dependent on the second. This is because only the second argument would be able to establish, without either circularity or inconsistency, what a phenomenalistic construal of the first argument would presuppose. That is that our perceptual experience consists entirely of representations; and it cannot be established as long as the case of the first-person observer is implicitly treated as privileged, as the first argument treats him in its naive version.

It is the second argument, then, that needs attention, and especially its factual premise that says that the content of our experience changes in ways to which no change in the object of that experience corresponds. From this it is supposed to follow that what we experience cannot be that object because what we experience has properties – being bent, in the stick example – that the object itself does not have. The underlying assumption here seems to be that the object in question is defined by a list of properties that belong to it as it is in itself and that, if we are to be able to say that we see this object, it must appear to us with just these properties and no others. The difficulty about this is that it makes no allowance for differences that are due to the varying conditions under which we perceive objects. We see an object – a chair, say – on one occasion when it is well lighted and on another when it is just an outline in the darkness; and by the terms of the previous argument, we would have to say that the color of what we see has changed, although the color of the object has not. In fact, no one would ordinarily think of describing such a situation in this way. We would not say that we first saw something green and then, in the darkened room, something black. We would not say that we saw something black at all, but rather that we could not see well and could not make out what color the chair was. Nor would it enter our heads to say that we did not see the chair but rather something else that was of a different color. The supposed blackness that on the representational theory would be the property of a sense datum is dealt with quite differently as a lack of illumination that makes it difficult or impossible to see what the color of the chair is. The assumption underlying all of this is that the conditions of observation affect the way objects look to us, but that this in no way implies that we do not continue to perceive the same object through these variations.[8]

The distinction between the way an object looks under a certain set of circumstances and the nature of that object itself is one with which we are all familiar. Objects, moreover, look the way they do under different conditions because they are objects of a certain kind and with certain properties; and they would not be the objects they are if they did not appear to us in these ways. For the most part, these regular and predictable variations have to do with such matters as conditions of illumination, proximity to the object, and so on; and since these variations tend to be pretty much the same for all observers, it is natural to incorporate them into our concept of the object in question itself. There are, of course, other variations that are functions not of external conditions of observation but of the condition of the observer himself. Some of these are well known, like the fact that pressure on the eyeball causes us to see double or that the taste of some-

---

8. As I understand it, this was the thesis of the "objective relativism" with which the name of Arthur Murphy was principally associated. See *Reason and the Common Good: Selected Essays of Arthur Murphy*, edited by William Hay et al. (Englewood Cliffs, N.J.: Prentice-Hall, 1963).

thing can be altered by illness or by something else that one has just eaten. Others are more idiosyncratic and far-reaching, like the effects on vision and the other senses of consuming lysergic acid or the hallucinations that accompany delirium tremens or certain forms of schizophrenia. The distinctive feature of such cases is usually held to be that in them the aberrant character of our experience is complete in the way it is in dreams. There is nothing in it that is not at variance with the actual state of the world – no context, in other words, of veridical perception, as there is in a case like that of the bent stick, that could be used as the point of departure for testing the aberrant appearance that turns up within it. In such cases, it seems that there is no overlap at all between the actual world and the content of our experience; and this makes it hard to see how that content could possibly be described otherwise than in terms of the mental intermediaries or representations with which I have been trying to dispense.

Inferences of this kind have been of great importance in the history of modern philosophy; and it would not be an exaggeration to say that the experience of perceptual illusion has provided the ultimate basis for the contrast between inside and outside that undergirds the dualistic conception of human being. What this preoccupation with the possibility of radical error obscures, however, is that the same being that is vulnerable to perceptual error is able to correct it, and to form for itself a concept of such error and of the disparity between experience and object that it involves. This would hardly be possible if the premise of the preceding argument that has to do with the completeness of the hallucination or system of illusory appearances were unassailable.

There are, moreover, a number of ways in which that completeness can be called into question. One way in which an illusory experience might fail to achieve this completeness would be if the person who is subject to it were to remain in some sort of effective contact with other people who do not share his hallucination. Another is the case in which that person retains some recollection of a previous time in his life at which things did not appear in the way they do now. If both of these conditions were met in a case of hallucination, that hallucination would not really be complete. This is because it would be possible for the person affected to get some leverage on his hallucination by raising epistemic questions about it that are based on his own former experiences and those of other people that are contemporaneous with that hallucination. By either of these routes it would be possible in principle for him to entertain the idea that what is in fact appearing to him is not what he might first have described it as being but, rather, something else that is appearing in a way he is unfamiliar with – so unfamiliar, in fact, that he is unable to identify these appearances as appearances of *that* object. In such a case, it may happen that he suddenly recognizes the object that he is *really* perceiving with the result that his sense of strangeness and aberrancy simply vanishes. An example of this might be "seeing" a mirage and then having it dissolve before one's eyes.

Another possibility is that even though no such sudden renormalization of the perceptual situation occurs, the person in question may be able to postulate an explanation – great fatigue, say, or a medication he has taken – for the unusual way in which what he is really seeing appears to him. In such a case, we learn in effect something we did not previously know about how things look to us in certain circumstances; and if these are repeated, we may gradually become capable of recognizing the object or objects that are appearing to us in this way. When such exceptional ways of appearing are naturalized in this way, there is no need to postulate any entities with properties other than those that belong to the ones that are actually present; and this is to say that the argument for the existence of representations that was based on these cases does not go through.

A more serious case is the one in which someone who "sees" things that are not there is himself committed to the description he gives of what he sees. If the commitment is strong, it could lead him to discount the testimony of others or his own recollections that conflict with what he now claims to be seeing. Such a person will not only say that it seems to him that he is perceiving pink elephants; he will also insist that there are pink elephants in the room with him. Having taken this stand, there is no reason for him to entertain the possibility that what he has described as "seeing pink elephants" is really to be understood as seeing something else that is simply appearing to him in an unfamiliar way because of some circumstance affecting the conditions of perception in this case. In extreme – presumably pathological – cases, such a person would be unable to assume a properly epistemic attitude toward his own perceptual claim at all or would at most be able to counterfeit it by offering bogus reasons for discounting conflicting evidence offered by others. The relevant point about such a case, however, is that this kind of pathological stubbornness about the way in which what he sees is to be identified offers no reason for anyone else to say that this person is in fact seeing anything other than what is in fact there. What has gone wrong has to do with an inability to utilize the epistemic resources afforded by our own past experience, and the testimony of others, and to use them in such a way as to isolate the hallucination as the deviant appearance that it in fact is. It may be that the exceptional condition by reference to which the fact of this aberrancy might be explained would also account for this inability.

However that may be, a failure of this kind does not really have any bearing on the question about the existence of representations. It may well be that if the conditions of perception – both in the environment and in the organism – were not reasonably stable, and as a result we had to deal with an uncontrollably variegated range of ways in which objects could appear to us, we would not be able to disengage the identity of such objects from their ways of appearing to us, as we can, for example, in the case of the chair that is perceived first in normal illumination and then in semi-darkness. The fact, of course, is that we are able to recognize objects for what they are through a quite extensive range of variations in the ways they appear to us. To the extent that we are able to do this, these variations do not provide any basis for the claim that what is before the mind is representations rather than things. Even in those cases in which the object has been so fractured by the special conditions under which we observe it – through a kaleidoscope, for example – that we cannot recognize it, this conclusion does not follow. What is really at issue here is not the existence of some special intermediary entities, but rather the limited range of the recognitional and classificatory capabilities that enable us to identify objects through all the variations in their modes of appearing to us. These capabilities need to be more fully characterized, and this is done in the chapters that follow. For now, however, the only point that needs to be made is that they are powers we possess and as such do not carry any commitment to special entities of the kind that representations have been thought to be.

It thus appears that neither of the arguments that have been used to prove the ubiquity of representations succeeds in doing so. What I now want to show is that an account of our experience in terms of representations would be redundant in the sense that even if it could in fact be carried out, it would only render in a far more laborious manner what is already accomplished by the language of ordinary perceptual objects and the ways they look under different conditions. This charge of redundancy is not, it may be noted, the one that is usually brought against such theories. Instead, the typical charge against them is that because they deal only in representations or ideas, and so cannot acknowledge anything that is not somehow mind-dependent, they must issue in some variant of philosophical idealism. But to criticize representationalism in this way is to accept the supposition that the concept of representation can retain its mental character even when it has been generalized in the manner previously described. I want to contest this claim and to argue that as a result of that generalization, the distinction between representations and what they represent unavoidably collapses. Because there is nothing with which they can be contrasted, it becomes impossible for representations to function as such, and as a result they become indistinguishable from the things they had been supposed to represent.

A theory that deals exclusively in representations can hardly conceive perceptual objects otherwise than in phenomenalistic terms. Any statement of empirical fact will, on such a view, turn out to be about the experiences – these would be so many representations – one would have in certain circumstances; and these circumstances themselves would have to be similarly explicated as certain constellations of experiences or representations. The complexity of these proliferating series of experiences is almost incalculable; but what is more damaging is the fact that it is utterly unclear how they could possibly yield anything that we would ordinarily recognize as a world. For one thing, the sameness of any perceptual object one encounters on two different occasions would always have to be explicated in terms of the similarity to one another of the visual and other experiences that come along at these different times. This chair, for example, would be a "family" of such experiences; and since every new member of the family – every incremental representation – would be numerically distinct from every other, there could, strictly speaking, be no such thing as seeing the same thing again. Thus, if I were to go back to a museum to view once again the painting I saw there last year when it was first hung, seeing this painting again would have to be understood as simply a fresh increment of experiences that are very similar to those I had in the past. As for the fact that the painting has been hanging there all this time, that would have to be interpreted in terms of possible experiences that I or someone else would have had when going to the gallery at any time during the intervening year.

I think it is clear that any such construal of the kinds of things we unhesitatingly affirm about things in the world is grotesquely inadequate. There is nothing hypothetical or merely possible about the painting that hangs in its place throughout the hours when no one is viewing it. Indeed, if that painting or any other object were no more than a family of experiences or representations, a question about what fills the intervals between these experiences would have no point. The painting I and others see when visiting the museum and the painting that hangs there throughout the night are one and the same, as they could not be if both were sets of experiences, some actual and others possible. What this comes to is that perceptual objects have a kind of identity that cannot be accounted for in terms of the qualitative similarities of representations. It is a thicker, perduring identity that is not pieced together out of series of experiences and that is largely unaffected by the breaks that inevitably occur in those series. From this it follows that those who suppose themselves to be living on the reduced rations that are all that phenomenalism allows are deceiving themselves. Although they claim to be dealing only in representations, the criterion of identity they in fact use is such that it is possible to see for the second time the same thing as before, which has been there all along. To the extent that they do this, the entities they call representations are being treated as things. The result is that the mosaic of representations that supposedly constitute the contents of the mind becomes indistinguishable from the array of objects that we ordinarily suppose ourselves to be in the presence of without the mediation of anything like representations or experiences. The paradoxical outcome of this kind of representationalism is thus that it reproduces just the version of perception that it repudiated so energetically in its inception.

One last point needs to be made in connection with the preceding discussion of error, and it is one that will growing in importance in the course of the argument of this book. What I have been trying to show is that the fact of perceptual illusion does not justify the philosophical inferences that have been based on it, and most particularly not the postulation of representations as the immediate objects of consciousness. To this end, I have argued that the objects that we seem to see do not require any special ontological status of their own and can instead be characterized in terms of the way the object that is actually there looks to us under a given set of circumstances. It is therefore not necessary to conceive the self as a substance of a special kind so that various kinds of perceptual debris can be housed in it. Even so, this line of thought does not account for the specific way in which we identify – mistakenly – the object that we do not recognize for what it is. There is, after all, no one kind of thing that an object must be assimilated to on the basis of the way it looks when there is a failure to recognize it for what it really is. That may vary widely and will typically reflect the preoccupations and expectations of the individual who makes this mistake.

The reason this is important in this context is that it has implications for the way that individual is to be conceived as a human being. I have said that I propose to construct a concept of human being by beginning with the simple fact of perceptual presence. My point now is that although the preceding discussion of perceptual illusion has shown that errors of this kind do not make it necessary to abandon this conception of presence in favor of a theory of representation, this does not mean that a false identification can be charged to the things themselves that are present or to the fact of their being present.[9] Instead, it must be attributable to the *entity* – the individual human being – to which what is present is present. The natural inference suggested by such an attribution might well be that I am committing myself to a theory of mental acts of which recognition would be the paradigm case. From this, it would be just a step to some conception of the entity – a mind, surely – that performs such mental acts; and then the question would be just how different this "mind" can be from the kind of inner domain against which I have been arguing. All I can say at this point in my argument is that this is not the route I plan to travel; and the

9. This is in contrast with something that Heidegger says in connection with his conception of a history of being. It appears to be his view that the ways in which being comes to be erroneously understood are to be attributed to being itself as its ways of hiding itself. The error involved here is, of course, an extremely high-level, philosophical kind of error, but the idea of explaining it as a disguise assumed by what we are mistaken about still seems paradoxical.

entity to which these recognitional powers are to be attributed will not be a mind but a human being. And far from marking a relapse into a mentalistic conception of human being, what I have just said about recognition is, in fact, a first clue to the distinctive ontological character of that entity for which I am using the term "ek-sistence." There will be many other such clues in these early chapters that have mainly to do with the concept of presence with which that of ek-sistence is intimately linked. In the latter part of the book, and especially in the final chapter, ek-sistence itself, will be at the center of the discussion, and these "clues" will be subsumed in a unitary concept of human being.

V

The argument presented in the last two sections was designed to show that the attempt to incorporate the understanding we have of ourselves as observers into the understanding we have of others as observed must fail. That attempt took the form of a conception of human being as a compound of body and mind, and of the mind as the container of representations that are the proximate objects of its acts. Implicit in this was the claim that, within the picture based on the observation of others, the first-personal element in perception – the understanding that the observer has of himself as an observer – could be accommodated as the inner landscape of the mind. But since the splitting of the observed human being into body and mind must also apply to the observer qua observer of others, it follows that the observation of others must itself be mediated by representations. This consequence must be unwelcome, if only because it means that the proximate object of the act of the mind that is involved in the observation of other human beings must be something – a representation – that forms part of the contents of that mind. This makes the status of the human being who is supposedly being observed doubly problematic, since it means that not only the mind but also the body of that person has turned out to be a matter of a constructive inference by which one human being postulates the existence of another. In these circumstances, neither the plurality of the parties to the observational transaction nor the symmetry of their relationship to one another can be taken for granted; and everything in effect tumbles back into the first-personal case that, in this radically modified version, becomes the new locus from which the issues that make up the philosophy of mind now have to be dealt with.

Such, then, is the paradoxical result of the attempt to favor what I have been calling the first picture – that of the observation of others – over the second – that of the self. It effects the subordination of the favored picture to the one that was to be subordinated to it. This result must call into question the whole idea of treating mental phenomena as being internal to human beings in any of the senses that have been explored. At the same time, however, there needs to be some explanation of how so implausible a view could become so deeply embedded in our ways of describing and thinking about ourselves that it seems almost self-evidently true. A clue to a solution of this puzzle may lie in some remarks of Heidegger's about the concept of a mental substance or, as he ironically puts it, a "spiritual thing."[10] The concept of mental substance is clearly modeled on the more familiar notion of a material substance or thing. One could even say that it is the latter turned inside out – or, better still, outside in – in the sense that the representations a mental substance contains within itself are what correspond to the properties of a perceptual object that present themselves to an external view. Again, the inner act of the mind that unites these representations takes the place of the substratum in which properties are supposed to inhere, and in both cases there is a perduring identity over time.

What a mental substance does not have, of course, is location in space; but Heidegger's suggestion seems to be that the "thing" model remains uniquely attractive in spite of this difference. Applied to the two pictures discussed in this chapter, this leads to the hypothesis that when it becomes evident that the observation of other human beings will never reveal a thought or a perception in the way it does a bone or a tissue, the only provision we know how to make for what will not fit into the body thing is to postulate the existence of a mind thing – another substance that is different from the familiar kind simply by virtue of not being in space and thereby accessible to the senses, as material substances are. This difference we then express through a violently extended metaphor of interiority that has also to be applied retroactively to the observing self as well as the observed other.

This whole exercise is an attempt to reconcile a primary implicit understanding that we have of ourselves as – among other things – observers and the quite different understanding, itself based on observation, that we have of other human beings. The final result of this attempt, however, is a distortion of the former by the application to it of a mode of conceptualization we have devised for the latter. But in that case, the moral of the tale is clearly that instead of pursuing further the largely chimerical problem of "other minds," we should return to the original contrast from which this account set out, and determine whether the discrepancies it involves do not lend themselves to some better resolution than the one that leads to the distinction between mind and body and to the theory of representation

10. Martin Heidegger, *Being and Time*, translated by J. Macquarrie and E. Robinson (New York: Harper and Row, 1962), p. 83. Heidegger's discussion of the concept of a mental substance can be found in *The Basic Problems of Phenomenology*, translated by Albert Hofstadter (Bloomington: Indiana University Press, 1982), p. 126.

previously outlined. More specifically, it seems that more attention needs to be given to the second picture and to the understanding it expresses of the first-personal case. It is this understanding that is distorted and well nigh lost through the kind of resolution that turns on the mind–body distinction. But clearly this would not have happened unless the symmetry of self and other had not somehow been misconstrued to begin with. In other words, the kind of "subjectivity" that was first imputed to the other and then transferred back to the self could hardly have had that distorting effect unless it had been in some way significantly different from what actually obtains in the first-personal case.

The question is thus whether the implicit understanding we have of ourselves as percipient beings can be more successfully developed than it has been within representational dualism. The real test of any alternative account that may be proposed is its ability to satisfy the conditions set by the facts of plurality and symmetry. These are, in effect, the twin constraints under which such an account must be constructed, and a word about each is therefore in order. The plurality condition defines the locus of an inquiry into these matters as falling within a public world that is shared by two or more human beings who function in the manner that the word "mental" is supposed to designate. The symmetry of the relation between these human beings means that each of them is there for the other – that is, each is able to recognize the other as human like itself and thus as a locus of mental activity, just as it is itself. Plurality was an explicit feature of the original contrast between observing and being observed. So, in a way, was symmetry; but a coherent conception of symmetry could not be achieved as long as the mental was supposed to be internal to the human being in question. The task is thus to see what can be achieved in the way of a theory of human being once we stop thinking in terms of minds and all their associated apparatus of inwardness.

In making the first-person case the point of departure for this inquiry, I may seem to be falling into the kind of subjectivism that has been the trademark of so much modern philosophy. This is far from being the case, and the difference is made by these two associated conditions – plurality and symmetry. Under these conditions, there can be no question of extracting the first person from the world it shares with other, similar beings. It is true that the first person has been in great favor among philosophers to whom neither plurality nor symmetry had any prima facie satisfactory credentials and who have had to summon all the resources of the philosophy of mind to determine whether they had any validity at all. But unless one accepts the epistemological premise of such arguments – that is, the picture of a mind alone with its array of representations – there really is no reason to asssume a skeptical posture vis-à-vis the plurality of human beings and the symmetry of their relations to one another. This is what the dis-

cussion of the argument from error earlier in this chapter was designed to
show.

At the same time as these points are made about the first-personal case,
it is important to understand that it remains the foundation on which all
constructive theory in this area of philosophy must rest. The reason is simply that this is an area of thought in which we are talking about ourselves.
The thought in which we engage, together with all the associated functions
of perception and imagination on which it draws, are themselves what that
thought is attempting to conceive. That would not be possible unless we
already had – each of us – a certain understanding of ourselves. Just as the
plurality of the instances of what we are inquiring into and the symmetry
of their relations to one another cannot sensibly be called into question,
so it is impossible to proceed on the assumption that we can remain utterly
oblivious to ourselves and to the character of our being as both observing
and observed. In other words, each human being is there for itself, as others
are for it and it is for others; and this fact constitutes a *donnée* that is prior
to and independent of any theory of mind or of human being. It is just this
prior, mostly inarticulate understanding that is to be brought to the level
of express conceptual formulation to the degree to which that is possible.

Such a role for a prior reflexive understanding that we have of ourselves
is not generally accepted by philosophers at the present time. From their
point of view, there is nothing special about a reflexive context of application for their theories that makes it different from others, and typically
it is not even singled out as such for special attention. Ostensibly, this procedure exemplifies a laudable avoidance of egocentricity and of the obses-
sion with self that is often imputed to modern Western philosophy. Unfortunately, if carried to its logical extreme, this procedure would entail that
there will be nothing to which the theorist, who is after all the same person
as the human being with whom his theory deals, must somehow remain
faithful, not even his own status as an observer of other like beings. The
result can only be that the first-personal case, which is really that of each
one of us, is assimilated in advance, not, as it is usually thought, to the same
status as that of all the others – for there would be nothing wrong with that
– but to that of a very peculiar third person who cannot also be a first
person. Such a being would in fact be a fragment broken out of the observing–observed circle – the observed without the observing and itself de-
prived of the power to observe.

Since the inspiration for this avoidance of the first person is supposed
to come from the practices of the natural sciences, a word may be in order
here about the status that natural science accords to the beings who carry
out their inquiries in accordance with the requirements I have been describing. These "beings" are, of course, simply we ourselves wearing our
scientist hats; and in the life sciences and elsewhere, they – we – become

the objects of inquiry as well as its subjects. This dual role generates a rather intricate dialectic. On the one hand, the absolute priority that is given to the ideal of objectivity makes it necessary that every scientific observation be susceptible of being repeated by the members of an open community of inquirers. In practice, this means that any observation of fact that is by its nature confined to a single individual is thereby disqualified for scientific purposes. This applies with special force to those that come under the heading of "introspection." This is supposed to be a function of the mind in which it turns away from the common world of objects and attends instead to itself as a private inner domain. Accordingly, each of us must school himself to offer for scientific purposes only such observations of himself as could in principle be equally well made by someone else. But it is clear that the same rule would have to apply to that someone else as well, and so on indefinitely.

The upshot of all this is that we are all to emulate those public personalities who have the disquieting habit of referring to themselves in the third person. It is as though observation of self could be legitimate only if I either go about it as though I were someone else or in fact hand off the responsibility for making such observations to someone else, and then that person to yet another, and so on. It should be noted, moreover, that in this compulsory third-person mode of discourse, the person who is a third person cannot also be interchangeably a first person, as is the case in our ordinary understanding of these matters. Instead, the first person, and with it the whole reflexive relation to self, is elaborately detoured around in a most peculiar way – peculiar, above all, because nothing testifies quite as eloquently to its reality as these rituals of avoidance. As a result, although scientific inquiry undeniably has a subject, every attempt that is made to close with it so as to define its character more perspicuously is referred to the new address from which it is doing business. There is something about this systematic elusiveness of the subject of natural science – its lack of any identifiable domicile in its own world of objects – that makes one wonder whether it is not implicitly claiming for itself what amounts to a transcendental status. A recent book dealing with these themes bears the title *The View from Nowhere*, and I cannot help feeling that that offers at least some confirmation for the suspicion I have just voiced.[11]

Even so, the self-understanding that is thus denied a role in such proceedings does not simply disappear. Indeed, the effect of its being treated in this way is just the reverse of the one intended. It is as though the self that is routinely subsumed under the theory were not the self that is the sponsor of the theory itself and as though the latter, by virtue of never being mentioned, were being assigned a unique and privileged position of

11. Thomas Nagel, *The View from Nowhere* (New York: Oxford University Press, 1986).

some kind. The result is that although this position is patently modeled on the understanding that an individual human being has of himself as, for example, an observer of other human beings, it is treated as though it were locationless and thus not identical with the situation of any such individual. The significance of this tacit distinction between an empirical self that is subject to the requirements of the theory and a transcendental self that is the author of the theory lies in the fact that it blocks the full application of the distinction between mind and body, as well as of the associated theory of representations to the being that is in fact its author and its source. To put the same point in a different way, it is as though the theory of a mind–body distinction had been designed as one that applies to the entities – the human beings – in the object domain of the human being who deploys that theory, rather than as one that treats the status of the latter as strictly equivalent to that of all other human beings and most relevantly of those that it observes. At any rate, any reflexive application of the theory that does occur is not allowed to call into question the assumptions on which the theory itself rests and, most important, the accessibility to observation of the other human beings to whom the psychological conception of mental states is to apply.

In the chapters that follow, these features – plurality, symmetry, and the reflexive character just described – are treated as a preanalytic ordering of the field that this inquiry seeks to understand. It is, accordingly, important to note that all three conditions postulate human beings as the primary entities that constitute that field. This is also what the account I present is intended to do, and its goal is the working out, in these terms, of a unitary concept of human being. It is, of course, imaginable that someone might reject one or another of these conditions and produce a theory of mind that is, for example, solipsistic if the plurality condition is the one rejected. Even so, there would always remain the issue of whether the author of such a theory really does or can reject the condition in question. Taken together, these conditions are intended to express something like a set of distinctions and assumptions that all of us implicitly accept in the ordinary course of things and that set a baseline for any philosophical inquiry that seeks to achieve a deeper understanding of these matters. If a theory were to be produced that rejected some or all of these conditions, it is unlikely that it could provide an answer to any questions we have about ourselves because those questions presuppose the validity of these conditions.

All three conditions are clearly involved in the contrast with which this chapter began between a picture based on my (anyone's) observation of other human beings and my (anyone's) understanding of myself (himself) as engaged in such observation. The theory of mind that was examined in this chapter is a theory that accepts these conditions at least in the sense of building on the distinctions they involve and of trying to find a place for all of them within the framework of mind–body dualism. That effort has been shown to be unsuccessful; and in this new terminology, the reason for that failure can be expressed by saying that this theory does not satisfy the symmetry condition and, through a lack of attention to the reflexivity condition, misses this fact about itself. The upshot of this failure is that we have to provide a new account that will avoid the failures of its predecessor and satisfy these three conditions. As things stand, then, plurality, symmetry, and a reflexive understanding of self as both observing and observed are essential criteria that must be satisfied by the concept of human being. What we do not have is that concept itself, and in succeeding chapters I undertake to provide that.

2

PERCEPTION AS PRESENCE

I

In the preceding chapter, an argument was advanced against a representational theory of perception. That argument called into question the contrast such a theory makes between an object of perception as the origin of a causal process outside the organism and that object as the content of an episode in our mental lives. It thus suggests that the commonsense view of perception – the view that has to be revised when the representational theory is espoused – may have been right after all in its claim that it is objects in the world that we see and touch and not, as the representational theory would have it, their mental proxies. Of course, what has been said on this point thus far falls well short of a satisfactory statement and defense of a nonrepresentational theory of perception. Accordingly, an attempt will be made in this chapter to sketch in the main lines of such a theory.

In proceeding in this way, I am following a strategy that is itself dictated by a surmise about the fundamental importance of perception as the primordial form of presence for any constructive philosophy of mind or, as I should now say, any theory of human being.[1] This view of perception does not appear to have been shared by many philosophers in recent years, and the prevalent assumption that the primary concern of philosophy is with language has encouraged the view that perception is a topic that belongs principally to psychology. But if that view is bound up, as I have tried to

---

1. It seems to me that only Maurice Merleau-Ponty has unambiguously given perception the place it deserves in an account of human being. See his *The Primacy of Perception*, edited by James Edie (Evanston, Ill.: Northwestern University Press, 1968).

show it is, with the conception of mental phenomena as occurring *in* human beings in the sense analyzed in the preceding chapter, then the outcome of those analyses must make any such assumption appear problematic. More specifically, it has been shown that the picture of mental phenomena as contained within human beings, whether in an ill-defined physical sense or in the sophisticated dualistic sense, cannot be applied either to the case of other human beings for which, I have argued, it was originally designed or to the first-personal case to which it is transferred without calling into question one or more of the three criteria of adequacy I have been using. We are, therefore, left with the unreduced fact that obtains in the first-personal case – the fact of the presence to us in perception of objects that are not in any definable sense internal to either our bodies or our minds but that at the same time are not "external" in the peculiar sense introduced by the representational theory. What this suggests is that perception generally has to be understood in terms of the presence to us of the different kinds of objects and events that we see and hear and touch.

This conclusion will hardly seem startling or unreasonable to common sense, but it is significant nevertheless because it reverses the assumptions on which the philosophical treatment of perception has traditionally been based. Instead of making the description of our own perceptual states independent, at least in principle, of these objects and events, this new conception would tie these states to them. It would do so in such a way that perception would no longer be understood as a relation – whether causal or inferential or both – between something in me and something that may or may not exist outside me. Instead, it would be the presence to me of the very entities that I am said to see and hear, and since they are certainly not inside me, their presence to me cannot be understood as an internal state of mine. But because the association of the mental with the inner is so firmly established, it is extremely difficult even to entertain a conception that breaks as sharply with it as does that of perception as presence. It has already been pointed out that the concept of mind itself can hardly survive this transition in any of its traditional versions and will have to be replaced by new idioms of thought. In any case, it is clear that the character of this presence is of fundamental importance for a philosophical account of perception and of the entities that are involved in it. There is a pressing need to define a status for it, and if none is available in our table of categories, a constructive philosophical interpretation of it will have to be attempted.

II

In moving away from representationalism toward a theory of presence, it will be helpful to begin by examining another very general approach to issues in the philosophy of mind that at least appears to move in the same direction. This approach is best known for the use it makes of the concept of intentionality – intentionality understood as the feature of mental states that directs them to objects. A conception of mental states that makes reference to objects their central and constitutive feature certainly sounds quite different from that of a self-contained mental content on which the representational theory of mind is based. Nevertheless, it is by no means clear that a construal of mental states as intentional acts breaks cleanly enough with the representational theory to be of much use in the present context. Historically, there has been a link between the two theories that derives from the fact that intentional acts have been supposed to be mental acts and have, accordingly, been understood as something that the mind does. What is more, the objects of these acts were originally conceived in a way that clearly identified them with intramental representations; and even when a distinction was made between the content of these acts and their extramental objects, the status of the latter remained problematic in various ways. Because the concept of intentionality thus emerged within a philosophical context that was set by the representational theory and by the dualistic concept of mind, there is a real question of whether an intentional theory of perception can make a place for a concept of perception as presence. Even now, when the discussion of intentionality has taken on a predominantly linguistic cast and the intentional act is either taken to be itself a linguistic act or is understood in terms of a linguistic model, some of the same tendencies that marked the older theories of intentionality have a curious way of turning up again. In these circumstances, it seems desirable to get a little clearer about the whole conception of perception as an act that is directed to an object so as to determine whether this act–object picture can serve the purposes of an account of perceptual presence.

When representative ideas or sense data are thought to mediate the relationship in which the mind stands to the "external" world, there is always a residual question as to how one should characterize the mind in which these representations are contained. In other words, what other attributes or functions, in addition to the states produced in it by the action of external causes, does the mind possess as its own intrinsic nature? If no answer could be given to this question, the mind itself would have to be regarded as simply the aggregate of the states that are produced in it, and this would subvert the container/contents picture of the mind and its states by identifying the one with the other. One way in which this can be avoided is by postulating a distinction between the contents of the mind that are produced in it by something acting upon it from outside and the mind's own awareness of these contents. The latter notion is that of consciousness as it was originally understood – that is, as the mind's reflexive relation to its own inner states.[2] It has usually been described as an act of the mind on the strength of a contrast with the passivity implied in the notion of receiving a sense datum through some sort of external action. Although the "activity" that was thus attributed to the mind was itself just as notional as the passivity with which it was contrasted, it came to be understood as an act of the mind that supervenes on the "impressions" it receives, and one of which we are immediately aware. It was conceived as being, in the first instance, an awareness of the sense contents of the mind, but it also had the character of an act of attention that might shift from one such content to another; and this could be taken as confirming the suggestion of voluntary control implicit in the concept of an act. On the basis of such considerations as these, a distinction between mental contents and consciousness as an act of the mind came to be generally accepted.[3] Very roughly, this act has the character of a viewing rather than of something viewed; and ordinary verbs that denote seeing were accordingly adapted, with fateful consequences, to the task of describing what was supposed to be taking place within the mind.

When consciousness is understood in this way, it is held to differ from the internal states of the mind not only because it is an act rather than a state but also because it is somehow diaphanous – a kind of *lumen naturale* that makes the interior of the mind perfectly transparent to itself. Another metaphor – this time, that of aiming at or being directed to something – has shaped the characterization of this supervening act of the mind as "intentional"; and these two metaphors have often come together in descriptions of consciousness in terms of "rays" that play on their objects. Just how those objects themselves are to be conceived has, however, been a vexed question. In the first modern theory of intentionality as the defining feature of the mental – that of Franz Brentano – no clear distinction was made between intentional objects and the contents of the mind itself, and so the former took on the same "immanent" or intramental character as the latter. Brentano, accordingly, spoke of the "intentional inexistence" of the objects of such acts; and the "physical object," as contrasted with the "physical phenomenon, " had no part to play in his account of intentionality other than that of being a presupposition of the dualistic theory of mind that he unquestioningly accepted.[4]

2. For a more detailed discussion of the concept of consciousness, see my *Heidegger and the Philosophy of Mind* (New Haven, Conn.: Yale University Press, 1989), pp. 14–15 and 21–7.
3. It is relevant here to note that Kant defines consciousness *(Bewusstsein)* as *die Vorstellung dass eine andere Vorstellung in mir ist. Vorlesungen Kants Über Logik* in E. Cassirer, ed., *Immanuel Kants Werke* (Berlin: Bruno Cassirer, 1923), vol. VIII, p. 350. Locke's use of the concept of "consciousness" in Chapter 27, "Identity and Diversity," in Book II of *An Essay Concerning Human Understanding* (Oxford: Clarendon Press, 1894) is also instructive in the contrast it makes between the soul itself and consciousness as its active functioning.
4. This aspect of Brentano's account of intentionality does not always receive the attention it

Later, a distinction between intramental contents and intentional objects was introduced; and in the most substantial modern account of intentionality – that of Edmund Husserl – the latter were declared to be meanings or noemata of which the intentional or "noetic" act was the vehicle.[5] A theory of this kind seems to have been designed to account for the conceptual upgrading of mental contents (or "hyletic data," as Husserl calls them) to the status of properties of perduring objects – what Husserl calls "constitution." Since the noema appears to be a species of representation, however, the object it constitutes can only be an *intentional* object, and it is intentional in a privative or deficient sense of that term. What this means is that because an intentional object is tied to the mental act in which it is posited, there is always a further and independent question of whether the object as such exists or not. This might seem to threaten serious difficulties for any theory of intentionality, since if, *ex hypothesi,* all the objects with which we have any kind of commerce are objects of some mental act, they will all turn out to be intentional objects in this deficient sense, and we shall be back in the labyrinth of representationalism. Husserl never addresses these difficulties; and his emphatic pronouncements about the idealistic character of his own philosophical position suggest that he may not have seen them as such. For those who do not share these affinities with idealism, however, a gap will always open up between an intentional object understood as a meaning of some kind and an object in some stronger sense, and the relation between these two objects will remain problematic.

This conception of the intentional object in what I have called its privative or deficient mode and the resulting contrast between two kinds of objects – intentional and nonintentional – have set the terms of the treatment of intentionality by linguistic philosophers. Since the latter treat intentionality as a logical property of certain sentences (and thus in effect equate it with intensionality), there is thought to be no difficulty about such a contrast between intentional objects and objects as such. The matter is dealt with by simply treating sentences in which no mental verb like "believe" occurs as though the objects referred to in them were not tied to anyone's believing in the manner just described. If that were the case, then it would indeed follow that the objects referred to in such sentences are not caught up in the toils of intentionality. They would stand free, in reassuring contrast with those that are, and the threat posed by the possibility that all objects might turn out to be intentional objects would disappear. On the other hand, if such matters of explicit linguistic form are

should, but it is clearly set forth in Linda McAllister, "Chisholm and Brentano on Intentionality," in Linda McAllister, ed., *The Philosophy of Brentano* (London: Duckworth, 1976), pp. 151–9.
5. These distinctions are developed in Husserl's *Ideas: General Introduction to Pure Phenomenology,* translated by W. R. Boyce Gibson (London: Collier-Macmillan, 1962), Chapter 9.

less important than what we all assume to be the underlying relationship between sentences and human beings, this purely logical contrast will seem less impressive.

On the philosophical point at issue, moreover, this contrast is inconclusive unless it can be shown how it is possible for statements to be made (and not just sentences written) outside of any context of belief. In this connection, it is of interest to note that when we express our own beliefs, we typically do so in sentences that are nonintentional in the sense just specified, whereas the beliefs of others are reported in sentences that are intentional because verbs like "believe" occur in them. It is conceivable that because we are familiar with shifting from the one mode to the other in this way, we assume that it is always possible to avoid dealing in intentional objects, and even that our own beliefs are implicitly privileged in this regard as long as we do not cast them in the self-referring form ("I believe that . . ."). But just as a decision by a speaker to use "know" rather than "believe" in expressing his beliefs cannot settle the question of whether what he believes to be the case really is, so the alternative of omitting the mental verb from a statement of belief can not be expected to determine the status – intentional or otherwise – of the objects of that belief.

If we return now to the case of perception, it is evident that an account of it given in terms of intentional acts makes the perception of an object a pairing of representations. One of these would be sensuous – a sense datum – and the other would be a meaning or *Sinn* – something like a concept of the object that is supposedly being perceived. Even if it were not contested that we understand what it would be like for such a meaning to "ensoul" (*beseelen*) a sense datum, as Husserl puts it, these conjoined representations would still have to refer beyond themselves to something that is itself not a representation but an object or thing. But if, again in Husserl's language, perceptual intentions turn out to be "signitive" or meaning-bearing intentions in the sense that has just been explained, it is clear that they could never be "fulfilled" in anything like a state of perceptual presence since every perceptual intention by which this could be effected would be just as signitive in character as the one it was to fulfill.[6] There is, in other words, no way in which the act character of these intentional acts could enable them to break through the circle of representations in terms of which their function has been defined.

In light of its uselessness for the purpose it was apparently designed to serve, the whole concept of an intentional act stands in need of reappraisal. One point worthy of note is that although the concept of such an act was

6. I owe this point to Hubert Dreyfus, who developed it first in his doctoral dissertation on Husserl. The relevant portion of that dissertation has been published as "The Perceptual Noema" in *Husserl, Intentionality and Cognitive Science* (Cambridge, Mass.: MIT Press, 1982); see pp. 107–8.

supposed to apply to all the modalities of mental functioning, such acts have been conceived primarily in terms of the model of vision and the metaphors it suggests. Among the latter, those that involve light have been especially prominent. Light is so intimately associated with vision that it has been common to think of vision itself as being like light in that it brings the things we see into a state of visibility. A common prescientific way of thinking about vision in fact represents it as issuing from the eye like a ray of light and as illuminating the objects on which it plays.[7] And although the physiology of vision discovers no such emanations, the control we exercise over the direction of our regard or look may confer a certain plausibility on this idea. On closer examination, however, examples like these prove to be less than helpful. It is true that we can close our eyes and thus not see something we would otherwise have seen, and also that we can shift our attention from one object to another. These are, in a perfectly authentic sense, acts of ours; but the fact that in one way or another they modify or terminate our visual perception does not in any way demonstrate that seeing itself is properly described as a mental act or that it is anything like a ray of awareness that comes from my side of the perceptual situation and lights up the objects that stand over against me. The reason is simply that turning one's gaze in another direction or closing one's eyes are acts of human beings, not minds. Moreover, even if one sets aside everything that involves the body as plainly as these do, it is by no means clear that there are any other acts involved in perception.

It thus begins to look as though any attempt to find an act, intentional or otherwise, with which the essential nature of the mind could be identified is a blind alley. It even seems likely that the idea of such a self-transcending act is itself a variation on the picture in which perception is construed as the mind's reception of something that functions as a proxy for the external object. When one thinks in terms of that picture and it turns out to generate the grave difficulties that have been described, a natural inference might be that since the mind does not receive its object in this sense, it must somehow go forth to meet it; and this is certainly one source of the idea of perception as an intentional act. But to reason in this way would be to go on postulating the old inside–outside contrast, in which anything that involves a relationship to something outside the body must be understood either as something coming into the mind or as something coming out of it to reach the other term of the relation. What is different is simply that now the "movement" is in the reverse direction. But if this is the way the idea of an intentional act is generated, it is no more surprising that we cannot detect this act than it is that the notion of the mind as the

---

7. See, for example, the discussion of the way children conceive the "looks" people direct to objects in Jean Piaget, *La représentation du monde chez l'enfant* (Paris: Presses Universitaires de France, 1947), p. 20.

inner locus of representations proves to be similarly lacking in empirical content.

One could, of course, argue, as Kant does, that one cannot find as an object what must be presupposed as a condition of experiencing objects generally, and that this is what explains the negative result of a search like Hume's. But even if this is so, a question remains as to *what* must be so presupposed and whether it has to be a mental act. Why, for example, should the undoubted element of activity in perception not simply be attributed to human beings rather than to minds? On that view, instead of trying to isolate a mental act as one element within the putative makeup of the mind as a whole, it might be more promising to think of any act that may be involved here not as bringing about perceptual presence as such but as itself conditioned by (and responsive to) the fact of such presence. There would be no use looking for any intentional act or "experience" in vision (or presumably in any of the other senses), and the kind of directedness on an object in which intentionality is supposed to consist would belong not to any part of us, whether mental or physical, that it would be possible to search for and identify separately but to a whole human being.

This line of thought is reinforced by the fact that the notion itself of a mental act is modeled on the ordinary commonsense notion of a view or look, that is, of the kind of look that we direct to some object in our vicinity. It is also pertinent here that both of these terms, "look" and "view," have been extended to apply to the appearance – the aspect – of some such object when it is viewed at a given moment and from a certain angle. It is this sort of look or view that philosophers who want to introduce the concept of the sense datum as a mental content have declared to be what one sees directly and immediately; and it is also supposed to be what certainly exists at that moment, whether or not the object of which it was, in the first instance, an "aspect" turns out to exist. The paradoxical element in all this is the fact that it is just these looks of things that, in their new character as mental contents, become the objects of yet another look or view. After all, they are themselves no more than hypostatized aspects of some perceived object or that object as reduced to the way it presents itself to a particular momentary view. It is as though the momentary aspect of some familiar object – its *facies* or *eidos* – had been magically peeled off it and were being treated as an entity in its own right.

A notable peculiarity of such entities that has often been remarked is that they do not have backsides or, for that matter, any other side than the one they present to the view directed at them. Because they cannot, in this strangely mutilated state, be viewed from more than one perspective, as ordinary objects can, they cannot *be* otherwise than as they appear to just that one view. It is these distinctly exotic entities, compounded as they are of elements abstracted from the ordinary concept of a perceptual object and the ordinary concept of the look we direct at it, that are to be the initial objects of an act of the mind and thereby compensated for the loss of their former dignity as full-blown objects. There is a strong element of redundancy in this account of the way this intra-mental apparatus reproduces the substance of what common sense had always affirmed until it was superseded by a representationalist theory of mind. In our ordinary way of thinking, things are viewed – that is, perceived – by human beings; but when aspects have been conceptually detached from their objects and become representations, they must appear to the mind in which they are contained as the objects of what Descartes called the "eye of the mind" and of its *inspectio sui* or consciousness. That same mind must then do its best to reach beyond this gratuitously diminished remnant of the world of natural perception. Since the best it can hope for in the circumstances is an intentional object – that is, another representation – it seems that the whole exercise has been in vain.

III

The idea of perception as an intentional act has now been examined, and it has been found to be heavily compromised by the very picture of perception with which it ostensibly breaks. More generally, it looks as though one should be cautious about espousing the whole act-object picture of perception. This is not easy to do because so much of the language in which we talk about perception seems to conform to that picture. We say such things as "I see the house" and "I hear the bell," and in doing so we at least seem to be reporting acts of ours that are directed to these objects. These are, moreover, well-established idioms of thought and discourse, and there can hardly be any question of simply eliminating them altogether. Nevertheless, until it is clearer how they can be understood as acts of human beings (along the lines suggested in the preceding section) and not of minds or of consciousnesses, there is a strong case to be made for exploring whatever alternatives there may be to an act-object approach to perception. Such alternatives would not treat perceptual presence itself as a mental act or as effected by such an act, although it might prove to be connected with acts of human beings in various ways that have yet to be determined.

The underlying assumption of the act-object model is that perception is self-conscious and, as it were, self-descriptive in the sense that the datum for the philosophical analysis of perception must always be something like the fact that is expressed by saying "I see x."[8] By contrast, the conception of

---

8. This is what Merleau-Ponty calls the *pensée de percevoir*, which improperly preempts the place of perception itself. See his discussion in *Phenomenology of Perception*, pp. 38 and 375. It is unfortunate that the translation of this phrase into English as "thought about perceiving"

presence that I propose to introduce in this chapter reverses this procedure and, instead of postulating an act that somehow reaches out to an object, begins with the perceptual object itself and draws attention to the ways in which that object shows itself and shows itself *to* someone.[9] This way of putting things may seen strange; but I think it is possible to give a clear meaning to these expressions and thereby, at least in a preliminary way, to the notion of presence itself. The great difficulty about presence is that our familiarity with it is so pervasive and profound that we allow it to remain implicit (and thus largely invisible) in whatever account we give of perception. In this section, I draw attention to a number of features of perceptual situations that in one way or another throw this patent yet elusive fact of presence into sharper relief and enable us to begin forming a concept of it.

One way of initiating this discussion, and of preparing a challenge to the act-object model as well, would be to raise the question of whether what is perceived is always an object of some kind and whether states of affairs might not be more plausibly regarded as what is perceived. This line of argument will be deferred until the next section, in which states of affairs and their role in perception will be examined. It will be argued there that states of affairs are not just objects of a special kind to which perceptual acts can be directed, and that they in fact break out of the act-object framework in a radical way that is centrally important to an understanding of presence. In this section, however, I go along with the common view that objects are, in some privileged sense, what is perceived. What I want to show is that even under this assumption, the fact of presence – the presence of objects in perception – is evident in a number of different ways that are independent of their becoming the objects of a supervening mental act of some kind. In other words, the hypothesis I want to develop is that the things we perceive wear their character as perceptual objects on their faces, so to speak, and that the ways in which they do so offer us our best clues to the nature of presence itself.

One other feature of the approach I am adopting needs to be noted at least briefly here at the outset. In substituting a concept of presence for the act-object model of perception, I am choosing to begin with the object and with the ways in which it shows itself to someone.[10] In order to allow

distorts Merleau-Ponty's meaning. A better rendering would be "the thought that one is perceiving." This would make clear that the "thought" is not simply "about" perception in some vague, undefined way and that, instead, the thought "I am perceiving" has pre-empted the place of the perception as such.

9. This is the notion that Heidegger believes to be expressed by the Greek verb *phainesthai*. The root meaning of the family of words based on the stem *pha-* is that of "showing" in the sense of bringing to light; and *phainesthai* is in the middle voice, which gives this showing the reflexive character that is central to Heidegger's use of this word.

10. *Being and Time,* translated by J. Macquarrie and E. Robinson (New York: Harper and Row, 1962), pp. 91–5. This point of departure – what Heidegger calls "beginning with the world" – is fundamental to his whole approach, but it will always be misunderstood as

the style of analysis that gets under way from this starting point to show what it can achieve without improper reliance on other models, it will be necessary to avoid making use of any prior conceptions of the "subject" to which objects thus show themselves. These are all too readily available and offer themselves helpfully at every turn in the argument. That help must be rejected, however, and to the extent possible, the eventual picture of the subject that is to emerge from this account must be built up of materials that become available through an analysis of the modes of presence of the things in the world that we perceive and, as successive chapters will show, also remember and imagine and otherwise think about. The only prior assumption about the subject of presence that will be made for these purposes is the one introduced in the last chapter under the three headings of plurality, symmetry, and reflexivity. By proceeding in this way, it is hoped, an understanding of the ek-sistence of human beings can be achieved that will replace established conceptions of subjectivity and will, at the same time, do justice to the radical interdependence of ek-sistence and presence.

With that said, it is time to turn to the features of perception referred to previously as clues to presence. To proceed in this way is not to deny that we have a global understanding of presence that is reflected, for example, as Heidegger suggests, in the contrast we make between the relation between a chair and the wall it is in contact with, and the relation between the wall or the chair and a human being who touches one or the other. We intuitively understand that the one kind of touching is quite different from the other; and the difference consists in the fact that in the one case, as Heidegger puts it, the wall does not "encounter" (*begegnen*) the chair (or the other way around), but in the latter is there *for* the person who touches it.[11] To understand, however implicitly, this distinction is thus to understand the presence of one entity to another, as well as the difference between the kind of entity to which something can be present and the kind to which nothing can be present. Nevertheless, this understanding is overlaid by so many other ways of conceiving mental fact that it is unlikely to be available for philosophical purposes unless it can be unpacked into more specific indices of presence. That is the task of this section; and if our global understanding of presence discerns it as something that holds between certain entities and not between certain others, attention will now be drawn to the variety of forms of presence and to the intermittent character of

long as his concept of "world" as a milieu of presence is not accurately distinguished from the usual concept of a totality of entities. It is also important to remember that there is a wrong way of beginning with the world to which we are all prone. This is what Merleau-Ponty calls "le préjuge du monde." Because the *zuhanden* character of the world is passed over, things in the world – the *vorhanden* – become the only model that a human being can use for understanding himself, and so his mode of being is conceived as that of a substance and not as that of an ek-sistent.

11. *Being and Time*, p. 81.

each of these within the life of an entity like ourselves to which other entities can be present.

The first and most obvious index of presence is simply the fact that perception itself involves different sense modalities. When sensations or sense data are held to mediate the relationship between the perceiver and the object that is being perceived, there is an easy way to deal with the fact that we have five senses and not just the one – vision – in terms of which perception is typically interpreted. It is simply laid down that there are many qualitatively different kinds of sensations and that the object itself is implicated in these differences only in the sense of having the causal power to act on the sensibility of the perceiver in a corresponding variety of ways. At the same time (and with dubious consistency) the object that has these powers is conceived in terms of its physical properties, and this is to say as a physical object that has been stripped of many of the properties – notably color – that it appears to have. If the concept of sensation is dropped, however, the different sense modalities can no longer be dealt with in this way. The object itself cannot be so readily separated from the specific sense modality in which it is encountered; it has to be dealt with, instead, in its character as a visual or a tactile or an auditory object.

But just what is it that we have in mind when we speak of a visual or a tactile object? Are tactility and "visuality" themselves properties of the objects we perceive? The standard answer to this question is that a visual object is something that one sees and a tactile object is something that one touches; in this way, the differentiation of visual from tactile is transferred from the object to the several different kinds of acts of perception. In practice, however, this differentiation by act appears to rely principally not on any insight into how an *act* of seeing differs from an *act* of hearing but, rather, on the fact that seeing and hearing depend on the functioning of different parts of the body – different sense organs. But since this functioning is understood in terms of the action of an external object on these same organs and the neural processes that are set off by that action, this really just brings us back to the concept of the object as detached, to the extent possible, from the whole context of perception and as related to it only in a causal manner. There is also, quite plainly, a not so virtuous circle in this approach to the matter since no scientific description of the functioning of our sense organs that does not already incorporate an understanding of the differences between, say, "rough" and "blue" will ever yield anything like that distinction in the form of a distinction between acts. The puzzle, therefore, remains; and it is to understand why and how these adjectives – "visual" and "tactile," among others – apply to the object that is perceived and not just to some putative intermediary in the perceptual transaction.

As an alternative to this not very promising approach, it may be helpful here to bring in Aristotle and his contrast between proper and common sense qualities.[12] The former are the properties of objects that are accessible only to a single sense. Color, for example, must be seen; it cannot be heard. A certain organ of sense is attuned to a particular property of its object, and any given sense modality is thus at once a state of the object and of the perceiver. On this view, the perceived object may be said to address, in some sense, the perceiver through the various sense modalities peculiar to its different properties. There are also sense qualities, such as size, shape, and motion, that are common to more than one sense; but there was no disposition on Aristotle's part to interpret this distinction between proper and common sense qualities as one between qualities that are in the object and those that are really in the subject, as happens in the modern distinction between primary and secondary qualities. In any case, one can say that in such a theory as this, the presence of such objects in one modality of perception or another is not to be understood simply as the state of the perceiver that is produced by the action on it of the object in question. It is rather the way – visual or tactile or whatever – in which the object itself is what it is *for* such a perceiver.

All of this is summed up in Aristotle's famous dictum that "the soul is in some sense all entities." A conception in which the soul or mind is what these entities – *ta onta* – themselves are is clearly very different from one that treats perception as a causal transaction that produces sensations. There are, admittedly, some elements of the latter view in Aristotle to the extent that he speaks of the form of an entity – the properties that make it the kind of entity it is – as being disengaged from the materials of sense and of this form, without the matter of the thing in question, as being *in* the soul. It is admittedly only an essentially metaphysical assumption that guarantees the identity of the form in the soul with the form in the object. Still, the effect of that guarantee, whether it is well founded or not, is to keep a gap from opening up between the presence of a form in the soul and the presence of the entity itself that we normally believe to have that form. To that degree, Aristotle's position maintains a distance from representationalism and from any doctrine that declares the object that issues from the synthesis of the materials of sense that is effected within the mind to have a purely phenomenal status. At the same time, one cannot help wondering what the idea that the form has been separated from its matter can really come to in empirical terms. It sounds a good deal like Locke's insistent reminder that Worcester Cathedral itself cannot be in my mind; and one suspects that it is once again the assumption that what is perceived

---

12. See Book Two of *De Anima* in *The Basic Works of Aristotle,* edited by Richard McKeon (New York: Random House, 1941).

by me must somehow be *in* me that is forcing Aristotle to espouse this peculiar notion.[13]

I have cited Aristotle's account of the different sense modalities as an early approximation to the thesis I want to defend – the thesis, namely, that the differences among sense modalities are so many ways in which the presence of entities is itself differentiated. What this means is that the same entity (and not just the qualitatively variegated products of its action on us) is present to us in different ways – as something seen and as something touched and as something heard. My justification for this proposal is the fact that every attempt to treat these differences as though they were so many decalques – whether distorted or undistorted is another issue – of a set of qualitative differences *in re* must wind up in the bog of representational dualism, as even Aristotle's position is in danger of doing. But if that is the case, then these different sensory modes have to be thought of not as being in us, in the manner of either sensations or forms, but as so many ways in which an object can be present to us. It is worth pointing out that on this view, for example, the old distinction between what is objective and what is subjective in perception – between what is in the object and what is in the perceiver – will have to be revised. Normally, what is subjective comprises not just the perceptual errors and illusions that were discussed in the last chapter, but also the normal variations in the way objects appear to us under conditions in which the objects themselves are assumed not to change. When these variations are treated as subjective, they are in effect declared to be occurring *in* the perceiver in a sense that effectively dissociates them from the object and thereby supposedly ensures its independence and objectivity.

But if, instead, one thinks of these sense modalities as the modes in which such objects themselves are present to a perceiver, then the variations that are so intimately bound up with them take on new significance. In place of the old contrast between the changes going on in the perceiver and the unchanging object, one would have to think of the several sense modalities in a different manner as the ways in which the presence of an object is realized. There will, accordingly, be a much closer relation between what we normally call the properties of an object and the perspectival and other variations through which these pass in the different sense modalities. There must, of course, still be a sense in which the former do not *change* simply because such variations occur; but having such a stable property – being triangular, say – would be understood in terms of its presence through one or more sense modalities to a perceiver rather than as an in-itself to which not even the kind of variation through which such properties pass in the various sense modalities could be attributed. This does not mean

13. *The Works of John Locke* (London: Thomas Tegg, 1823), vol. 4, p. 390.

that a phenomenalistic account of perceptual properties is to be adopted, but rather that the "being" – in a sense of this term that will be explained in the next section – of an object and its properties is to be understood in terms of presence.

Another index of presence has to do with the orientation in which an object is perceived. In its simplest terms, this means that an object must be viewed from one side or another and cannot be viewed from all sides at once. At any given time, therefore, certain parts of it will necessarily be hidden from view while others are visible. Similarly, when one object is visible, others that are behind it along a given line of sight will be wholly or partly blocked from view.[14] What is arguably subjective about this is the fact that what is hidden and what is exposed to view vary from one perceiver to another. Expressed in psychological terms, this is taken to be a difference between the sensations one or another observer receives and the way the gaps in each observer's supply of sensations are filled by inferences that enable us all to live in what is pretty much the same world, in spite of the evident differences in our mediated access to it. Understood in terms of presence, however, these perspectival variations are so many ways in which the perceived object shows itself, and shows itself to one person and not to someone else. One observer and another may also perceive the same object and, in many cases, the same parts of that object; but there will be at least a slight difference between what is included in the visual field of one observer and of the other. These differences in what is exposed to view and what is not are, in effect, indices of presence in its plural, finite, and shifting character. These perspectival variations are also functions of, and coordinate with, the location of the observer to whom the object shows itself. Far from being extramundane or transcendental, that location is a place in the same space as the object itself; and it is the place occupied by the body of the observer, although, as will be shown in Chapter 6, we must be cautious about straightforwardly identifying the latter with the body as it is conceived by the natural sciences. If this body were to move and take up the position formerly occupied by someone else, then what would show itself and not show itself would change, and the object would now present itself to this observer's view in the way that it did to that of his predecessor in that location.

This perspectival variation is so universal and so familiar to all of us that there is little chance of its giving rise to misapprehensions about the objects

14. It is interesting to note that in his much discussed *The Ecological Approach to Visual Perception* (Boston: Houghton Mifflin, 1979), Chapter 5, J. J. Gibson describes facts of this order in a way that acknowledges the identity of the object that has been obscured with the one that was visible a moment before. In general, his firm situation of perception in an environment – an *Umwelt* – has clear affinities with Heidegger's conception of Being in the world.

in question. It is regularly taken for granted and allowed for, and it is understood that it in no way calls into question the identity of the objects that are common to many observers. It hardly deserves to be called "subjective," therefore, if subjectivity is supposed to be a source of error and disagreement that may even in some cases prove intractable. Nevertheless, these unproblematic cases are worthy of note precisely because they involve differences from perceiver to perceiver that do not call into question the identity of the perceptual object. It is also important to note that in the accounts we give of these differences, the identity of the common perceptual object is presupposed; it is not, in other words, as though its constancy had the status of some sort of inferential construction out of sense data or representations or any of the other entities that have so often been assumed to be the primary contents of perceptual experience. It is this object that presents itself to the view of one perceiver somewhat differently from the way it does to the view of another, and it does so in a setting of other objects that also have differential conditions of visibility. But if the character of a given perception is specified by reference to the aspect of the object that it captures or misses, then that object sets the milieu within which perception itself takes place. That could hardly be the case if the status of the object were that of a construction out of perceptual contents and if the perceiver were conceived in a transcendental mode that denied him any location in the same space as the perceptual object.

There is still another feature of our perception of objects that is closely related to the matters of orientation just discussed. When we see something, there are not only other sides of that object that are not visible from the place where we stand; the object also has an "inside" that, unlike the sides that are hidden because of the angle from which we perceive this object, is not open to view at all, no matter where we stand in relation to it. What we in fact see is always in some sense the "outside" or surface of an object, although this is always the outside *of* that object and not something other than the object itself. There is, of course, wide variation in the way these terms apply to different kinds of objects. There are objects like buildings that can be viewed from the outside but also from the inside; there are transparent objects that do not seem to be closed to perception in the way that opaque objects are; and there are objects like the human body that normally cannot be entered in the way a building can but that can nevertheless be viewed from the inside by means of special equipment. Even in a case for which no such procedures are available – that of a stone, for example – we can break open the object and expose the inside to view. In this way, it might seem, the invisibility of the inside could be shown to be just a special case of the unavoidable unavailability to any given point of view of certain of the outsides of an object. In the case of objects like stones, of course, we gain access to the inside only by breaking them open, with the result that instead of one opaque object, we have two or more and, therefore, a new outside and a new inside for each of the latter.

Our inclination may be to conclude that the inside of an object can simply be identified with what we see when it is broken open and made accessible to view, but there is something queer about this. For one thing, it is as though we were saying that the inside of an opaque object is like a collection of snapshots in a closed album, all pressed tightly against one another until the album is opened. This would be a phenomenalistic conception of objects that understands what is hidden in them entirely in terms of a contingent unavailability of the *views* we get of them when they become visible. But if the inside of an object is not just a view or a set of views waiting to be put on display, then the contrast between the inside and the outside is one that cannot be satisfactorily spelled out in phenomenalistic terms, and will have to be conceived in a way that involves some more radical contrast between what is present and what is not. This suggests that the outside that presents itself to our view should be counted as another index of presence. An outside or surface in this sense is a facies – the face of an object or the object as it faces some observer to whom it shows itself, but it shows itself only as something that at the same time does not show itself.[15]

Still another index of presence came to the attention of philosophers mainly as the result of an argument about causality that Kant sets forth in the First Critique. His concern there is to show that the causal relation between events is one of the conditions of the possibility of experience as such, and in the course of his argument he makes a contrast between the experience of walking around a house and that of seeing a ship go downstream. In the first case, the order of the perceptual experiences we have as we move around the house can vary freely. Depending on the direction in which we move, we shall see the back of the house first and then the front or the other way around, but this variation makes no difference that affects the character of the object we perceive. What Kant wants to establish in this way is that the case is quite different with the order of experiences we have in the case of the ship, and he wants to show that the necessity of the order in which these experiences come is constitutive of the concept itself of a natural event. For our purposes, however, the relevant part of his analysis is the part about the house; and what that example shows is that the order in which the perceptions of the house come tells us something not about the house as the object that is being perceived but about the way it becomes present to some observer. Kant called that order "subjective" and the order of perceptual experiences in the case of the ship "objective,"

15. On this point see Martin Heidegger, "Der Ursprung des Kunstwerkes," in *Holzwege* (Frankfurt am Main: V. Klostermann, 1980), p. 41.

since the latter must be the same for all observers of the ship's passage, whereas the former can vary freely among those who perceive the house. For my purposes, however, this free variability of the order in which an object is perceived is significant as one of the indices of presence to which I want to draw attention and not as a subjective element that has to be deleted from the domain of objective fact.

There is another respect in which what I have said about this index of presence needs to be contrasted with the wider assumptions that inform Kant's treatment of these matters. Kant's line of thought, it must be remembered, develops out of his representational theory of knowledge and of mind – the very theory that was rejected in the preceding chapter. Using the terms made available by that theory, he attempted to prove that the contingent psychological laws of association cannot be the only forms of order among our mental representations. It may be that in developing this line of argument he was really, as some now believe, undermining the representational theory itself. If so, then there would be no need to contrast the kind of objectivity that, on his view, must characterize phenomenal objects and events with some elusive thing-in-itself. Even so, it can hardly be denied that in many respects Kant's position remains within the orbit of the representational theory.

To cite just one example, the alternative he envisages to the kind of order that is effected by the categories and the forms of sensibility is a "rhapsody of sensations," a chaotic state of mind in which there would be no principles of identity and coherence among sensations and therefore no experience of stable phenomenal objects. There is an unclarity here as to whether Kant thinks this rhapsody of sensations is really an imaginable state of mind even though it violates all the conditions that would make it an "experience" in his sense of that term. To the extent that it is supposed to be that, Kant would be committed to the possibility of a mental state in which one would be aware of sensations as sensations, independent of any linkage to objects. A supposition of this kind is fundamental to the theory of representative ideas, but it is one that I want to avoid in my account of the indices of presence. Accordingly, that account is developed in a manner that, unlike Kant's, makes no use of the concept of sensation or representation. The order that can vary freely, without prejudice to the integrity of the object in question, is the order in which parts of that object come into view and not the order in which sensations follow one another, as is the case in Kant. Even if no distinction could be made between an order like that in which a house is viewed and that of our perceptions of a ship's movement, there is no implication in my account that a disorderly mass of sensations would survive as an imaginable mental state. Thus, the difference between the two accounts is that in the one – Kant's – the subjectivity of the order of appearance of an object is grounded in a more fundamental kind of subjectivity that characterizes sensations as the units of experience of which this sequence is held to be made up. In the other, there are no units of this kind to which our mental state could in principle be reduced; and the distinction between the subjective and the objective is therefore one that is made within our being in the world, and not within a form of mental life that is logically prior to the perception of a world.

IV

It is time now to examine the assumption that what we perceive is, in the first instance, objects of one kind or another. This matter has been extensively discussed among philosophers; and there appears to be a widely shared disposition to think that the perception of objects is indeed fundamental, and that the perception of states of affairs derives from it.[16] This disposition goes with a more general view of the world as an aggregate of objects, facts and states of affairs as creatures of language and therefore not attributable to the world as such or even properly describable as being *in* it. In what follows, an alternative to this general approach will be presented; and I will try to show not only that the assumption about perception that it involves is false, but also that this fact has strongly negative implications for the act-object model of perception as a whole. It is, of course, not part of this undertaking to suggest – absurdly – that objects are not perceived at all; it is only the priority that has been claimed for the perception of objects over that of states of affairs that is in question.

In spite of the popularity of the view that there is such a priority, it has surprisingly little to recommend it. For one thing, if I see a house, I must also see that there is a house somewhere in my field of vision, and surely I can also be said to see that the object I am looking at *is* a house. In neither case is there any reason to think that the state of affairs in the that-clause is somehow derivative from a more fundamental apprehension of the object that abstracts from the fact that there is such an object before me and that it is an object of a certain kind. Again, if on this view it is permitted to say, for example, that I see a red house, then it is evidently being presupposed that I am familiar with what is involved in a house's being red. Since this is the gerundial equivalent of a proposition that says that the house is red, it is hard to see why one should suppose that there is some priority that attaches to the attributive as contrasted with the predicative form of this apprehension. Those who hold this view sometimes point out that we can see something without knowing what it is that we are seeing, and this is certainly so. It does not follow, however, that such cases should be de-

16. See, for example, Frank Jackson, *Perception* (Cambridge: Cambridge University Press, 1977), Chapter 1.

scribed as "nonepistemic seeing" and that, for this reason, their object does not have to be expressed in the form appropriate to a state of affairs.[17] Typically, even if I do not know that what I am seeing is a house, I do identify what I see, at least implicitly, in some way or other – perhaps incorrectly as a mote in my eye or correctly but unhelpfully as the big thing over there. But in that case, what I am claiming to see is, in one way or another, a state of affairs; and so we come back to the point from which we set out. Unless one is prepared to claim that I can see something without having any belief about it at all and without identifying it in any way, seeing something without seeing that something is the case is not possible.

In these examples, the perceptual states of affairs that were cited were expressed in the grammatical form of noun clauses preceded by verbs of perception that ostensibly denote acts ("I see that . . . "). In grammatical terms, therefore, these states of affairs are being treated in much the same way as are the objects of perception in sentences like "I see the house." On the basis of this similarity, it might be argued that even if it is states of affairs that are perceived, this fact does not force us to abandon the act-object model of perception but only to expand our working conception of the object of these acts so as to include states of affairs. Against this view, I shall try to show that far more than a grammatical change is involved when we enlarge our definition of the "object" so as to include states of affairs. Instead, this modified conception of the perceptual object can be shown to issue in a view of perception as presence that renders superfluous the whole notion of it as a mental or intentional act.

It has been noted that the act-object model of perception is bound up with the assumption that perception has to be conceived in the terms in which it figures in perceptual reports of the form "I see x" or "I see that p." There are, certainly, occasions when we are explicitly asked to say what we see or hear, and to such questions we typically reply in this same idiom. When the question is put in this form, however, there is typically an implication that the situation presents some special feature that may mislead the perceiver, and when we answer "I see such and such," we accordingly wait to learn what we may have missed or gotten wrong. In the more normal case in which a question about what we see or have seen is asked, neither the question nor the answer draws attention to the seeing as such, and we simply report what we see or hear without bothering to use any perceptual verbs. At a baseball game, for example, someone who was distracted and missed a play may ask us "What happened?" and in reply we may say something like "He dropped the ball." It would be strange to reply to such a query by saying, "I saw him drop the ball." That is not what (relevantly) happened, and

17. Such a concept of nonepistemic seeing is developed by Fred Dretske in his *Seeing and Knowing* (London: Routledge and Kegan Paul, 1968), Chapter 2.

normally, unless what we say is contested or we expect it to be, no perceptual verbs at all are used in reports of this kind. This is of interest because it suggests that perception may not be, in any primary way, an act addressed to an object in the sense indicated previously. Instead, at least in these examples, it is impersonal in the sense that what is perceived is something in or about the world that can be (and perhaps is best) conveyed without any express indication of the sense modality or even of the person – the "I" – that may be involved. In other words, when one sees something, what is seen can be (and normally is) understood in a way that does not involve any reference to the "who" or the "how" of that perception.

This "anonymous" character of perception stands in marked contrast with the account of it in terms of an act and its object; and the next order of business, accordingly, is to see where a view of perception that builds on this character may lead and what its strengths and weaknesses may be. This way of proceeding will undoubtedly seem incongruous to those who are convinced that only an act of some kind – our perceiving something or our perceiving that something is the case – can confer a specifically perceptual character on either an object or a state of affairs. And yet the assumption that states of affairs can, for these purposes, be treated in the same way as objects passes over the fact that states of affairs or facts are not easily accommodated in the world conceived as an aggregate of objects. The reason for this is clearly that states of affairs have a logical form that simply does not fit into the kind of spatiotemporal slot there is in the world for an object or a thing. This is what has led many philosophers to conclude that states of affairs are artifacts of language and do not belong in the world at all.

There is another way of dealing with the contrast between objects and states of affairs, however, that does not generate the puzzles that go with this rather extreme conclusion. This line of thought takes its cue from the linkage between the form of states of affairs – something's being something – and truth. Anything that has such a form is susceptible of being true or false; and this is to say that simply by virtue of this form, a state of affairs stands in a relation to the possibility of such a determination and, at least putatively, to something or someone that can or could make it. What this suggests is not that states of affairs must be taken out of the world and set down somewhere else – in language, for example – but rather that states of affairs are precisely the form of the world itself in its relation to something that can discriminate between what is and what is not the case. If that is so, then it would follow that, as elements in states of affairs, things in the world do not need some act that supervenes on them if they are to be perceived or thought of. What finds expression in talk of states of affairs is just this – that these objects have, as it were, already broken out of their self-contained mode of being as things and have become present to something in some modality or other of perception or thought. But in that case, the act in the act-object model of perception comes too late, and the further increment it adds to what is implicit in the state of affairs that is the ostensible object of this act is redundant. In other words, such an act is not needed in order to establish a relation between, for example, a potential perceiver and a state of affairs, and it is not needed because such a relation is already implicit in the state of affairs itself. Indeed, if we compare the picture that this way of thinking about the matter suggests with the act-object picture, it would not be that of a mind that is shooting arrows of intentional reference in the direction of something in the world, as in the latter picture, but rather of something in the world that manifests itself to another entity that, just by virtue of that fact, can be said to perceive it.

The linkage that is being proposed between perception and states of affairs would be seriously misunderstood if it were supposed that on this view something's being part of a state of affairs is equivalent to its being perceived. Obviously, there are far more states of affairs than are being perceived at any given time, and I am hardly suggesting that the form of a state of affairs as such can be used as a criterion separating what is being perceived from what is not. It will be shown, moreover, in the next chapter that the concept of presence is broader than that of perception, and it is with this broader concept of presence that the notion of states of affairs is being paired rather than simply with that of perception. I do propose to argue, however, that there is a close linkage between presence and truth; that it is in perception that things are, as one might put it, bodily present; and that when a question of truth arises and it is thus a matter of showing that a given state of affairs obtains, perceptual states of affairs are in an important sense privileged. If that is the case, then the truth claim of a proposition that does not express a current perceptual state of affairs would nevertheless be bound up with some eventual or possible perception and with the presence it involves. But the basis for this claim must first be established by a discussion of the import and function of the verb "to be." In the course of this discussion, I shall argue that that function is to bring presence itself to expression. In this chapter, this thesis will be developed as it applies to perceptual states of affairs. In the next chapter, its bearing on their nonperceptual counterparts will be taken up.

The verb "to be" – the "is" and its syntactic variants – figures prominently in propositions that report states of affairs. Its existential use – the "there is . . ." – has been extensively discussed by philosophers since Kant, and the dominant view of its import is that it is not predicative in any extralogical sense. On this view, "is" (or "exists") is not, as Kant put it, a "real predicate," and what it expresses is the fact that the class denoted by the concept used to designate the subject of such a proposition is not empty.[18] Thus, if we were to attempt to say of something that is already

---

18. In this connection, see Heidegger's essay "Kants These über das Sein" in *Wegmarken* (Frankfurt am Main: V. Klostermann, 1967), pp. 273–308.

agreed to be a thing of a certain kind (and thus a member of a certain class) that it is (or exists) or, more egregiously still, that something that we refer to by using a proper name exists, the result will be mere redundancy. Negatively, at least, this line of thought is quite powerful, and at the very least it effectively cuts the ground out from under the interpretation of being or existence as a property of particular entities – in other words, the interpretation that underlies the traditional ontological account of existence as something that is added to essence to form an actual entity.

By itself, however, this does not show that the verb "to be" has a purely logical function if by that is meant one that says nothing about the world. For one thing, even if the "is" does not denote a property of particular entities in any ordinary sense of "property," in saying something about a class that is denoted by a concept, it also says something about the world – namely, that it contains or does not contain entities of a certain kind.[19] Even more important is the fact that in saying this about the world, it must also implicitly relate these entities to whatever has that concept; and in the first instance, that will be the being that makes this statement about them. That would ordinarily be a human being since human beings are also the only entities we know of that can make explicit determinations of truth and falsity. What this suggests is that the verb "to be" has an extralogical import, but one that is of a very different kind from that postulated by classical ontology. It is not that of designating the being of entities, as though it were one of their properties, but rather that of bringing to expression the relation in which the entities that make up this state of affairs stand to something that can make determinations of truth and falsity. That relation, I have argued, is implicit in all states of affairs, whatever the verb that occurs in the corresponding proposition; but the verb "to be" would uniquely and directly express just this feature of all states of affairs.[20]

Against the background of this conception of the function of the verb "to be," I now want to argue that the positive function of the "is" in "There is . . ." is to bring to expression what I have been calling presence. To begin to make this claim more plausible than it may seem at first, a few terminological points about the word "presence" need to be added to those made in the preceding chapter in the discussion of representation. The word "presence" is in general use, and its philosophical use develops di-

---

19. I owe this point to a paper on facts that was read by Professor Fred Sommers some years ago at the University of California at San Diego.

20. Of course, if one were prepared to espouse a Platonistic ontology in which essences and kinds are independent of the thoughts in which they are entertained, and of the thinker of those thoughts as well, then the relation between the entity that is the subject of the verb "to be" and the human being who perceives it or thinks of it would be just an incidental psychological matter and could accordingly be given short shrift in any logical analysis. This is still the way logically inclined philosophers seem to prefer to proceed even though they are not Platonists in any other respect.

rectly out of the familiar sense of its Latin root – that of "being before (someone)." "Before" here has a spatial rather than a temporal meaning, but this is not the spatiality of location in some narrow sense. In Latin, to say that someone is present (*praesens*) is not just to locate him in a certain place at a certain time. It also implies that there is someone else to whom he is present. What the word envisages is thus not just a matter of two people being in the same place, as defined by some physical criterion; to be present is to be before someone in the sense of being in sight or in view, and perhaps reciprocally so, as is implied in the sentence *assum praesens praesenti tibi*. All of this carries over to our own use of the word; and as in Latin, it also applies to things other than persons and with the same implication of their being immediately at hand and thus in view. There are, of course, other uses of the word – bureaucratic ones especially, as, for example, in schools – in which the original face-to-face character of presence is occluded, but it certainly does not disappear altogether.

All this points to a close affinity between presence and the function of the verb "to be" that was just described. On the view being proposed, that function would be to express the relation in which the entities referred to in a statement of fact stand to the entity for which they are there. There are, certainly, undeniable points of similarity between presence and the verb "to be," especially in the form "There is. . . ." It was shown in the last section that presence is relational in the sense that the mode in which the object is present points to a vis-à-vis to which it is present. In its adverbial use, "there," too, is explicitly indexical (and thus relational) in that it points to something and locates it, at least roughly, in terms of some relation in which it stands to the person who uses this expression on a particular occasion. When one says "There is . . . ," as in "There is a car in the garage," that expression retains an indexical force that will be more or less apparent, depending on how close the statement is to being a perceptual report. It is true that this indexical function of "there" may be considerably attenuated in many occurrences of the expression "There is." To say "There is . . ." is certainly not always to imply that whatever one is referring to is in view and thus present at the time of the utterance. On the other hand, even when the word offers no spatial indication, its function does not therefore become purely logical, whatever that might mean. At the very least, it "points" to the world as the place where something is or is not to be found, and it does so typically in the context of background understandings about the route that would have to be taken in that world in order to come into the presence of whatever is under discussion.

The suggestion that a relational character that is common to both is the basis for the affinity between presence and "There is . . ." will be disquieting to many. Something is, after all, present *to* someone; and if it were to turn out that the relational character of "There is . . ." ties it to some observer, the consequences would be, in the eyes of many, both far-reaching and un-acceptable. If all existential statements were tied, by virtue of the relation implicit in them, to the existence of the entity that is the other term in that relation, this would, arguably, amount to the kind of subjective idealism in which the existence of a perceived object is bound up with that of the being that perceives it. If this is not acceptable, then what "There is . . ." asserts cannot be relational in anything like the way presence is; and to say this is to say that what it asserts is the existence of the object in itself, apart from any such relation.

This difficulty must now be addressed, but that can be done only by moving the discussion some distance beyond perception and into the wider concept of presence that is to be more fully elaborated in the next chapter. When we speak of a relation, we normally have in mind something that stands in this relation to something else; and it is assumed that we can give a description of both these "somethings" as they are, independent of the relation in question. There is a question, however, as to whether this can be done in the case of presence. If something is present to me and I am the other term in the relation in which this presence is supposed to consist, the relation would presumably be one between the object in question and my body or one of its parts. The difficulty is that this relation itself could just as easily be what is perceptually present to me, and this raises the question of what it would then be present to. It is at least not easy to see how I could be both an object that is one term in this relation and that to which the relation as a whole is supposed to be present. It is as though I wanted to conceive myself as one term in a relation, as a term in a relation to this relation, and so on indefinitely. As these relations proliferate, how-ever, I would surely have less and less sense of myself as being anything like the stable term that can be identified independently of these relations into which it enters. But in that case, the whole picture of presence as a relation between terms of this kind begins to look more and more dubious.

What is the alternative to such a relational view of presence? This is a question I am not yet in a position to answer, but what has been said so far suggests that such an answer might require a concept of human being that is different from any of those that permit the traditional distinction be-tween terms and relations. More specifically, it may turn out that such a concept ties a human being to the world rather than the world to him and that it does so in a way that is different from anything that can be rendered in terms of the concept of relation as it is ordinarily understood. If that is so, then a human being as an ek-sistent would not be a term of the required kind because he could not be conceived independently of the world that is present to him. If it turns out that such a new concept can in fact be introduced, it would carry with it certain modifications in the concept of the world with which we habitually work; some of these modifications were sketched earlier in this chapter. But there is nothing in this involvement of a human being with his world that could serve as the entering wedge for any sort of subjective idealism. That involvement – the bond that connects ek-sistence with presence and thus with being – would have to be consistent with the world's being the way it is, independently of its being present to me or to any other human being. In this sense, it would have to make a place for what we refer to as the "being-in-itself" of the world.

This notion of the in-itself has been at the heart of much of the resistance to the concept of perception as presence. It has a long (though not necessarily illustrious) history, and the presumption in its favor has been and continues to be that it represents a rock-bottom postulate of common sense, as well as of philosophical realism, from which we depart only at the risk of our sanity. There is, however, a noticeable peculiarity in many of the arguments in which it is invoked. Berkeley drew attention to this feature of philosophical realism when he pointed out that it is as impossible to conceive something that is unconceived as it would be to perceive something that is unperceived.[21] It is, therefore, impossible to give an example of something that exists in-itself – that is, apart from any relation to a thought or perception addressed to it – without violating this independence just by virtue of offering it as an example. Berkeley made this point in an unhelpful way, however, that derives from his assumption that whatever is either perceived or conceived must, by virtue of this very fact, be "in the mind." This idea of the mind as a receptacle that things are either in or not in is one that fatally distorts the discussion of the issues raised by the notion of the in-itself. Instead of assuming that presence in any of its forms is a matter of the mind's somehow containing the entities that are present to it, we need to distinguish between such entities themselves and their being as understood in terms of the states of affairs in which they figure and of the verb "to be" as expressing the presence of such entities.

Properly understood, the question about the in-itself is not one that concerns the putative location – in the mind or in the world – of the objects we perceive. Instead, it is a question of whether an acknowledgment of the being-in-itself of the entities that make up the world constitutes a counterexample to the independence in terms of which the in-itself is being conceived. The answer to this question is pretty clear once it is understood that the independence of the in-itself is not a matter of its not having been sucked up into a mind that functions as a kind of cosmic vacuum cleaner. There is no point in trying to isolate the in-itself from the perceptions and thoughts by which it would be acknowledged. The reason is that all the attempts we make to affirm or even hypothesize the existence of an object that is unper-

21. George Berkeley, *Three Dialogues Between Hylas and Philonous* (Indianapolis, Ind.: Bobbs-Merrill/LLA, 1954), p. 42.

ceived and unknown have a manifestly self-defeating character. As an example of such an attempt, we might imagine a diamond buried deep underground on some distant and uninhabited planet – something, in other words, as unlikely ever to be present to anyone as can be imagined. But it is surely evident that whatever is proposed in this way as an example of something that lies wholly outside any form of presence must be thought of by the propounder of the example, as well as by those to whom it is offered. The terms of reference may be vague, but to the extent to which they can be said to refer successfully at all, as of course they must if the example is to have any force, they bring the thinker and the thing thought of into what we ordinarily call a relation. One might, of course, try to evade this point by replying that the example just offered – that of the buried diamond – could have been replaced by countless others, and that the undefined objects of these possible examples must exist – that is, there must be such entities – even though the examples were not given and a relation to these unnamed entities thus was not constituted. It is quite easy to show, however, that this maneuver is no more successful than its predecessor, and for the same reasons. It tries to separate the "There is . . ." from any modality of presence, perceptual or extended, to anyone; but the very utterance in which this separation is asserted effects the opposite just to the degree that it achieves a successful reference to the entities in question.

It is this feature of the concept of the in-itself that Hegel had in mind when he coined the expression "in-itself for us" and made it clear that it was not intended as the contradiction that it must be on the traditional interpretation of the in-itself.[22] That interpretation asserts the independent existence of an object and does so in a way that implies that the being of this object – the fact that there is such an object – has nothing to do with its presence, whether in perception or in thought, to whoever declares that it exists. It is almost as though the idea were to make it appear that in its character as in-itself, the object in question could speak for itself, so that there is no need to acknowledge its being-for someone, that is, its presence precisely as in-itself. It is as though in trying to separate being from presence, we were attempting to deny that it is we ourselves who are applying the concept of being in-itself to something that must evidently be somehow present to us. This attempt begins to look pretty quixotic when one considers that the force of an assertion in which the notion of the in-itself is applied to something is precisely to deny that it makes any difference to it that it is perceived or judged by someone. In other words, to describe an object as being in-itself is to envisage it in such a way as to make a clear distinction between it and the being that so envisages it. But that contrast

22. G. W. F. Hegel, *Phenomenology of Spirit*, translated by A. V. Miller (New York: Oxford University Press, 1977), p. 56.

itself can be made only by the latter; and so, as Hegel says, it is for that being – that is, for "us," understood as anyone who has complied with the requirements that go with this contrast – that what is in-itself exists as such.

There is a related point here that may help eliminate some of the perplexity that is often caused by theses like Hegel's. It is often assumed, mainly on the strength of connotations carried by the word "for," that the point of drawing attention to the implied context of judgments about things that exist in themselves must be to assert some form of dependence of those things on the subject "for" which they are said to exist. This assumption is in fact wholly unwarranted and seems to rest mainly on a confusion of "for" with "in" along lines that have already been explained. It may also owe some of such plausibility as it has to an unavowed postulation of something like an absolute standpoint from which the existence of things in themselves could be acknowledged. The advantage that goes with such a standpoint is that because it is absolute, and thus eternal and unchanging, there need be no concern that if the in-itself proved to be somehow tied to it, it would then be exposed to all the hazards associated with any finite standpoint. In fact, however, it is possible to affirm from such finite standpoints everything about the independence from them of things in the world – their in-itselfness – for which we wrongly suppose an absolute being to be required. We can even assert that these things would remain what they are even if there were no one at all to perceive them or to think of them. In such judgments, the independence of the existence of the object in question from the standpoint that acknowledges it is explicit, and it is asserted by or from this standpoint itself. But even without such explicit assertions of independence, the import of the "There is . . ." that expresses presence is not such as to acknowledge the existence of what there is only in some sort of linkage with itself as an episode in the life of a finite being.

V

A number of objections can be made to the account I have given of perception as presence. In this section I take up three of these, which I judge to be the ones potentially most damaging to my argument. Of the three, two argue that my account is simplistic and misleading by reason of an implicit assumption that no difficulty arises about *what* it is that is to count as present. The charge both objections make is that I have made it seem as though perception were simply a matter of opening our eyes on a scene in which familiar objects declare their presence to us in an unambiguous manner and we duly acknowledge them as what they so unmistakably are. In the one case, what I have failed to deal with is held to be the element of epistemic uncertainty that so often qualifies our perceptual apprehensions. In the other, the trouble is thought to be due to the purely conventional – and thus in some sense arbitrary – character of the system of classification in terms of which we assign identities to the objects themselves that are said to be present. What both these objections seek to establish is that presence is not unmediated and that when the quite fundamental character of the mediation that is required is understood, the whole idea of presence as I have described it begins to look rather fishy.

By contrast with these objections, which move on more or less the same philosophical terrain as my own account of presence does, the third objection is based on conclusions that have been reached by the natural sciences about perception and especially about the properties that the objects we perceive really possess. These conclusions are very different from the view taken of these objects by common sense, and the charge is that a theory of perception as presence that accepts the latter as unproblematically real or objective can stand only if it is prepared to reject the whole scientific theory of the natural world. Since this is judged not to be a tenable option, a theory of perception that has this consequence must be just as untenable.

To begin with the first of these objections, there can be no doubt about the uncertainty that so often characterizes our perceptual apprehensions. We often perceive things that we are unable to identify or about which we are at least somewhat uncertain. We are sure that we are seeing or touching something, but we are unable, at least for the time being, to say what it is. We might, for example, be inclined to suppose that it is a camel that we see approaching from a great distance; but this is only a conjecture of ours, and whatever it is that we are seeing – that is, therefore, present to us – might be any one of several other possibilities. Even if it is indeed a camel that is so present, then it is not present as a camel in any way that does not depend on our making a lucky guess; and this guess or conjecture or belief itself will surely have to be viewed as being something very different from what I have been calling presence. It is not, after all, something that is just put there before us; it is rather something that, as we say, we have to come up with ourselves. But in that case, it looks as though perception must essentially involve, at least in such cases as this, an element of what can only be called belief; and what is present to us will be so only through the mediation of a belief. There is even the danger that since belief is supposed to be a mental act, we shall have come back to the act-object model of perception.

These considerations receive added authority from the fact that uncertainty is by no means confined to more or less exceptional cases. For one thing, as has already been noted, a perceptual object can never be given in its entirety at one time. Perception is, instead, discursive, and this means that it discovers its object incrementally. By itself, this does not mean that we are constantly being surprised, as we turn corners in our perceptual exploration of an object, by coming upon something different from what we had expected. It does mean, however, that by reason of its discursiveness, the perception of objects is necessarily anticipatory in character and that it remains, accordingly, susceptible to error since the possibility of surprises can never be wholly discounted. This makes it appear that perception must be, as its Latin etymology suggests, more a matter of *taking* than of being given, and it is at least not clear how a theory of perception as presence can accommodate this fact.

This objection clearly makes a point that needs to be taken seriously, but an approach to perception through belief has its own difficulties. Most notably, when perception is conceived in terms of belief, and belief, in turn, as involving the use of a concept to identify something, there is a strong tendency for the intuitive side of perception to wither away altogether.[23] It may, of course, maintain itself in the form of an array of sense data that are supposed to be what the concepts involved in belief are applied to; but enough has already been said about the intramental form of presence – that of sensations to the eye of the mind – that is the only one that such a view can permit. By contrast, the objection I am now considering treats perception straightforwardly as a process of belief formation that is to be explained causally as a function of sensory stimulation, but without any postulation of sensations or sense data as mental entities of a special kind. On this view, there would be no need at all for a concept of presence, and perception would be assimilated in a radical way to belief and, typically, to language as well, as the medium in which belief is expressed. It should also be noted that when this route is traveled, the first-person understanding of perception is effectively suppressed in favor of a causal model of belief based on the third-person case. That is a steep price to pay; and before agreeing to it, one would do well to take another look at the conception of presence that is, negatively, driving this argument.

It is almost as though it were expected that if an object is to be present to someone, it should carry a name tag that identifies it as a thing of a certain kind. Because things do not oblige us in this way, and because conflicts arise as to what something is that cannot be immediately resolved, presence comes to be treated as though it were in some essential way a matter of what people come to believe (and say) as a result of sensory stimulation. In fact, however, the experience of disagreement and error in identifying objects should point us in the opposite direction. If something I have identified as a camel turns out to be an elephant, I have to revise the description of my earlier perception and acknowledge that what I saw *was* an elephant and not a camel – in other words, that it was an elephant that was present to me, although I failed to identify it correctly. It follows

23. For an account of perception in which this seems to happen, see George Pitcher, *A Theory of Perception* (Princeton, N.J.: Princeton University Press, 1971).

from this that something's being present to me is not at all a matter of what I believe, whether correctly or incorrectly. It is prior to and logically independent of the beliefs I may form about the thing in question. It is, in fact, prelinguistic in the sense that what I say or think about that thing neither makes it present to me nor affects it in any other way.

To this it might be replied that I am assuming a case in which the identity of an object does eventually come to be known, and it is thus possible to project that identity backward to the time before it was established – the time in which it was quite uncertain what it was. There are, however, other cases in which such uncertainty is never resolved and we do not find out *what* the thing we saw really was. The real issue concerning uncertainty and presence must, therefore, be how what is present can be described in such a case as this and how an appeal to belief along the lines set forth previously can be avoided. To this, the answer can only be that even in such a case, what is present would not be wholly indeterminate. Even though presence is not realized through identification, it does not occur without any accompanying recognition or identification of what is present by the human being to whom it is present. At the very least, something could surely be made out about the size and shape and color of the unknown object or of the part of it that is visible; and two people who might have made different conjectures as to what it really was might be able to agree on at least this much. They might also agree that the other elements in the identity of this object – the ones that are not apparent under these conditions – have, under these conditions of uncertainty, at best the status of possibilities. Typically, of course, people who are uncertain are not interested in paring back their descriptions of what is present to them in this way until they reach something that is at least unproblematic. Instead, they make conjectures as to what the socially relevant identity of such an object may be – conjectures that may go well beyond the aspects in which that object, whatever it is, is present. In that sense at least, perception is indeed a matter of taking rather than of being given; but it would not be perception unless what is so taken were also given, at least in principle, and this means being present to the taker.

The second objection, like the first, is concerned with the question of how what is present is to be described, but the difficulty it brings out stems from the fact that presence is prelinguistic and thus, in principle, independent of the categories of any particular language. In the various examples that have been given of things that are present, however, I have relied on the English language and its classificatory categories for the purpose of naming such entities. In these circumstances, it is fair to ask whether in so doing I am claiming that English is somehow privileged, and that its classificatory grid is the naturally right one when it comes to determining what there is and thus what is present. If that were the case, such a claim would be hard to sustain, though no more so for English than for any other language. But if there is an indefinitely large number of ways in which the world can be divided up into entities and if, further, there are no natural kinds or "transcendental signifieds" that make one system of classification the uniquely right way of identifying what is present, then, it can be argued, the conception of presence itself takes on quite a different aspect.[24] In these circumstances, to say that such and such an entity is present can hardly be regarded as a simple report of something that is prior to and independent of language. It is less like reading off the identities of the objects that are simply given as such and more like introducing an independent set of criteria that pick out certain kinds of objects, which are then said to be what is present. So, far from being mere transcriptions of some "natural" or prelinguistic system of classification, these criteria will turn out to be peculiar to a certain language and, more generally, to the form of life it codifies. Perception is, therefore, not the presence of entities in the simplistic sense that has been proposed here, but rather something much more like the constituting, in the medium of language, of the system of entities that we call a world. And if we were to try to describe the world out of which these entities are generated as what is present without relying on any particular set of such criteria for this purpose, this would amount to an impossible and self-defeating attempt to use all such sets at once or none at all, and the only proper description for what this would produce would be "chaos."[25]

Doubts about these skeptical conclusions may be initially suggested by the way the idea of presence and of truth itself is made to depend on the availability of unit referents that have been prelinguistically designated as such. It does seem somewhat perverse to appeal to a discredited metaphysical theory of real essences as the standard by which to judge the legitimacy of determinations of what is to count as the same and what as different for a theory of presence. Then, too, one cannot help thinking that even though there is nothing uniquely valid about any single system of classification, it does not follow that all such systems are equally arbitrary. That appears to be the premise, however, on which the critique of presence relies, and so it is committed to the thesis that there is no limit to how fluid and accom-

24. It is in a way such as this, I take it, that Jacques Derrida's polemic against what he and his followers refer to as a "metaphysic of presence" is to be understood. At any rate, it represents my best effort to formulate the notion that is suggested by their not exactly pellucid utterances on the subject.

25. The name of Nietzsche is at the center of the discussion of these issues, and I have tried to deal with them in "Nietzsche's Philosophy of Culture: A Paradox in 'The Will to Power,'" *Philosophy and Phenomenological Research,* vol. 51, no. 3, 1991, pp. 557–72. There is also an excellent discussion of the same issues as they arise in Nietzsche in Jurgen Habermas, "Zu Nietzsche's Erkenntnistheorie," in the same author's *Zur Logik der Sozialwissenschaften,* 5th expanded edition (Frankfurt am Main: Suhrkamp Verlag, 1982), pp. 505–28.

modating the world can be in its relation to a language that seeks to divide it up into unit entities of various kinds. Against this view, there is the fact that, at least on the scale and calibration in terms of which events and objects are mostly accessible to creatures constituted as we are, there are discontinuities and uniformities that cannot be simply dismissed as figments of linguistic convention simply because they have no special ontological status. These afford us many "natural" points at which to designate a break between one event or thing and another; and it is not enough to respond to this observation by drawing attention to the fact that these contrasts and discontinuities are just the ones that are recognized in our language, as though that somehow proved that they owe their prominence and their appropriateness as lines of cleavage within the perceptual mass to this recognition. It would be a strange logic indeed that inferred from the fact that a distinction is made in a given language that it is not a distinction *in re* as well. And yet something like this seems to happen when, for example, it is suggested that nothing can count as an ending or as a beginning until it is so designated in some language. It is surely relevant to point out to those who reason in this way that dying is not a linguistic event and that it is an ending quite apart from its being so recognized in a language.

Apart from such reflections as these, the best answer to this objection is to show that even though the concepts we apply to the description of what is present have no claim to be regarded as founded on natural kinds or real essences, they can nevertheless be perfectly adequate vehicles of truth and can, therefore, as I shall argue, serve to express the fact of presence. This can be done by conceding, for the purposes of argument, everything that that the objector says about the element of linguistic and logical convention that informs the concepts we use to characterize even the most ordinary and familiar things we perceive around us. In other words, it need not be contested that these objects represent a kind of selection from among many others that are defined by different logical conventions even though, to the unsophisticated eye, these might appear to designate the "same" things. If we have settled on just these objects, however, and if the concepts that denote them are even minimally well defined, they will be such as to carry with them certain truth conditions that have to be satisfied if statements about these objects are to have a claim to acceptance. If the object is, say, an acacia tree, and what I want to say about it is that it is in bloom, it is normally possible to make the observations that will establish the truth or falsity of this statement, even though no special claim is made about the status of the properties to which the semantic elements in this statement refer. In these circumstances, it is hard to see what would stand in the way of our also accepting the statement that there is a blooming acacia tree outside my window in the sense of "There is . . ." that is equivalent to that of presence.

At this point in my counterargument, the logical instincts of a philosophical interlocutor are likely to be aroused even if he is not predisposed in favor of the point of view from which the original objection was made. Out of a general feeling that things are moving a little too fast, such a person will typically point out that the observations I or others make underdetermine the truth of any given factual statement like the one in my example because they are at least imaginably consistent with some other state of affairs that either precludes or has nothing to do with the acacia tree's being in bloom. Accordingly, if for some bizarre reason we had a big stake in there not being such a tree blooming outside my window, we could probably protect the denial of this statement against empirical refutation by various logical expedients.

The point to be made by such an intervention is to remind us that verification is by no means as straightforward a matter as my example seems to assume, and that is indeed the case. Incidentally, however, it also serves notice as to who is really running the show when the truth of various beliefs is at issue. It is the transcendental subject – the owner and operator of all this logical and linguistic apparatus – who decides what is to be admitted to credence and on what terms; and the thought that inspires this reminder may be that even in a trivial and unproblematic case like my example, it is just as well not to let this issue of where ultimate sovereignty lies be finessed. That, of course, is what the whole conception of presence may well seem – deplorably – to do when it makes it appear as though objects in the world announced themselves without first having routed their claim through the proper court of higher instance. What is implied in all this is the thesis that no state of affairs to which complex logical conditions attach can ever be anything but the outcome of an independent commitment to a certain mode of description – in other words, that it cannot just be what I see and what is thus present to me.

I have already stated that it is no part of my argument in this book to deny that the human being to whom something is present must be able to identify that object in some appropriate way. What I do want to deny is that this constitution of objects should be described in a transcendental manner, as though it were somehow antecedent to the emergence of any particular world of objects. Instead, I would argue that there is never a time when perception is simply a "rhapsody of sensations" without any of the elements of continuity and identity that objects of whatever kind presuppose. It is when we think of perception in such terms as these that it becomes most natural to attribute whatever order does emerge from this chaos to a projection upon it of principles of identity by something or someone that is not domiciled within (and that cannot be conceived in terms of) the milieu that it so constitutes. This description would apply to a mind or consciousness and its acts; but it does not fit a human being, since a human being is conceivable only in a specific natural milieu. It is also human beings that are able to move and act in that milieu and to manipulate the objects that it contains in various ways; and it is this capacity that is centrally involved, so I want to argue, in the discrimination of one (kind of) object from another. Those discriminations are not fixed once and for all; and as they change and develop, the world we live in becomes more (or less) finely differentiated. Even so, unless we repudiate altogether a particular kind of object that we formerly acknowledged – phlogiston, say – our world must find a place within it for everything that we so discriminate, even if we cannot understand how this is possible. There is, in other words, a certain commitment involved in our designations of kinds of objects by virtue of which we cannot simply cast them off when other kinds compete for their places in the world and then reinstate them when we have a use for them again. But the central point I want to make here is that the criteria of identification are not laid down in logical paradigms elaborated in a transcendental space. They are distinctions that emerge first at the level of what one does or can do with or about something. This point will be developed further as the concept of a human being as one that presupposes presence but is not exhausted by it is progressively refined in later chapters.

There is another assumption that tends to be made when the transcendental account of the discrimination and identification of objects is preferred to the one just sketched. This is the view that perception can only supply the raw materials for the logical operations that establish what something is, and that it is therefore inappropriate to speak as though the object whose identity is constituted by such operations could show itself at the level of perception. If adhered to rigorously, this view would require a sense datum theory of perceptual experience because everything that does not wear its identity on its face, as a sense datum is supposed to do, would have to be the work of thought and of language and could not be "given." But in that case, the entities that make up my visual field could never include a complexly constituted entity like the president of the United States. Or rather, the entity that is in fact the president of the United States would figure there only in some reduced capacity – as the tall man at the podium, for example. The trouble with this is that there is no way to arrest this process of cutting back the identity of something to the point where its presence in perception becomes unproblematic by the standard that rules out the presence of the president of the United States. If a slide in that direction is ruled out by the conclusions that have already been reached about representations, then there is no good reason to accept the impoverishment of perception in which it would issue. By parity of reasoning, it follows that the case against presence that is made on the basis of these linguistic considerations fails to make its point.

I turn now to the objection that appeals to the authority of modern natural science against the account of presence that has been given here. This argument denies the independent reality of perceptual objects – more precisely, the reality of these objects understood as possessing the full complement of properties with which they normally appear to us. To take color as the most obvious example of a property of this kind, the scientific claim is that the commonsense distinction between, say, red and green finds a place in physical reality only as the difference between different wavelengths of electromagnetic radiation; and neither this radiation nor the molecules that make up the objects from which it is reflected are conceived to have color understood in commonsense terms as a property. Colors must, therefore, have the status of effects produced in us by the action of electromagnetic radiation on our sense organs and nervous systems. But if this is the case, then the objects that are supposed to be present to us in perception are, in the guise in which they appear to us, not really parts of the world at all. In these circumstances, the notion of perception as the presence to us of objects in the world would have to be given up.

There is much in this line of thought that is at least as philosophical as it is scientific in any specific sense; and it is evident that at many points it has a close affinity with the theory of representative ideas that was elaborated by the philosophers of the seventeenth century who were also the founders of the scientific worldview. This is palpably the case as long as the mind remains, for the purposes of a "scientific realism" of this kind, the essential *alibi* – the "elsewhere" – to which anything that is denied a place in the real world can be consigned. Views of this kind have already been examined and rejected, and it is not my intention here to go back over that ground again. The kind of scientific realism I am concerned with here is, in any case, expressly antidualistic and physicalistic, so the question that needs to be discussed at this point is a narrower one that has to do with the compatibility of a theory of perception as presence with the conceptual requirements of modern physical science. The issue is whether there are any real grounds for holding that the so-called secondary properties – color, sound, smell, and so on – cannot be assigned the kind of objectivity that is thought to be so unproblematic in the case of physical properties.

In dealing with this issue, it needs to be remembered that there is a distinction that applies to colors and sounds and other secondary properties between, say, something's being really red and its being only apparently so. This distinction between "objective" and "subjective" is usually ignored in scientific theories of perception and replaced by a much broader concept of subjectivity that makes color as such a mere appearance rather than a property of objects. The question that needs to be raised about this wider concept of subjectivity is whether the notion of subjectivity and appearance that it invokes, after setting aside the one that usually applies to colors and sounds, is really intelligible. The source of the difficulty here is that, on the most natural construal of what such subjectivity might involve, it cannot apply to colors. Being subjective usually means being uncontrollably idio-syncratic and variable, and yet the objects that on this view are said only to appear to be colored appear so regularly and to almost everyone – so reg-ularly and so universally, in fact, that we have no hesitation in declaring them to *be* so. Even when we become convinced, on the strength of the scientific argument, that they cannot really be colored, that conviction does nothing to alter the way they appear to us. And yet it is just this universally shared view of color as a property of objects that is being rejected as a mistake.

In such a case, when a whole range of judgments that are held to be obviously true by everyone is declared to be false, it is natural to want to know what kind of mistake it can be that everyone makes and in fact goes on making even after they acknowledge that it is a mistake, at least if their use of traditional color words is to count as evidence of their beliefs. More specifically, one would like to know how it would be possible to avoid this insidious error. But for this it would be necessary to understand what is to count as really being colored, as against merely appearing so; and on this point the scientific theory typically does not have much to say. Here the contrast with the older representational dualism is especially marked since the latter held that what was really and truly colored was something in the mind – a sensation – and that the mistake of which common sense was guilty consisted in believing that this same quality – color – that belonged to a sensation was also a property of something outside the mind. Whatever difficulties there may be about this way of defining the nature of the error, it at least acknowledges that something is in fact red – namely, a sensation, something in the mind – and it thereby sets up a contrast between what really is and what only appears to be colored. This cannot be said of the physicalistic formulation of the same thesis because it does not acknowl-edge that anything really is colored, not even our sensations.[26] All it says is that objects merely look colored, without giving any indication of what it would be to *be* colored or in what respect looking colored falls short of being colored.

In the absence of further explanations of this point, it seems as though, in asserting that objects only appear to be colored, scientific realism is using a notion of appearing borrowed from common sense, but without supply-ing the element of contrast that is essential to the empirical concept of appearance described in the previous chapter. In the scientific use of this concept, the term that is paired with that of appearing in the common-

26. This is the view defended by C. L. Hardin in his book *Color for Philosophers: Unweaving the Rainbow* (Indianapolis: Hackett, 1988), p. 111.

sense understanding of colors – the notion of something's being colored
rather than just appearing so – is left altogether indeterminate. There is,
for example, no suggestion in this argument that when someone says that
an object is red, he will be misled by this belief in some empirically speci-
fiable way and that, as a result of this belief, he will expect this object to
look different to him in some imaginable set of circumstances – the "normal" included – from the way it actually will.

It is precisely this implication that gives the commonsense concept of
color properties its empirical content; but any such implication is precluded from the start by the fact that, on the scientific view, the object as
it really is – the object as lacking color – is not accessible to perception at
all! It cannot, therefore, serve as the norm in relation to which aberrant
color experiences come to be identified as such, and this constitutes a
fundamental difference from the case of the colors that common sense
attributes to objects as the real colors to which various apparent colors are
contrasted. To say that something only appears to be colored is, therefore,
quite different from saying that a red object appears black in certain circumstances. In the latter case, the real color is the color we see in certain
normal perceptual situations; but the real noncolored object of science
does not stand in any such relationship to what we actually see. Nevertheless, to the extent that the scientific use of "appears" is understood on the
model of the commonsense use, we would have to be able to give an empirical meaning to the contrast between being and seeming in the former
case as in the latter; and yet this is just what we cannot do. We are thus
forced to conclude that if the appearing that is in question here is to count
as a mistake of some kind, then it is clearly not an empirical mistake and
it has nothing to do with any feature that the perceptual object might
exhibit or fail to exhibit.

In the absence of any empirical content that might differentiate appearing colored from being colored, it begins to looks as though the claim
that objects only appear to be colored and really are not will have to be
interpreted in some other way if it is to stand at all. One such alternative
interpretation would be to say that this thesis has to do with objects not as
they figure in perception but as they are to be thought about or conceived
for the purposes of scientific theory. On this view, in attributing properties
like colors to objects, common sense would be making a mistake at the level
of theory rather than an ordinary empirical mistake. Such a move would
be very much in the spirit of the extreme rationalism that assimilates perception to thought by arguing that intuitive or experiential distinctions are
just confused versions of conceptual distinctions. But if the commonsense
view of colors is itself a theory, then it will have to be judged the way all
scientific theories are judged, since perception has no truth other than that
of thought. If this theory turns out to be a bad one from the standpoint of

its scientific utility, then it will deserve to be rejected on these grounds alone. In this same rationalistic spirit, it is sometimes even suggested that the language of theoretical science may one day completely replace the descriptive vocabulary in which we currently express the deliverance of perceptual experience.[27]

Sometimes an attempt is made to soften the contrast between a theoretical blunder and a perceptual illusion by describing the commonsense view of colors as a "projection" of a subjective quality – color – upon the objective world. This makes it sound as though at some point we had become confused and had somehow transferred these qualities from one domain to another. The trouble with this idea is that if we really had in some sense misplaced these subjective qualities, it ought to be possible to reverse the transfer so effected once we understand what a bad idea it is and thereby make things look once again the way they really are – that is, colorless. This is, of course, just what we cannot do, and so the idea that we have somehow got things mixed up lacks any empirical content. But beyond that, if the commonsense view were simply a bad theory and one that we could simply dispense with altogether, it would be impenetrably obscure how, even after we accept different frequencies of electromagnetic radiation as the only realities that our color words stand for, we are able to go right on distinguishing, for the ordinary purposes of life, between red and green objects, without the aid of theory and in strong agreement with one another. This distinction and others like it are clearly not replaced by the new scientific ones, even though the latter explain many things that cannot be explained simply in terms of our ordinary color concepts. But for all the explanatory value of the concept of electromagnetic radiation, there is no way in which one can show, by even the most exact analysis, that a certain frequency of radiation must produce a color experience of one kind rather than another. What this shows is that the integrity of the commonsense distinction is not affected by the discovery of the correlation of wavelengths of light with certain colors. It remains independently available to us; and so, far from being just another theory – a bad one – that is replaced by the theory of electromagnetic radiation, this perceptual distinction between colors is the indispensable empirical fact that is presupposed by any scientific theory of colors.

There is thus good reason to think that the claim made by the scientific theory that objects only appear to be colored is not really coherent in its own terms, and that it cannot make sense of the notion of things appearing colored without proceeding to a much stronger form of representational dualism. Apart from these objections, however, there is a real question as

27. This suggestion has been made by Paul Churchland in his book *Scientific Realism and the Plasticity of Mind* (Cambridge: Cambridge University Press, 1979), Chapter 3.

to why we should think that we have a stake in the belief in question – the belief that objects in themselves have no colors or any other nonphysical properties. The reason that is usually given is that this belief is an essential postulate of physical theory, but it seems to be no more than a well-established prejudice. It is certainly true that the concepts with which physics works are those of electromagnetic radiation and its different frequencies, and not our ordinary everyday color concepts. What is not clear is why the procedures of physics in this regard should not be viewed as simply a matter of abstracting from a certain range of properties in favor of others that have greater explanatory value. To abstract from something does not require that it be viewed as nonexistent or merely illusory so that a monopoly of "reality" accrues to the properties to which a certain type of inquiry transfers its attention. And yet this is just the inference that is regularly drawn by scientists and philosophers from the superiority of physical properties for many of the explanatory purposes of natural science. It seems that no serious thought has been given to the possibility that things in the world have both kinds of properties – primary and secondary – or to the way their compresence within the same objects might be conceived.

These considerations suggest some wider conclusions about the competence of natural science to deal with perception as the primordial condition of its access to the object domain with which it deals. Even when the roles of language and theory are fully acknowledged, the ability to perceive objects and make perceptual discriminations among them must form part of the standing repertory of competences of anyone conversant with the truth of things, whether scientific or otherwise. But if the world is an aggregate of physical objects, as science declares, what kind of a relation among such objects could a perceptual relation be? That it would be a causal relation is clear, but a causal theory of perception has traditionally postulated that the effect produced by something that acts on our sense organs is a sensation. A thoroughgoing scientific realism cannot, however, allow sensations to be mental states, as they have usually been supposed to be, because that would be to acknowledge the reality of something that lies beyond the range of its own inquiries. Sensations, therefore, must be identified with certain neural processes, and as such they are absorbed without remainder into the functioning of the body as a physical system.

But then what becomes of perception as a distinctive relation in which things in the surrounding world are present to me? The simple but rather astonishing truth is that there is no room for such a relation in the scientific account of what we are. Presence, whether conceived in commonsense "realistic" or representational terms, just has no place in the ontology of natural science. It hardly need be said that there is something strikingly anomalous in this state of affairs. How are we to distinguish, under these circumstances, between our sense organs and our other bodily organs? And how are we to distinguish between one kind of sense organ and another if "seeing" and "hearing" are just words for the neural processes that occur in different parts of the body or the brain? Is the difference between them describable simply in the language of neurology? And what about neurology itself? Is it not an empirical science and thus dependent on observation, and is there any way in which the neuroscientist could equate his observations of some feature of neural tissue with an event in his own brain? The answers to these questions are obvious, and they can only mean that the scientific study of the human nervous system relies on something that finds no acknowledgment in its official concept of perception. That concept has been abstracted from another understanding of what a human being is, and this prior understanding cannot be repudiated by the science that covertly relies on it.

3

PRESENCE AND ABSENCE

I

If perception is the foundational fact for a philosophical account of presence, perception and presence are nevertheless far from being coextensive. A little reflection on a number of familiar facts about our mental life can help us to see why this is so. When I see an airplane fly low over my house, I may actually have it in view for only a few seconds, but after it has disappeared I may still go on thinking about it, for whatever reason, and later in the day (or the month or the year) I may recall this incident and give an account of it to others. Normally we say that on such subsequent occasions we recall what happened at the earlier time; and memory, as our ability to do this, is held to be one of the great departments of mental activity, alongside perception and some others that we have yet to take up. *What* I remember is that an airplane flew low over my house; and with due modification of the tense of the verb, this is also what I perceived earlier. At the time of remembering, of course, the plane is no longer in view; it may be thousands of miles away or it may even no longer exist. But although it is absent in the sense that it is at least no longer visible, in this absence it is nevertheless, on these occasions of remembering, what I am thinking about. It is accordingly, as we say, present to my thoughts. There is thus, at least in the idiom of everyday life, a recognized sense in which things can be present even when they are absent.[1]

---

1. This phrase – "present to my thoughts" – combines both the ontological element that is contributed by the notion of presence and a psychological one that is implicit in the idea of "thoughts."

Although it is the task of this chapter to explicate the understandings implicit in this way of speaking, it has to be acknowledged that there is something paradoxical and even contradictory about absence as a modality of presence. The reason is that, typically, the notion of presence makes sense to most people only when it is explicated in terms of perception. After all, a perceptual object can appear and disappear and reappear; and in so doing, it gives an intuitive meaning to the notions of presence and absence as these apply to it. Nothing comparable, it seems, can be pointed to in the case of objects that we merely think about, for they remain absent throughout the time we spend thinking about them. Then, too, instead of being initiated by something that announces its presence to us, thought seems to be self-starting and self-contained in a way that makes it hard to conceive otherwise than as something that goes on "in the mind" and thus in effective isolation from anything that could be described as present in any mode at all. Everything thus seems to point to the conclusion that since in thought the object that is thought of is not present, thought itself must be a matter of using symbols or images – in short, representations – in lieu of that object. Under these conditions, the only real topic for inquiry is the character of the representations that are involved in Thought as the broad psychological rubric under which all these matters have been dealt with.

In spite of the persuasiveness of this representational view of thought and the treatment of absence it entails, it can be shown, I think, that, as my example suggests, absence itself is a kind of presence, and that the relation to us of an object that we think about does have something in common with that of an object we perceive. At its deepest level, this matter turns on the fact that presence and being have been virtually identified with one another; and this would suggest that since the concept of being is differentiated by temporal and modal distinctions, something similar must be the case for presence. Otherwise, presence (and, by implication, being) would be confined to the present tense, and the example with which this chapter began makes it clear that this cannot be the case. That was an example in which something *was* the case, and other examples of things that *will be* or *could be* the case would not be hard to provide. These are variations on the "is" of being that register temporal and modal differences, and for each of them there is a psychological concept like "memory" or "expectation" that is supposed to express what is going on in our minds when we are dealing with things in the past or the future. But because the psychological account of such matters has treated them as forms of representation, the idea that the things we are thinking of must themselves be somehow present in their absence has found little favor. To this must be added the further difficulty that if being and presence are to be yoked together, as I have proposed, it would seem that what corresponds to absence must be nonbeing; and the prospect of having to accept that what is not the case – whether "no longer" or "not yet" or "not at all" – is nevertheless present in its very absence is enough to make any philosopher quail. And yet it is just such seeming paradoxes that have to be accepted and, to the extent possible, resolved if Heidegger's close association of being as presence with time is to be espoused.

In order to do this, I must show that every attempt to give a psychological explanation for this presence in absence that will make it seem less paradoxical must fall short. In this connection, the strategy followed in the preceding chapter can offer valuable guidance. In the case of perception, it was shown that the efforts that have been made to postulate some kind of mental machinery from which the perception of something would issue have proved fruitless and leave as their residue only the state of affairs itself – the "There is . . ." – in which perceptual presence is realized. Something very similar holds for presence in absence; and I will argue that memory, for example, has to be understood in terms of another nonpsychological state of affairs for which the appropriate expression would be cast in the past tense. What is expressed by the past tense – the "There was (or there has been) . . " – is not, however, just a fact that happens to be a past fact; it is also a disclosure of a past state of the world to the person who remembers, and as such, it is a modality of presence.

In order to support these claims, I will take up three major modalities of presence in absence in this chapter. In each case, a psychological or language-based conception will be replaced by an account that is ontological in the same sense as the treatment of perception in the preceding chapter. These modalities of presence in absence are differentiated by the kind of absence they involve; and these different kinds of absence are, in turn, closely bound up with temporal distinctions. There is a difficulty here due to the fact that presence has not only been virtually identified with perception but has also been conceived in terms of what is present in the temporal sense of the word. As a result, we confidently infer that where nothing is present in this sense, as in the case of memory, presence of any kind is automatically excluded and some other account of what memory involves must be adopted. Nor are assumptions about the incompatibility of presence and absence confined to the case of memory and the past. The natural complement to the past is the future – those states of affairs that will obtain one day but do not yet do so. Here again, the idea that things that may not yet exist could be present in any sense seems hard to swallow; and the linkage between future events and the possibility of acting in such a way as to keep them from occurring poses another grave problem for anyone who wants to claim that they can be present in their absence.

It has already been pointed out that just as the varieties of absence are closely related to temporal distinctions, so they must also be understood in terms of the different kinds of nonbeing and thus of negation to which they correspond. Because nonbeing – something's not being the case – has given philosophers so much trouble, they have tended to follow the lead of Parmenides in denying to it any uneliminable role in their accounts of the nature of reality. At the present time, this repudiation of nonbeing is usually effected by reducing it to negation as a logical function and then by treating the latter as an artifact of discourse that is to be judged by its pragmatic value rather than by any ontological import it may have been thought to have. At the same time, the tense system of ordinary language may be replaced by an "eternal present" tense that abstracts altogether from the differences in temporal location that make some events past and others present or future. The effect of this modification is to make it unnecessary to think of some events as *no longer* the case and of others as *not yet* the case. In this way, we are able to dispense entirely with an extralogical conception of nonbeing in favor of a plenitude of being – the world as a four-dimensional aggregate of tenselessly actual entities.

The trouble with this procedure is that it obscures something that is fundamental to human being and to having a world – the finitude of presence in all its modes and the consequent need for a term of contrast with which "presence" can be paired. Thus, what is the case needs to be contrasted with what was the case and with what will be the case and also with what could be the case. The concepts of negation and nonbeing have been fundamental to the making of these contrasts; and when they are denied any ontological significance in favor of a single "objective" plenum of being, the effect is to obliterate the character of finite ek-sistence as having a world, not to speak of the linkage between being and presence. This, in turn, presupposes that human beings have already been reduced to the same status within the world that natural science accords to all entities. It then becomes plausible to claim that the notion of an ontological status for nonbeing is simply a survival of a prescientific mentality in the talk that human beings emit and that, as such, it is something that can be eliminated with no great effort. By contrast with such an approach, I will try to show that the contrast between being and nonbeing is grounded in that between presence and absence, and that having a world is possible only in terms of a contrast between what is and what is not the case in the many forms it takes. The point here is not just that the absence of what is no longer the case is quite different from the absence of what is not yet the case. It is also that the truth of the negations that express both of these forms of absence (and others as well) constitutes the presence in absence of the entities that are being referred to.

This examination of the modalities of presence in absence will begin with memory, which will be shown to be more appropriately understood as having a past. What any one of us is able to remember is, of course, only a tiny fragment of the past; but I shall try to show that the presence in absence of our own past lives – that is, of what we are ordinarily said to remember – is a necessary condition for our having a past in any more comprehensive sense. But if in memory we address particular episodes in our own past, we are also able to think of matters that lie well beyond the boundaries of our own lives. We think of things we have never seen and that we "know" of only through the accounts others have given of them. "Thought" is the term we typically use to designate what I have in mind here, and I shall use it for this purpose but without capitalization, so as to preserve the contrast with Thought as the overarching term for all our modes of commerce with what is absent. It should also be noted in this connection that this wider background of absence in which the objects that are present to me at any given time are embedded forms the horizon of my experience in the sense of what surrounds and delimits what is present to me. Since we typically have never perceived these objects, we can refer to them only under general descriptions; and there is thus a question as to how this fact could be accommodated within a theory of thought as presence in absence.

Thus far, I have been describing the modes of presence in absence of what is or has been actual. It would seem that the natural complement to these discussions would be an account of the future and of the presence in absence of what will be actual. There is an important ambiguity, however, about this actuality-to-be of the future and, as has already been noted, it is due to the special linkage between the future and action that can prevent what would otherwise come about from actually taking place. In the light of this complication, it seems best to defer a discussion of the future until it can be placed in the context of human action, as it will be in Chapter 5. Even so, the form of absence that is distinctive of the future evidently has much in common with that which is characteristic of what is merely possible. This is what we usually think of as the province of the imagination. There can be no doubt that imagination is an element in both action and the relation to the future that action presupposes; but it is also independent of the context of action, and it is as so independent and as the presence in absence of what might possibly be the case that it will be considered here.

Overall, what I hope to show in this chapter is that absence as an authentic modality of presence does not lend itself to any of the psychological or linguistic interpretations, that a representationalist approach to it has suggested. The character of the argument will be somewhat different in the case of each modality of presence in absence that I take up. In the case of memory, the principal emphasis will fall on the kind of temporality that memory presupposes; and in the case of thought, it will be on the attempt to make language do the work of representation. Finally, the discussion of imagination will center on the role of nonbeing as possibility and also on the contribution that imagery has been supposed to make to imagination.

In spite of this procedure, however, it should be evident that many of the points made with respect to one of these modalities of presence in absence may apply to the others as well, even though I may not always take time to point out their wider relevance.

There is another general feature of presence in absence, and its relation to presence as such, that needs to be noted at least in a preliminary way. It has been pointed out that what is absent is often directly continuous with what is present to us in perception. Although this kind of continuity forms the constant background for the presence of the objects that I perceive, only certain objects and certain events are picked out, as it were, from this vast domain of absence to form the more highly particularized field of what is present in absence at any given time. If, for example, I am considering selling the house in which I live, then real estate agents whom I might possibly consult or matters relating to the improvements I have made since buying the house may well form the context in which the house is present to me. This is what is usually referred to as the "subjective" aspect of Thought. It has to do with the way this or that object or event claims our attention at a given time and then yields to others in a pattern that does not appear to have anything to do with the things in question themselves, and a great deal to do with us and our present preoccupations.

The term that we most commonly use to designate this succession of extremely variegated and often incongruously juxtaposed items that Thought comprises is "stream of consciousness." The mentalistic implications of that designation are clearly apparent, and there is a pressing need to find an alternative to it. Thought is not, after all, the flotsam and jetsam carried along on some private river system but, rather, a way in which we have a world. Accordingly, what we need to understand is why this or that object or event or fact rather than some other emerges, at a certain time and in a certain context, from the wider background of absence into presence in absence.[2] For that, however, we would need a concept of the entity to which other entities can be present. The specific makeup of the field of presence in absence could then be understood as a function of the active interests of the being to whom they become present in absence. This is by no means to suggest that they become present in absence in response to a summons that I issue to them or that I simply *choose* that they should be

---

2. There is a question here, on which I do not touch, as to whether this absence should be said to comprise everything there is – that is, the whole world. Heidegger is committed to the view that if anything is uncovered, then the whole world is uncovered as well, though mostly in the mode of absence. See "Vom Wesen des Grundes" in *Wegmarken* (Frankfurt am Main: V. Klostermann, 1967), p. 52, where Heidegger states that "human Dasein exists in such a way – as an entity situated among entities and comporting itself toward entities – that entities in their entirety (*im Ganzen*) are always manifest (*offenbar*)." This resembles Leibniz's doctrine that each monad represents the whole world, though with differences of salience and clarity.

present in absence. What it does imply is that any account of what is present in absence at any given time must reckon with the agency of the being to which it is present – with what that being is up to and with the context that is evoked by that form of agency. To touch on this aspect of presence is to introduce into the discussion matters having to do with the particularity and selfhood of the being(s) to which entities are present, and these are matters for the understanding of which no groundwork has yet been laid. As will gradually become clear, however, considerations of this order will be central to the concept of ek-sistence that has to be paired with that of presence in a theory of human being.

II

It was noted earlier that the traditional philosophical approach to presence in absence has taken the form of a theory of representation. The way this works is particularly clear in the psychological account of memory. Even though it is implicitly acknowledged that there is some sort of identity between what we have perceived and what we later remember in a case like my example of the airplane, it is held to be equally clear that what is present to thought (or "before the mind") when we remember something that we perceived earlier cannot be either the airplane itself or its actual passage over my house. What is so present must accordingly be something like a memory image – more grandly, a memorial representation – and thus itself a denizen of the mind. As such, it comes into being as a more or less remote consequence of some earlier perception, and it then represents what was so perceived. But clearly, such a representation can no more be the thing or event it represents than a picture can be what it is a picture of. It follows that the event that is remembered, and whatever it is that is in the mind when we are said to remember it, must be distinct from, and logically independent of, each other; and this is hard to reconcile with our ordinary beliefs about remembering. In order to resolve this tension and show how the nonidentity of a representation and its object can be reconciled with the fact that a memory is a memory *of* a certain past event, various explanations have been offered. Unfortunately, the inferences and associations that have to be postulated in these explanations raise as many questions as the original explanation in terms of representations does.

One indication that this tension has yet to be resolved is that it is extremely difficult to characterize memory and the way it works in a noncircular manner, and this means without making use of an unreduced – that is, a nonrepresentational – concept of the past in the course of one's account of memory itself. Later in this section, it will be shown that this inconsistency typically arises through an unacknowledged exploitation of the contrast between what one remembers oneself and what other people are held to remember along the lines of the contrast between the two pictures set forth in Chapter 1. What needs to be explained now, however, is why this unreduced concept of the past makes philosophers and others who are concerned with memory so uneasy. The reason for this uneasiness appears to be the fact that when I remember something, I do so, as we say, "in the present," but what I remember took place "in the past" and the objects in question may not even exist at the time of the remembering. Memory thus apparently involves a relation between something present and something past, but in this case the relation between the two has a notable peculiarity.

In the sequence of events in the world at large, later events, including those that take place in any given present, follow upon and are produced by earlier events; and whatever difficulties we may have with the concepts of causation and of time, we think we roughly understand this sort of sequence. One thing we think we understand about it is that when an event has taken place and has, so to speak, done its work by producing certain effects, the state of the world that succeeds it has its own reality that can in principle be described without reference to the prior event. But when the later event is one in which the prior event is *remembered*, this logical segmentation of the time order appears to be violated. Not only is the "direction" of memory puzzling because it seems to go from the present to the past and from the later event to the earlier; there is also the fact that in such a case a present event appears to be linked to a past event in a way that makes the latter an essential element in the description of the former.[3] This strikes many people as extremely strange.[4] A past event that is over and done with would, on such a view, become the object of a mental act of some kind that occurs in the present, and it would thereby itself enter into the description of a later event in a nonoptional manner. Because anything of this kind appears to entail the possibility of something like time travel, it is held to be inconsistent with the requirements of the scientific worldview, and strenuous efforts have been made to remove such an anomaly from the theory of memory. If successful, these efforts would show that

3. It may almost seem as though the logic of the verb "to remember" invites us to make just this assumption, since it is like that of "to know" and unlike that of "to believe" and cannot therefore be properly used unless what is "remembered" actually took place. But because it is always possible to use "remember" improperly, although in good faith, the mere fact of its being used cannot settle anything about the past.

4. Bertrand Russell once offered as an example the case of a people that had suddenly come into being with a full complement of "memories" of a past it had never had. The possibility of such a case was supposed to show the logical and ontological distinctness of what occurs in the present as a "memory" of some past event and that past event itself. For those who accept this example as it stands, any suggestion that a past event may be essential to the characterization of a present event of remembering must seem profoundly misconceived. See Bertrand Russell, *The Analysis of Mind* (London: George Allen and Unwin, 1921), pp. 159–60.

memory does not have to be thought of in this way and that it can, in an appropriate reconceptualization, be incorporated into a scientifically and logically acceptable theory of the world process.

It would hardly be an exaggeration to say that the history of these efforts and the history of philosophical and psychological thinking about memory pretty much coincide. In a general way, the theories of memory that have been advanced are designed to overcome the unmediated character of our relation to the past and to replace it with an account in which memory is shown to be part of a causal order of events that does not involve any problematic linkages of later events to prior ones. As we will see, those events can be conceived in either mentalistic or behavioristic terms, but in either case the succession of events that link past and present is understood in a way that makes these events logically independent of one another. This is to ensure that the present in which the remembering occurs could take place even if it had not been preceded by the events that in fact led up to it and, more specifically, even if it had not been preceded by the event that it ostensibly represents. What this comes to is the thesis that remembering is causally but not logically or ontologically linked to those past events. Unless this logical independence is maintained, it is argued, the possibility of specious memories – memories that misrepresent the past – would be excluded at the outset. The reason is that when such a memory occurs, it must be possible to show that nothing in this specious memory or in the reference it makes to the relevant part of the past can, as an event that takes place in the present, determine or in any way logically control the character of any past event.

In this respect, the theory of memory is designed along the same lines as the representational theory of perception; and in both cases the under-lying motive is to allow for the possibility of error. In the case of perception, the required separation is effected by assigning the representation to the mind and the object it represents to the external world. In the case of memory as well, the representation is supposed to be "in the mind"; but because what is remembered is typically an "experience" of some kind in one's own past, and as such would have to count, at least for a represen-tationalist, as itself a (past) state of mind, the separation between the two that guarantees their logical independence from one another is effected by somewhat different means. It is done by conceiving the mind as though its contents at any given time were as effectively isolated from its contents at any prior time as they are from what lies outside the mind altogether. Remembering thus takes place in the present, just as it does in the mind, and what the picture of its being *in* the present is supposed to convey is its logical independence of what is *in* the past.

The practicability of conceiving memory in this way varies with the form of memory to which one applies it. If it is a question of remembering *how*

to do something – play the piano or repair a carburetor – then to remember
the one or the other will arguably just be to play the piano or repair a
carburetor. Memory in this sense would be the survival of a modification
that our behavior undergoes when we learn to do something, and it could
be described as such without any reference to the past occasions on which
this behavior was learned.[5] In those cases in which we remember *that* something happened in the past, however, the applicability of this schema becomes much more problematic. It might be thought that if, in place of
such a behavioral theory, a mentalistic approach to memory were adopted,
the prospects of its being able to deal with remembering that something
was the case would be more favorable. This is because, when remembering
is treated as a mental rather than just a behavioral event, it can be conceived
as the presence in the mind of images or fainter replicas of the sense experiences we had on the past occasion that is the object of our memory.
The presence of these images in our minds is supposed to be itself the
outcome of psychological processes initiated by that original sense experience, and these processes all go forward in time in an unproblematic way.
As it turns out, however, there is not nearly as much difference between
the behavioral and the psychological interpretations of memory as there
might appear to be. They are in fact equally inadequate to the task they set
themselves, and for the same reason. This is that they both miss an essential
aspect of memory because they are unable to make a place for the kind of
temporal reference that is involved in memories like those that have just
been described.

In order to show that this is so, it is necessary to draw attention to the
relation in which these theories themselves stand – as theories – to the
processes with which memory is being identified by them. This relation is
itself a special case of the relation in which one human being stands to
another whom he observes or thinks about, and some of the intricacies of
that relation have already been explored. In these theories, the memory of
the human being who is their object is envisaged in terms of a process that
is initiated by a perceptual episode and that continues either through the
fainter revivals of that episode in the form of images or through progressive
modifications in the behavior of the person in question. In either case, the
process that is so postulated goes forward in time; and the governing presumption is that each of the stages through which it passes can be adequately characterized in terms of the features that come into being in the
present in which it occurs. Accordingly, the fact that someone else – the
human being the theory takes as its object – remembers something would

5. It seems very doubtful to me, however, that "remembering how" could be completely
   independent of "remembering that." Typically, even a person who has solidly acquired a
   skill would on occasion correct his performance and, in so doing, might well recall his
   learning of the detail in question.

seem to be accounted for in a way that does not violate the logical conditions defining this temporal order in the way that memory would do if in fact it could simply "double back" to a past event qua past, as common sense seems to suppose it can.

Nevertheless, there is a difficulty for such a theory as this, and it stems from the fact that *as a theory* it violates the restrictions that it places on the objects to which it addresses itself. These are, of course, human beings, the beings for whom the claim is made that they are capable of sustaining a kind of commerce with the past for which there is, at least, much less evidence in the case of other animals. At the same time, a theory is a way in which some part or aspect of the world is envisaged by the human being who espouses it; and a theory of memory is a theory that presents human beings in a certain way to the human beings who hold it. At the same time, any general theory about human beings must also be applicable to those human beings who hold it and, more specifically, to them in their capacity as holders of this theory. If one can hold this theory only by standing in a relationship to the past that is not allowed for in the theory itself, this condition would be violated. And this is in fact the case. This theory of memory explains our remembering by making connections between present behavior or imagery and past events of certain kinds; and it therefore presupposes that it is possible for those who espouse the theory to deal with those events themselves as distinct from the changes they bring about or the images of them that survive in the minds of human beings. One might, of course, try to make the theory self-applying and interpret the thoughts in which it is formulated by those who hold it as either their present mental contents or some bit of learned behavior on their part. Such an attempt would certainly fail, however, because its effect would be to break the connection between the present and the past in the case of the theorist, as previously in the case of the objects of his theory.

The status of a theory of memory that has canceled out its own relation to the past is a curious one, to say the least. One may suspect, however, that it is not really possible to do this, and that all that really happens is that the indispensable reference to the past is transferred once again. In this case the shift would not be, as it originally was, from the object of the theory to its subject, but from the latter to the theory itself in some discarnate form in which it is not supposed to be any actual human being's view of anything and thus, in effect, to an extramundane and infinite knower. If transfers of this kind do not seem attractive, then the inference must be that they should not have been initiated at all. Instead of resorting to a theory in which such transfers play an essential role, it would be better to acknowledge freely that even ordinary human beings who do not construct theories of anything have the capacity for unmediated temporal reference, however paradoxical this may seem to their more reflective brethren. It also looks as though a theory like the one just discussed places its objects in the wrong kind of time – a time that is logically segmented in a way that cannot possibly accommodate temporal reference, either in its familiar everyday forms or in the guise in which it turns up in theories of memory.

Although a discussion of the linguistic form of representationalism has been reserved for the next section, it may be useful to see how what has just been said applies to language as the bearer of memory. It is sometimes suggested that to remember something essentially involves the use of language – more specifically, saying to oneself or to others that something took place or was the case at some point in one's own past. Saying something is, of course, an event that occurs in the present, and it is this saying that is supposed to represent the past fact or event that is thereby remembered. Whether it is accompanied by any imagery or not is an independent issue; and it is not required, on this view, that images of the past event be an element in the remembering that takes place in the present. In any case, a linguistic mode of representation enjoys significant advantages over representation by means of images. For one thing, it would be extremely difficult for images to express unambiguously just what was remembered. The same image could serve as the representation for any number of memories without there being any way of deciding, simply on the basis of what is found in the image itself, which of these it expresses in a given case. Another advantage is that a statement dates the fact or event it reports by the tense of its verb and thus establishes, by itself, the pastness of what is remembered. This is something that no image or picture can do for itself; and the "feelings of pastness" that have been postulated in order to provide images with the temporal reference that they do not themselves contain are therefore not required when remembering is conceived in linguistic terms. In a sense, such a conception can be said to effect a purification of our understanding of remembering through a sharper definition of its semantic content.

At the same time, however, these very advantages raise questions about the representational character of memory in this theory. It is trivially true that when someone makes a statement, his doing so – his locutionary act – is an event that takes place in the present; and to that extent, it is certainly distinct from the fact or event that is remembered. But if one considers *what* is said in such an act and the latter as the saying of what is said, it is not so clear that a distinction between the past event and what takes place when we remember something can in fact be made. For if remembering is a matter of saying to oneself something like "The airplane flew low over my house," then these words are, of course, being uttered – whether aloud or silently or even "mentally" does not make any difference – at this moment; but in saying them, the speaker is also saying *that* the airplane flew low over his house. In this respect, what he is doing is something that cannot be described in a way that does not expose this reference to the past. It is also something to which all the physiological and acoustical (or graphological) properties of a speech act – the very properties that make it appear to be a quite unmysterious event in the natural order – are irrelevant. The point is that when we abstract from all these properties of the speech act, what remains is simply what is usually called its "propositional content." There will be a good deal to say later in this chapter about this term, and especially about the problematic notion of "content" that it introduces. All that needs to be pointed out here is that in my example this content would most naturally be regarded as being the fact itself that the airplane flew low over my house. That way of conceiving the matter would yield the idea of a present that discloses that something *was* the case, and this seems to be the conception of memory that is implicit in our unsophisticated ways of describing it. It is also just such a present that resists incorporation into the logical schema of world time.

The representational theory requires something very different. It requires that we split such a fact as the one just cited into two parts: the fact or state of affairs itself, safely back there in the past, and a proposition that represents it in the present and in the mind. It justifies this requirement on grounds that are by now very familiar. This is the fact that memory is at least as liable to error as perception is, and yet the account that has been given here of memory in terms of presence in absence may seem to be designed only for cases of veridical memory. On the basis of what has been said up to this point, it is indeed far from clear how the concept of presence in absence can be applied to those cases in which we "remember" things that in fact never took place. It may, therefore, appear that an acknowledgment of the fallibility of memory must lead us back by another route to an endorsement of the logical and ontological distinctness of the present from the past about which I have been raising questions. By following this same line of thought, we might also be led to an account of how we determine what really occurred in the past that bypasses the conception of presence in absence altogether in favor of a view that gives pride of place to language use and to the sorting out of evidence through the use of logical criteria of various kinds. On this view, the occurrence of a "memory experience" would be at best one element in the much more complex process of determining what actually was the case; and that experience itself would have to be described in a way that is completely noncommittal with respect to the truth or falsity of what it says about the past. It is evident that in these circumstances the distinction between *my* past and *the* past would lose much of its importance since the same evidentiary procedures would govern the determinations we make with respect to both the one and the other.

In fact, however, one can accept the vulnerability to error of memory without adopting the view of it as just one of many "experiences" that come along and have to be assessed with a view to determining their epistemic value. One obvious objection to such a view is that it unrealistically assumes that it must always be possible, in principle, to make these independent determinations of past fact without reliance on the unmediated rememberings that they are supposed to confirm or disconfirm. It is, however, very doubtful that this is possible. There are, clearly, many facts that we "know" *only* on the strength of our remembering them; and in such cases, we are committed to both the description of what we are doing as remembering and to the truth of what is remembered without being able to separate one from the other. In these circumstances, what *is* remembered is what *was* the case; and because the present event – the remembering – is itself the disclosing of the past event, we cannot stand outside the one and the other and take note of their independence in principle from one another. In these circumstances, it does not seem possible for the person who remembers to describe the remembering in a way that abstracts from the truth of what is remembered.

It might be replied to the foregoing argument that it relies too heavily on the contingent fact that we are often unable to find evidence that corroborates the testimony of memory and must therefore simply rely on the latter as it stands. The suggestion is that it would be more appropriate to draw very different conclusions from this fact – conclusions that have to do with the gappy and inaccurate character of much of our knowledge and not with paradoxical referential capacities that human beings supposedly possess. In effect, what this comes to is the thesis that not only may any given individual's memory prove unreliable and thus need to be discounted, but that memory generically should be treated as though it were no more than one of many witnesses that can be deposed with respect to something that is supposed to have occurred, and by no means the most respectable. A picture thus begins to emerge of a being that is conceived almost entirely in terms of its logical powers and that could in principle decide all such matters on the basis of evidence alone, without having to rely at any point on unmediated memory.

Suppose, for example, that our situation were to change in such a way that it would always be possible to find evidence that bears on the same matters in our past about which we claim to remember this or that – evidence that can decide the truth or falsity of these memories. This would be very different from the actual state of things in which, for example, my memory that I drove to work by one route rather than another is often no more in keeping with such evidence bearing on this fact as there may be than is its opposite. In any case, let us suppose that by means of newly available evidence, it could be established that I drove via A Street rather than B Street even though I "remembered" driving via B Street. Perhaps one of my tires has an idiosyncratic tread pattern, and this pattern has been found in some dirt left on a section of A Street by a dump truck an hour before I left for work. That might well persuade me to accept the conclusion about my past to which it points even though this evidence jogs no corresponding memory of mine. Normally what I would then do is place this fact about my past in a context provided by others that are otherwise available to me – recollections, say, of my leaving the house or of arriving at work that morning. Consistently with our assumption, however, there would have to be adequate evidence bearing on the truth or falsity of these memories, too, without any reliance on still other unsupported memories, whether my own or those of others.

The question this raises is how anyone who proceeds in this way could acquire the concept of the past that he evidently must have if he is to be able to sort out and place in their proper relations to one another all these past facts. Just as a representational theory of perception affords no explanation of how the concept of an external world could be acquired, so a conception of the construction of the past out of evidence that is all rigorously present, with no reliance on memory as anything other than a present datum or experience, must be deeply problematic. The only way epistemic operations concerned with past fact can be coherently conceived is against a background of a prior familiarity with other past facts. But if that is the case, it follows that there can be no point in attempting to play the skeptic vis-à-vis the reality of the past in the manner of Bertrand Russell. If we are to have a concept of the past at all, we are all dependent (and not just contingently so) on the deliverance of unmediated memory in a form that would be appropriately expressed not so much by "I remember . . ." as by "There was. . . ." Otherwise, we would have to assume that a concept or representation of the past is available to us in some a priori manner that serves merely to pose the question of whether anything corresponds to it or not; but it is precisely this noncommittal availability that is so deeply implausible. It is implausible because it would require us to have a concept of a hypothetical past independently of any commitment to a real one.

The alternative to such a view is to acknowledge that, in spite of all the fallibility of memory, we are irreversibly committed to the reality of the past and that we are indeed in the presence of the past as a distinctive modality of absence in a nonoptional way. From this it follows that the undoubted fact that we are often mistaken in what we claim to remember does not entail the logical independence of the present from the past. When I discover that a memory of mine is mistaken, I often substitute for it another account of what *really* happened. Even if I am unable to do this and have to leave that part of the past blank, it is still the past that I am concerned with, and I certainly believe that *something* happened at the time in question even though I am not now able to determine what it was and in fact may never be. In this way, the past provides a context for the present that persists throughout the revisions of our memory beliefs that take place; and each revision of past fact unavoidably involves us in the renewed claim that *this* really was the case. We may be compelled again and again to revise our claims about the past, but if there is something rather comical about this pattern of assertion, backing down, and reassertion, it does seem to be our lot. We do not for a moment suppose that when this occurs, the past itself changes. What happened in the relevant part of the past was the case, independently of my remembering it or not. It does not, in other words, *become* the case that the airplane flew over my house when I remember that it did. In any case, it is to the past as the continuing subject of these assertions and revisions that we are committed. As the reference of our rememberings and their revisions, moreover, it qualifies the presentness of our memories and our thoughts about the past generally as decisively as does a fully determinate remembering.

It seems fair to conclude, on the strength of the considerations that have been advanced, that the attempt to understand memory in terms of any form of representationalism cannot really succeed. It fails, as has just been shown, for the same reason as did the older forms of representationalism: the sealing off of the present from the past by logical conditions defining the temporal order. But in the case of language it also fails for a special reason, namely, that language cannot be made to conform to the conditions that define the status of a mental representation. A representation must be distinct from what it represents, but those elements in a speech act that would satisfy that condition are the ones that are extraneous to its semantic and referential content. What remains is not two terms – a representation and a past fact in a problematic relation to one another – but, rather, the past fact/event itself as disclosed to someone in the present; and it is this disclosure that makes it appropriate to speak of memory as a form of presence in absence.

One further point needs to be made before leaving the topic of memory. In the preceding discussion, I availed myself of both the psychological terminology of memory and the ontological idiom of "having a past." Since the goal of the whole exercise has been to replace the former with the latter, at least for philosophical purposes, it should also be pointed out that there is a need for something like a psychological conception of memory quite apart from its simple convenience and familiarity. Just as in perception, in memory there is a side that we usually call "subjective" or psychological but that might be better described as simply the idiosyncratic and occasional character by which presence in absence is so strongly marked. These idiosyncrasies are not just a matter of a susceptibility to error that is even more pronounced in the case of memory than in that of perception. It is, rather, a matter of the way the presence in absence of the past is embedded in the special character of the life of an individual ek-sistent. For example, when we speak of remembering something, it is often implied that we had previously forgotten what we now remember. In such a case, there is a temporal sequence in which, first, I do not remember what happened and then succeed in recalling it. There are also other things that happened in the past that I cannot recall at all. Sometimes I know that this is the case and can at least struggle to recover what I have lost, but even more often I also forget (or never take note of) my own forgetting. It is at least imaginable that we could have a past in a way that would not be characterized by such sequences of failure and recovery. Perhaps it is even possible that our memories might be free of error altogether. But even if that were the case, there is one thing that would not change as long as we remain active beings. It would still be the case that one part of our past is relevant and available at a given time to whatever we are about and another not. There would, therefore, still be sequences in which certain features of our present situation "call up" certain parts of our past, or the other way around, and it is by capturing the way these sequences qualify the presence in absence of the past that the language of remembering and forgetting performs an essential function. The alternating play of these different modalities of ek-sistence (and thus of presence and of presence in absence) is what corresponds in a theory of presence to what we usually call "subjectivity," but it may be hoped that it is free of the serious liabilities that have traditionally been associated with that term.

III

In moving from memory to thought as another modality of presence in absence, we immediately notice a significant difference between them. We can be said to remember only what has been a part of our own lives at some time, but what we can think of is not so limited. It follows that we cannot remember anything we have not ourselves perceived, but we can think of things we have never perceived, as well as of those we have perceived. The former are, of course, far more numerous than the latter, and thought ranges over this extensive domain of absence with a freedom and a spontaneity that have often been remarked on. We can, it seems, think of anything we please; and it is almost as though, in thought, the whole world were somehow ideally present to us even though the overwhelming bulk of it is, and can only be, absent.

At the same time, however, it is just this freedom and independence from both perception and memory that make it seem so problematic to try to apply the concept of presence in absence to it. That the things we think of are generally absent may pass uncontested; but how is it, one may well ask, that something we have never perceived and may never perceive can qualify as present to us in any sense at all? The obvious answer to this question is that we supplement our own limited perceptual familiarity with the world with borrowings from what other human beings have seen and reported. We do this so regularly and so unhesitatingly that we often have no clear sense of what derives from our own past experience and what from that of others. There is a great deal to say about this contribution that other ek-sistent beings make to our lives and we to theirs, and there is reason to think that the vicarious presence (and presence in absence) that is the issue of this epistemic cooperation deserves much more attention than it usually receives. It is, however, a matter that I have reserved for a possible sequel to this study, and so I shall not enlarge on it here. One implication of this relationship in which we stand to one another is plain enough. That is that language must play an essential role in any such vicarious presence in absence since it is only in and through the communicative use of language that it can be achieved.

This is undoubtedly right as far as it goes, but if what interests us is the ontological character and implications of presence in absence, that may not be very far. Contemporary discussions of thought and of its relation to language certainly do not make any place for presence in absence, vicarious or otherwise. More generally, they tend not to be concerned with the question of what human beings are doing when they think. Such attention as has been given to the question of what thinking itself is – for example in the writings of Gilbert Ryle, where it is more or less equated with intelligent behavior – typically leaves the ontological status of thought in an amorphous state.[6] It seems likely that the reason for this is that philosophers have become accustomed to dealing only with the publicly offered product of thought, and since this product consists of sentences, it is easy to slip into the assumption that, at least for all legitimate philosophical purposes, the only thing thought can be is the production of these sentences themselves or of the utterances in which they figure.[7] In other words, thought as a process – that is, as something that goes on in an individual human being at a given time – can only be the assembling of these same sentences together with an occasional private rehearsal, once they have been put together, as a preliminary to public utterance. In this sense, then, the old distinction between the mental activity in which thought was traditionally

6. This seems to me to be true of the accounts of thought given by Gilbert Ryle in his *The Concept of Mind* (New York: Barnes and Noble, 1949), Chapter 9, and in his *Collected Papers* (London: Hutchinson, 1971), vols. 2 and 19. The same might be said of the very different treatment of thought by H. H. Price in *Thinking and Experience* (London: Hutchinson's University Library, 1953).

7. This thesis is emphatically stated in A. J. Ayer, *Thinking and Meaning* (London: H. K. Lewis, 1947). It is interesting to note that what is at least superficially the same view was held by Homer, who regularly identifies thought with speech. See R. B. Onians, *The Origins of European Thought* (Cambridge: Cambridge University Press, 1951), pp. 13–14.

supposed to consist and the words and sentences that were regarded as merely the vehicles that express thought as so conceived and make it available to others has to be given up. This distinction has been replaced by the thesis that the thought that supposedly takes place in the mind itself presupposes language and is, in fact, a special covert modality of speech. It thus appears that to the degree that the philosophy of language would countenance a conception of thought in terms of presence in absence at all, it would have to insist that this must be achieved in language. It is also implicit that the "language" we are talking about here is language as it is understood in naturalistic terms, without any special ontological subtleties.

A closer look at this thesis may call into question some of the assumptions on which it rests. If, for example, you were to ask me what I am thinking about at this moment, I would normally answer you by framing a sentence containing certain words. Since sentences are held to be not just the expression of thought but the thought itself about which the inquiry is being made, the fact that my answer is itself a sentence – a bit of language – takes on a significance that may seem to settle the matter without further ado. But if you were to be a little more cautious and ask me whether, in thinking about the matter in question, I was in fact speaking these or any other words to myself before I uttered them aloud, things would become a good deal less clear. This certainly seems to be a question that I ought to be able to answer in the affirmative if thinking is always saying something. After all, if in thinking of something I, like everyone else, must always use words to frame sentences that express what I am thinking, then I should be able to recall what these words were a moment later in response to a question like the one I have just imagined. But typically, no such answer can be given, and we have no sense that in giving an answer we are *repeating* words that we just uttered to ourselves.

It is true that words can figure in my thoughts as, for example, when I am preparing a talk or deciding what the best formulation would be for a certain point in an article I am writing. It is thus possible for us to think *of* certain words and sentences, and we often do so; but this in no way demonstrates that we think *in* words. *What* I am thinking when I think of such words is typically not something that I say to myself in some further utterance. To tell someone what one was thinking is, accordingly, not a matter of quoting oneself, as though "I thought . . ." were like "I said, '. . . ,' " and everything depended on the exact words that were in fact used by the person in question. At best, the analogy would have to be between thinking and indirect discourse in which there is no claim about what the actual words were, but even this would have the disadvantage of implying that words were in fact used. It may be that, if we could not use words or form sentences at all, we would not be able to think either, at least in any meaningful sense. If that is the case, then it would indeed follow that the entities and states of affairs we could think of would be the ones for which there are words and statement forms in the language we speak, and so in this sense, thought would indeed depend on a language we share with others. But even if that is the case and no "private language" is possible, it does not follow that thinking is speaking in the sense of actually using words or word images or that speaking does not itself presuppose presence in absence as a more primordial disclosure of the entities we think about.

Even though no words are actually spoken when we think about something, defenders of the view that identifies thought with language use may still want to postulate some sort of internal or mental speech as what takes place when we think. There have, for example, been those who argue that thought is a kind of "mental word." If this means, as it appears to, that we think *in* mental words and not just that we can think *of* words that, as objects of thought, could be described as "mental," there seems to be no evidence for this and a good deal that goes against it. If an argument is needed on this point, one can point out that some thoughts are so complex that the length of the sentence that would have to be spoken *in foro interno* would far exceed the length of time in which the thought occurs. To this it might be replied that speech can occur in drastically abbreviated forms that permit very long sentences to be "spoken" very quickly. This point is fair enough, but it really supports the view I am defending and not for the one that identifies thought with speech. One need only reflect on the fact that the kind of abbreviation involved here can be so drastic that nothing, or almost nothing, is left in the way of recognizable features of normal, fully explicit speech. What is most significant about this fact is that it has no distorting effect on thought at all, as one would surely expect it to have if the thought were identical with the speech act itself. The fact that this is so, and that there is no limit to the departures that can occur from ordinary speech, must surely call that identity into question. Alternatively, it forces one to construe it in a way that makes it compatible with these facts, and that means in a way that identifies speech not with the words that are spoken but with their semantic and referential import. But in that case, it can be shown that the proposed identity of thought with language use becomes altogether innocuous.

The reason this is so has to do with the nature of language itself. When an assimilation of thought to language use is attempted, the underlying motive is usually to fit the speech acts with which thought is identified neatly into a naturalistic framework. But as a type of event that is understood in terms of the use of the vocal apparatus (or the writing hand) together with the physical effects so produced, such acts must fall short of being locutionary acts – utterances that say something – unless we can explain how semantic and referential properties accrue to sounds and marks. It is sometimes suggested that there is no real difficulty about this. Words, it is said,

are like money; and like money, they have properties other than their physical ones.[8] We who use them avail ourselves of these semantic and referential properties in pretty much the same way we do of the monetary value
of the pieces of green paper in our wallets; and so it is quite possible to
describe what we do with words in terms of what the words themselves do.
It is as though we could "farm out," for example, the reference to entities
we have never perceived to its linguistic vehicle, thereby avoiding having
to impute some mysterious power to ourselves by virtue of which such reference is possible.

All this may seem plausible as long as one assumes, as we do in ordinary
life, that we know what money and words are. In an established monetary
or linguistic system, the "properties" of the one and the other may indeed
be said to be an unproblematic given for any individual human being who
participates in the systems. It is clear, however, that this is not the perspective that gives rise to philosophical questions about words and their properties. Those questions are generated when we contrast the familiar social
perspective just described with the way objects are conceived by the natural
sciences. From that point of view, words have to be treated as phonetic and
acoustic phenomena, and there simply is no place within such a mode of
conceptualization for the semantic and referential "properties" that seem
so patent in ordinary life. But if this naturalistic conception of objects can
treat words only as sounds or marks that are differentiated by certain phonetic or other physical properties, then there really is a problem about the
status of their semantic and referential functions that cannot be settled by
simply appealing to our commonsense understanding of the latter. More
specifically, it seems unlikely that these semantic and referential functions
of the words we use could be isolated from the people who use them, or
what these words "do" from our own nature as ek-sistent beings.

The real trouble here lies in the assumption that there is something
called a "word" that stands in a relation to something else that is not a
word. This assumption can be made only by identifying a word with its
sound or its visual shape. Of course, an ink mark or a sound treated as an
acoustic event is not a word at all, and so the first term in this relation is
evidently misconceived. If we are to speak in terms of relations at all, we
have to say that it is precisely this relation to something that is not a word
that is internal to the concept of a word. Even then, the idea that this
relation is established by an ultimately arbitrary stipulation is hardly compatible with the view that identifies thought with speech. If we say that a
sound stands for a thing because we make it do so, it is evidently being
presupposed that we have a familiarity with the (kind of) object for which

---

8. I take this idea from a talk given by Professor Michael Devitt some years ago at the University
   of California, San Diego.

a particular sound is being made to stand – a familiarity that must be prior to and independent of the use of that sound for the purpose of referring to it. But how, it may be asked, is this familiarity itself to be conceived? Even if it is assumed that simple ostension plays a part in it, in order to know the meaning of a word we would still have to be able to think of the objects denoted by that word even when they are not perceptually present, and this would be different from using that word. This is to say that we must be able to *think* of those objects independently of the word that designates them. The only way to square this with the thesis that equates thought with some form of speech would be to render that whole claim trivial by conceding that speech cannot be treated, for these purposes, as consisting in the mere utterance of sounds that in some miraculous way do everything else by themselves. In that event, we would in effect have conceded that we can think of the same states of affairs that we express in language in a way that does not require speech of any kind.

Although thought and speech are not one and the same thing, and although we are able to think about something without formulating a sentence that expresses that thought, there can be no question about the importance of the linguistic-logical modality that thought assumes; and attention must now be given to it. One purpose this will serve is to make clear that the use of language to express thought itself presupposes the extra-linguistic character of thought that has just been discussed. My first concern, however, will be with the relationship between thought and thing as it has been understood in the philosophical tradition. In a philosopher like Aristotle, for example, the treatment of thought was decisively influenced by ontological assumptions that tie thought as something that takes place in the mind to things outside it through the substantial form that is common to both. With the emergence of the concept of representation in the modern period, however, thought came to be understood as something that goes on in the mind in full independence of the objects with which it is concerned, and without any prior guarantee of a correspondence between thought and thing. With regard to the way this representation is effected, there have been a considerable variety of views about the nature of the concepts or general representations through which it is achieved and their relation to what we perceive. The empiricist view that concepts are constructions out of impressions of sense was an attempt to supersede a realism of natural kinds that was sometimes associated with a theory of innate ideas. With the discrediting of empiricism on the grounds that it could not deal satisfactorily with the specifically logical features of thought, the representations that thought involves came increasingly to be conceived in explicitly linguistic terms.

It has already been explained why the logical-linguistic approach to thought lends itself so naturally to the conception of thought as representation. The reason is that thought in the medium of language, in either its auditory or its visual mode, involves the production of sentences and thus of something that seems manifestly distinct from the objects that are being referred to in such sentences. But because this sense of the separateness and distinctness of thought from its objects derives largely from the sounds and marks that occur in overt speech or writing, and not from the disclosive function of a sentence, it is clear that there is something incoherent in the concept itself of a representation. After all, what makes thought distinct *from* its object cannot be that which makes it a thought *of* just that object. Attempts have been made to deal with this difficulty by applying the content-container metaphor to thought as expressed in a sentence. On this view, the shape or sound of the sentence would be the container, and the content would be what makes a reference to an extralinguistic object and says something about it. Although the metaphorical character of this contrast is plain enough, it is seldom noticed; so the inappropriateness of the picture it invokes to the function of language it is supposed to illuminate passes unnoticed as well.

It is in the account of propositions as the content of sentences that this difficulty emerges most clearly. The concept itself of a proposition is introduced for reasons that are well known. One of them is the fact that different people can say (and therefore think) the same thing in different languages, and that the same people can do so at different times. Evidently, then, although thought understood as discourse is a process taking place *in* the person who thinks at a certain time, what is thought – its content – must be accessible to an open class of intelligent beings with whom that person may communicate. It cannot, therefore, be just an element in the inner life of one such being. To these considerations must be added the old concern with the possibility of error. Although our first inclination might be to say that it is just the object itself, out there in the world, to which a thought is ultimately addressed, there can be no guarantee that such an object exists at all. And yet if it turns out not to exist, it would seem paradoxical to conclude that the original thought must be somehow altered or diminished by that fact. A thought that turns out to be a misrepresentation of the way things are does not, after all, simply crumble into nothingness; so some provision must be made for it that will account for its residual status.

In all these ways, then, the theory of propositions as the content of thought abstracts from the mental processes of each person those identical elements of meaning by virtue of which those processes refer to the same entity and make some assertion about it; and these elements of meaning are then postulated as what all these mental acts of many persons at many different times converge on. This content has the form of a proposition because what is thought must be susceptible of being true or false. This means that it has the form of a sentence; but where in a sentence in a natural language there are words drawn from the vocabulary of that language, in a proposition there are only language-neutral meanings and a syntactical form that relates them to one another. Propositions are in fact something like ghostly sentences – that is, the abstract commonalities of sentences in natural languages that say the same things about the same objects.

The trouble with this whole account of propositions is that, as often happens in such cases, although propositions are supposed to mediate our access to extralinguistic states of affairs, they appear, once they are introduced, to function as a substitute for these states of affairs with which we were nevertheless assumed to be somehow familiar. It looks very much as though I must either conclude that the only world with which I am entitled to claim any familiarity is one that is made up of propositions or I shall no longer be able to think of the original thought as stopping short at the proposition it involves and as leaving the further connection between the proposition and the object to take care of itself. Unless one is a Platonist and is prepared to conceive the relation of these radically disparate terms to one another as a kind of *methexis* of the concrete in the abstract, the idea that it could so take care of itself does not seem to make much sense. But in that case, I would have to think of the thought itself as in some sense passing through the proposition on its way to whatever makes the latter true or false. This amounts to saying that the explanandum has to be drawn into the account we give of the explanans – the theory of propositions – in order to solve a puzzle on which the latter casts no light at all. But if we have to think of the thoughts that are the explananda of this theory of propositions as doing the work that the latter evidently cannot do, why should any form of mediation between such thoughts and their ultimate object be necessary?

These redundancies built into representational theories are too familiar by now to require further discussion. The real question they raise is whether there is not some way in which we can dispense altogether with the mediation that propositions are supposed to afford and return to the common-sense view that *what* we are thinking of, when we think, is not some abstract entity but, rather, the actual concrete entities out there in the world to which we so confidently refer. It has already been noted that any such suggestion is typically viewed as incongruous because it would involve inserting actual entities like cathedrals and mountains – examples of the kinds of things we think about – into the process of thought itself or into the mental domain in which the latter takes place. But we have already seen that there are excellent reasons why the notion of such a domain should be given up altogether; and if a differentiated concept of presence can replace that of representation, this objection will not carry much weight.

Clearly, if it were based on the concept of presence, a view of thought as addressing itself to things in the world would not entail any incongruous transfer of an object from one domain – the world – to another – the mind. And so, on these grounds at least, it is hard to see why an abstract propositional substitute for the actual entities the mind cannot accommodate is needed.

A more promising alternative to this triadic scheme – thoughts, propositions, things – would be to consider whether there may not be an affinity between the presence in absence itself of the objects of thought and the logical structures of the sentences we produce about them – an affinity that would make the mediating role of propositions superfluous. This suggestion would be consistent with the line of thought that I have been developing in the account of the presence of objects in perception and of their presence in absence in memory. In other words, if "There is . . ." and "There was . . ." express two fundamental modes of the differentiation of presence, it makes sense to consider whether other logical forms that sentences may assume do not, in a quite general way, also serve to express further differentiations of presence, and thus of presence in absence as well.

The thesis I have been developing is that states of affairs are the presence (and the presence in absence) of objects to us. As applied to thought and to the statements in which thought finds expression, this thesis becomes the claim that states of affairs are what statements express and also what makes them true (or false). In this sense, statements are modalities of presence, although they are not, as the preceding discussion shows, the only way in which objects can be present or present in absence to us. Accordingly, the different logical forms of statements, as well as their tense structures and modal variations, express the ways in which objects can be present in absence to us. It also follows that thought is not only not *about* propositions understood as intermediaries between thought and things; it is most certainly not *about* statements or sentences either. In the form it takes as expressed by these statements, it is itself the *being* of the objects with which it is concerned in that sense of "being" in which it signifies all or any of the modes of embeddedness in a state of affairs of the objects about which a true statement can be made. There is even a sense in which, simply by virtue of its character as presence, a state of affairs might itself be called "true." This would certainly be a very different sense from the one that applies to statements because the latter can be either true or false and a state of affairs can certainly not be false. It could nevertheless be argued that as what makes a statement true or false and thereby lifts objects, so to speak, into a domain of truth, a state of affairs has a valid claim to be so described. What is clear is that an object by itself has no claim to be called true, and that it is only as embedded in a state of affairs that we are familiar with it at all.

If the line of thought I am developing here is to be at all plausible, it must confront a number of serious objections. One of these has to do with the specifically logical form of the sentences in which thought is expressed; and it points to the difficulty – many would say impossibility – of finding anything in the world itself that could be said to correspond to it. But if logical form has to be conceived as something that is projected upon the world *ab extra*, and if its design is more or less arbitrary and subject at most to pragmatic constraints, the case for conceiving states of affairs as the presence to us of the objects they comprise would be seriously compromised. For one thing, since the whole apparatus of distinctions we use for categorizing the world as a system of objects of various kinds would have this projective character, the world itself would offer no clue to what is to count, for example, as a subject and what as a property or predicate. So nothing in the world could indicate what the logical form of either states of affairs or statements expressing them must be.

At bottom, this is the same line of thought that was considered in Chapter 2 in connection with perception; and the answer that was given there is equally valid against it in its application to thought. Once again, it is the view of the world as an aggregate of objects, rather than of facts or states of affairs, that makes it necessary to conclude that the domicile of the logical forms in terms of which states of affairs are constituted can only be in language. This idea did not have much to recommend it when it was confined to perceptual experience, and it has even less when it is applied to objects that are absent in the various ways that are being distinguished in this chapter. What are we to make, for example, of the claim that the past and the future, as well as the present state of the world, are aggregates of objects and, as such, devoid of anything that would require a sentence to express it? Julius Caesar was, if one likes, an "object" of a certain kind; but to insist on treating him as simply one object in an aggregate of objects is to prescind from the fact of presence – in this case, of presence in absence. That fact is presupposed by any knowledge we claim to have about him, and it can only be understood as constituting a state of affairs. Even the fact that there was such a man at all, as well as anything he did or suffered, must be expressed in the form of a sentence in the past tense. Nor does this requirement arise solely out of some contingent need or desire to put what is so recalled into words. The case is, rather, that our relation to the objects embedded in these past facts is such that only a sentence in the past tense, or some functional equivalent thereof in English or another language, can bring it to expression. We can, if we like, construct "eternal sentences" that make use of a supposedly tenseless present, and thus make it appear as though temporality could be objectified as position within a spatiotemporal continuum. So conceived, the position something occupies in the time order would have nothing to do with the temporal relation in which it stands to the fashioner of such sentences about it. What this turns out to mean, however, is simply that this relation can be hidden behind the linguistic fiction of a tenseless present. In one way or another, what is so hidden – that is, the pastness of the states of affairs we are concerned with, and with it our temporal relation to the various parts of such a continuum – must eventually manifest itself if only as what these linguistic strategies were designed to conceal. And in the wider context so exposed, Caesar will again have to be understood to be someone who lived long ago.

Another point to be made here is that this notion of something's being "in language" is ambiguous: It can mean either language as saying something or language as itself an event in the world. Since only the former can possibly serve as the domicile of logical forms, and since the relationship between such acts and the states of affairs in the world that they express looks quite different in the absence of propositional intermediaries, what objection can there be to saying that the logical form of the former is the form of a state of affairs in the world? This, of course, leaves open the possibility that nothing in the world uniquely requires one logical form as the only one in which it can find expression. Even so, this fact, if it is one, by no means justifies the idea that has recently found such wide acceptance – the idea that absolutely anything goes in the language–world relation and that, in the absence of anything that could be called correspondence between the two, there can be nothing that deserves the name of truth.[9] Even if we have to think of ourselves as in some sense designing the sentence forms we use without a template in the world itself, the only thing that counts is whether the statements we make using these forms can have determinate truth values; and nothing has been brought forth that vitiates this possibility.

A far more serious objection bases itself on the fact of error. It hardly needs to be said that thought is even more prone to error than perception is; and we have seen that just as the fact of error has inspired representational theories of perception, it has also led to representational theories of thought. As in the case of perception, what such theories achieve is something quite different from what they ostensibly intend since the intermediaries they introduce block the very access to things in the world to which they are supposed to serve as bridges. This paradoxical outcome can also

9. There appears to be an unavowed longing on the part of those who draw these dire conclusions for some way of talking about things that would be ratified by the things in question themselves. But since no such way of talking is possible, the only alternative is thought to be that anything goes in the language–world relation. On this point, see the critique of Derrida by Peter Dews in his *Logics of Disintegration* (London: Verso, 1987), pp. 4–11.

be observed in the case of the concept of belief, which plays a prominent role in such theories. Much of what I am calling presence in absence would usually be described in ordinary psychological parlance as belief. For these purposes, belief is understood to be a mental state or a "propositional attitude" that is logically distinct from the state of affairs that it affirms. The advantage of this separation is that when our "beliefs" prove false, as they often do, we can alter them without having to say that something in the world has concurrently changed. If we replace belief with presence in absence, however, there will be a difficulty about the way we are to describe retroactively what was the case before our error was discovered. After all, we can hardly go on describing that prior state of the world as the presence in absence of objects that have turned out either not to exist or to lack the properties we attributed to them. Retrospectively, therefore, it seems that I must introduce something like belief into my description of what has turned out to be only a putative presence in absence. There is also the fact that the concept of belief appears to admit of degrees much more readily than the concept of presence, and this makes it possible to deal with cases in which we are somewhat uncertain and are not prepared to commit our-selves unconditionally to there being something of a certain kind. This means that when there is disagreement, and when different beliefs about the same matter are held by different people, it is a good deal easier to describe such a situation in terms of belief than of presence in absence since it is not clear how something could be present in absence for one person and not for another who is similarly circumstanced. But if in re-sponse to all these considerations I were to introduce an element of belief into my account of thought, I would clearly have gone over to an utterly different paradigm in which thoughts are, in the first instance, something that belongs to me – something in me – rather than something's being present to me. In that case, all that will be left of the language of presence will be a *façon de parler*.

These advantages of a psychological model of thought as belief over any conception of it as presence in absence may well seem so conclusive as to make it foolhardy to contest the issue any further. Even so, before we ac-quiesce in this conclusion, the concept of belief itself may stand in need of a little scrutiny. It is usually counterposed to that of knowledge; unlike believing, knowing that p entails that it really is the case that p. To describe oneself as believing that p is, accordingly, to follow a counsel of caution since in normal circumstances an assertion that implies nothing about the world is unlikely to be wrong. Could I always describe my thoughts in this reflexive, self-descriptive way and leave the determination of whether or not I also *know* what I describe myself as believing to some court of higher instance? The strong emphasis that is now placed on the collective and public character of all inquiry might make it appear that I not only could but should do just this. The trouble is that all the other (human) participants in such cognitive undertakings are in the same situation that I am in; and if they are held to the same requirement in this matter as I am, they will not have any more authority to upgrade my believing to the status of knowing than I do. It thus begins to seem as though the truth that differentiates knowing from believing must accrue to our beliefs in a rather mysterious kind of independence from those beliefs themselves. So mysterious, indeed, does this whole distinction between believing and knowing become that one may doubt whether anyone ever believes anything in the sense that is laid down in this distinction, and even more whether such a concept as this of belief is at all suited to serve as the master concept for describing the life of an ek-sistent entity.

More concretely, although the use of the word "believe" does serve to convey to others a certain caution with which an assertion is being made, there is not the slightest reason to suppose that it names a mental act of a special kind, any more than "know" does. In ordinary parlance, my "belief," say, that the cat is on the mat cannot be distinguished from the cat's being on the mat; and this is clearly indicated by the vacuity of such a statement as "The cat is on the mat and I believe it," not to speak of the palpable strain produced by statements like "The cat is on the mat, but I don't believe it" or "I believe the cat is on the mat, but it is not." What the first sentence shows is the redundancy of the belief component when it is in harmony with the preceding assertion, and what the other two show is that the belief clause cannot express anything intelligible if it is at variance with the assertion of fact in the other clause. Nor is this point a merely linguistic or logical one in some sense that would confine it to the occasions on which we expressly formulate our beliefs. If, as we say, I "believe" that the cat is on the mat, there is not the slightest reason to suppose that, in addition to the cat's being on the mat, a mental act is occurring that would, if it were put into words, come out as a belief clause like the ones in the sentences just presented.

What has been said may be enough to render problematic the concept of belief on which we so readily fall back in these contexts, but it still leaves the fact of error unexplained in terms compatible with the presence-in-absence conception of thought. Suppose that the cat is really not on the mat at all, and suppose that I learn this when I come back into the room where the mat is. Now what is present to me is the cat's *not* being on the mat, but what am I to say about its prior presence in absence as on the mat? In the case of a perceptual error, I can say that what I saw *was* something quite different from what I had supposed it to be, even though I did not recognize it as such; and I can deal with the fact of the error itself by treating it as a failure of my recognitional and classificatory powers, without having to postulate any qualitative residue for which the mind would be the only plausible receptacle. In the case of an error about something I was not perceiving, however, I cannot proceed in this way. I cannot say that the mat without any cat on it was what was present in absence and that I simply failed to recognize it; and I can't say this because the notion of recognition simply does not apply to something one is not perceiving. My only recourse in these circumstances seems to be to say that the supposed presence in absence a few minutes ago of the cat on the mat was really just a belief of mine – something purely subjective, something occurring in my mind in full independence of the cat and its actual whereabouts.

This is indeed what we typically do, but there is a difficulty inherent in it. The trouble is that such a description subtly alters the prior situation to which it is addressed by overriding the redundancy of belief that was just discussed and disregarding its effacement in the presence in absence of the object in question. In its place, we postulate retroactively a full-blown psychological state that is sufficient unto itself in the sense just explained: a belief that happened to be paired with a state of affairs at variance with it. One thing does seem clear: The motives for our proceeding in this way have nothing to do with fidelity to the way things were "psychologically" at the time of the error; and it is only what we have learned about the cat, and not about ourselves, that dictates this new description. It also seems clear that this description involves just as much of a misrepresentation as it would to claim that whenever I appear to have made a mistake of this kind, it is always the world that has changed; in other words, the cat was on the mat, but it moved. Were I to take the other alternative and declare that I was really in a belief state that could have been described without implying anything about the world, this, too, would be a misrepresentation – not of the state of the world but, rather, of the person in question. To use an example, it is as though one were claiming that such a person's state would have been properly described as one of *believing*, say, that Europe, where he has never been, is on the other side of the Atlantic when the only thing this would have conveyed is a lack of certitude that he did not in fact feel.

It may be that the change that occurs when, as we say, we discover our error is one that cannot be dealt with by saying either that the change took place only "in me," with the replacement of one belief by another, or, fantastically, that there was a change in the world as well as a change in me. Instead, the change that occurs is of a distinctive kind that involves both the world and the self. There is a change in the self, if one likes to put it that way, but it is in the self as an entity to which other entities are present, and present in absence. The change occurs because the world is different from what it "was" – the quotation marks show that we have disqualified the claim implicit in the word they single out – although it has been all along as we now understand it. We deal with this peculiar situation by revising our description of the self as it was at that earlier time and imputing to it a "belief" in which the disqualified state of the world is encapsulated; and in this way, we make the state of the self at that time compatible with the state of the world. It is as though, in order to avoid opening up a gap between the self as it is now and what is the case in the world, we were prepared to sacrifice a former self (or at least part of it) by treating it as a container for beliefs and thus accepting a status for it that sets it logically apart from the world.

What especially needs to be noted here is that in doing this we are appealing to something as the governing standpoint from which the past self is redescribed – something that itself does not at all fit the model of belief. That something is the fact that we are not only liable to error but able as well to detect and correct it; and in this case, that would mean we are revising our description of our past state in light of the fact that the cat is not on the mat. What is important is that there is no way in which that fact about us can receive proper recognition within the model of belief under consideration. When the concept of belief is introduced in the way that has just been described, it presupposes a wider context that transcends it in the sense that it – the wider context – cannot be understood in terms of still further beliefs. If, as is sometimes done, we were to generalize the picture of the self as a container for beliefs and, in so doing, extend it to the self as it is at present, that contrast would be eliminated. Clearly, however, if we place both the past and the present selves on the same footing as containers of beliefs, we thereby undercut the basis on which we demoted a state of affairs – the cat's being on the mat – to the status of a belief and made it an element in the content of that former self. This would be a high price to pay for our use of the concept of belief, and it makes sense to try to determine whether there may not be a way of dealing with error that does not require so much of us.

The thesis I am defending is that the fact of error does not justify the introduction of beliefs as conceptual representations at the level of thought any more than it did that of sense representations at the level of perception. This is not to deny that our susceptibility to error at the one level and the other has implications for a theory of presence in absence. For one thing, it shows that presence in absence can no more be considered as spontaneously and infallibly self-declaratory than presence itself could be; and this means that an element of process and correction is involved in it that draws on the critical powers of human beings and thereby, in the language of this book, associates presence with ek-sistence as the mode of being of an entity that has a world. More concretely, just as perceptual presence presupposes the classificatory system that the human being uses to identify the entities in its world, so thought as presence in absence cannot be characterized in abstraction from the logical controls it exercises over the presence to it of objects as articulated in states of affairs. But all this may be conceded without thereby espousing the standard theory of mental representations that is supposed to enable us to deal with the fact of error or the concept of belief that derives from it. The practical utility of that concept as a signal to others of how they are to take what we tell them is not in dispute here, any more than that of many other mentalistic terms like "remember" was in earlier chapters. What is being challenged is the representational interpretation of thought that results when these mentalistic concepts are generalized in the manner described earlier.

What, then, is the upshot of this discussion of error as a recurrent feature of thought? It certainly cannot be claimed that the ultimate sources of our propensity to error have been discovered – that is, how it is possible for error to occur at all. That is a large independent question that I have not even attempted to answer. Finally, nothing has been said thus far about how the fact of disagreement between different people can be integrated into such a conception. But if the main conclusion of this section stands and the primordial fact that thought is susceptible to error does not by itself compel us to resort to a theory of belief, there is reason to think that these matters could also be successfully resolved.

There is one further respect in which this account of thought may appear to be vulnerable to objections. It has to do with the role of language in presence in absence and with language in its positive aspect as the medium in which we are able to draw on, for the purposes of thinking about them, someone else's account of things we have not observed ourselves. When we do this, it is only through the general import of the words used in that account that what they describe can become present in absence to us. There is a difficulty here for any view of thought as presence in absence, since it is not clear how something other than a particular entity could be present at all. But if words are meaningful, as has been supposed, by virtue of the general representations or concepts associated with them, this element of particularity remains unaccounted for.

Fortunately, the elements of an answer to this puzzle were set forth long ago by Bishop Berkeley, though in an idiom that requires some modification. In the controversy about the generality-particularity of ideas that was set off by Locke's *Essay*, Berkeley argued that there could be no idea of a triangle in general – that is, neither scalene or equilateral – and that generality accrues to some particular triangle idea by its being made to stand for all other triangle ideas that are, of course, equally determinate in their own ways.[10] This answer assumes that when we think of triangles or anything else, what we are thinking of must be "in" the mind and is therefore an

10. George Berkeley, *A Treatise Concerning the Principles of Human Knowledge*, in *The English Philosophers from Bacon to Mill*, edited by Edwin A. Burtt (New York: Modern Library, 1939), pp. 510–22.

"idea." It is possible, however, to avoid the liabilities this assumption entails by dropping Berkeley's mentalistic idiom. One can simply say that just as it would be impossible to draw a triangle that would be just a three-sided plane figure and indeterminate in all other respects, so there is no reason to suppose that triangles we think of could lack more specific properties. What we can do, however, is simply ignore any properties, other than being a three-sided plane figure, that a given triangle, whether actual or imagined, may have.

It is that "ignoring" that plays a constitutive role in the form of presence in absence that is mediated by general descriptions. By comparison with the objects of perception and even of memory, the objects that we think of via verbal descriptions are present in absence in a peculiarly reduced mode that corresponds to the terms in which they have been described to us. This is because presence in absence in the mode of thought involves the work of a classificatory capability that brings particular objects under general headings. It is the object itself (and not something in the mind) that either has or does not have the feature in question; but since every object belongs under indefinitely many headings, it cannot be that object itself that brings itself under any particular heading rather than another. That is the work of the entity to which things are present and whose mode of being is that of ek-sistence. When on the basis of such a classification the objects in question are present in absence to someone who has never observed them, it is as though they had been "cannibalized" out of other objects that are familiar. They remain nevertheless abstract because they have not been provided with a full complement of properties. But although generality accrues to a particular of whatever kind through this abstractive process of classification, the properties in terms of which it is described remain the properties of a particular, and its partial indeterminacy will yield to full determinacy if and when this thought is fulfilled in perception.

IV

In the preceding sections, two different kinds of absence have been shown to lend themselves to two corresponding (and, again, quite different) modalities of presence in absence. These two cases have something important in common because in both memory and thought the states of affairs that are what we remember or what we think, are or have been actual, and so it is Thought as a vehicle of truth that we have been dealing with up to this point. There is still another form of absence, however, that may not seem to be compatible with any claim to truth at all. "Imagination" is the word we use to designate the function of the mind that is supposed to be involved here; and, instead of being concerned with what is or has been actual, imagination addresses itself to what is not the case and may never have been – that is, to states of affairs that no one either perceives or remembers and sometimes to entities that do not exist and, for all we know, may never exist at all.[11] In these circumstances, it is hard to see how anything could be said to be present in absence to us when we imagine. Imagination, after all, involves no "There has been . . ." any more than it does a "There is . . ." or, for all we know, a "There will be. . . ." The most it could claim to express is a "There could (or might) be. . . ." The absence that imagination involves thus appears to be simply too unqualified by any contact with what is or has been the case for it to be eligible for any modality of presence.

Plausible as this summary rejection of any affinity between imagination and presence may seem, it can hardly be denied that when we imagine, we imagine something and not nothing. There is, accordingly, a temptation to conclude that there must be something that we so imagine. There are well-known difficulties with such an inference, however, and the standard philosophical ways of providing an ontological status for this nonactual "something" are of little help. Typically, a kind of pseudo object is postulated, which is supposed to be what we address ourselves to when we imagine something that is not actual. In one version, the talk of imagination as a pictorial faculty is taken literally, and what is present to the mind when we imagine something is supposed to be an image or mental picture of something that does not exist but could possibly do so. Clearly, however, one cannot simply nullify the distinction between a picture or image of something and that thing itself, and an account of the former cannot suffice for the latter. Another alternative is a theory of objects that do not exist but do "subsist"; this means that they have a kind of timeless, nonactual reality in a realm of possibility to which we have access through some special form of intuition.

Many objections can be made to both of these theories, but the fundamental mistake both make is their attempt to provide, for imagination, a functional equivalent of a normal object. By doing so, they lay themselves open to the tongue-in-cheek objection that these exotic objects will simply take up too much room in an already crowded world. This objection may achieve a certain rhetorical effect by casting the partisans of possibility in the role of reckless landlords who rent out more space than is actually available. If it does, however, that will be due to the fact that just as being itself has been misconceived as an object or superobject of some kind, so the according of an extralogical status to nonbeing is mistakenly thought to entail the addition of some (peculiar) entities to the complement of real

---

11. It is, of course, possible to imagine things that are actually occurring or have occurred. When we do this, we make up for the deficit of information about such events by picturing to ourselves what they might probably or possibly be like. The notion of possibility is thus still very much involved.

ones that make up the world. But if being is properly understood as presence, and this means as a state of affairs – as something being something – rather than as an object, then nonbeing will have to be reconceived along the same lines. Nonbeing will then be understood as paired with being as presence and as involving the same entities; it will, in fact, constitute the finite and thus exclusionary character of any state of affairs in which certain entities are present to us. In other words, just by virtue of the *being* such-and-such of those entities, many things that might otherwise have been the case are not so; and nonbeing is the disclosure of this exclusionary character of being itself. As such, it is a new and more radical modality of absence that is coordinate with presence (and thus with being) in all its forms. My thesis is thus that entities can be present only in an implicit contrast with what they are not and with what is thus not the case, and that this contrast is presupposed even when, as in the case of memory, it is in the first instance a past actuality that is directly involved.

These considerations can be further developed in a way that brings them into a clearer relation to the topic of possibility. If, as has been argued here, entities are present only as elements in states of affairs, and if the being of something is to be understood as what brings it into presence as the domain of truth, then there is at least one possibility with which a state of affairs must always be paired. That is the possibility of its not being the case that there is such an entity at all, or that it has the property it has or stands in the relation it does in the actual state of affairs. If an entity cannot *be* anything otherwise than in a contrast with its *not* being so, every state of affairs will have an associated "could" by virtue of which it *could* not have obtained at all. For most purposes, this "could" is doubtless a very weak one, but that does not diminish its significance. Unless it were applicable, it seems clear that no stronger "could" could ever replace it; and entities would no longer present themselves as being what they are in terms of a contrast with what, alternatively, might be the case. In this sense, there is good reason to say that what is not the case must be disclosed (and thus present in its own distinctive mode of absence) if any actual entities are to be present.

This idea of a pairing of being and nonbeing receives support from another quite different set of considerations having to do with the logic of the causal relation. Under the influence of an implicit actualism in logical theory, it had been assumed that the causal relation between p and q must be something one can read off from the different permutations of the truth values of p and q in the actual world. If that were the case and if, consistently with this assumption, the world, whether as an aggregate of objects or of facts, were actual through and through, there would be no place in it for possibility as something that is not the case but might or could be. As a result of work that has been done on the logic of the causal relation, however, it has been established that such a construal of the causal relation is untenable.[12] The reason is that that relation involves an uneliminable element of counterfactuality. If p – something's being such and such – is the cause of q, then it must be the case that p *would* bring about q even though neither p nor q is the case. In other words, the causal relation between p and q is *not* something one can read off from the truth values of p and q in the actual world, even when the latter includes the actual past and the actual future. Instead, the assertion that there is such a relation involves a claim about what would happen if p *were* to be the case even though it may never be; and this is to say that possibility is uneliminably involved in causal relationships.

Nor is it just the causal relation as such that is linked to possibility in this way. It is also evident that an understanding of what any given object is cannot be achieved in abstraction from the ways in which it acts and reacts in causal transactions with other objects of various kinds. But if this is the case and if those transactions themselves cannot be analyzed in purely Humean terms – that is, in terms of actually observed or observable regularities of sequence – without erasing the distinction between causal and purely accidental pairings of events, then it follows that our knowledge of things in the real world involves some sort of familiarity with possibilities. In other words, because the causal relation involves an implication as to what *would* happen if something else occurred, and does so without thereby entailing any prediction that this will – as contrasted with "would" – actually occur, an understanding of a causal relation between two events, and thus of the objects involved in that relation, requires an ability to envisage something nonactual and in that sense merely possible. It would follow from this that, to the extent to which we conceive, say, an apprehension – whether in perception or in thought – of some such object in terms of presence, the presence of any ordinary actual object would incorporate within itself the presence in absence of the possibilities that are implicit in the causal linkages that pertain to this object.

It seems clear, then, that in presence being and nonbeing – the world as it actually is and the world as it is not – are not simply paired so as to lie, so to speak, side by side with one another without there being any closer nexus between them. That would have the effect of reducing all possibility to what is called "logical possibility" – the mere absence of internal incoherence in the concept of something. Clearly there are stronger connections between what is the case and what is not than this notion permits. In the actual state of the world, some things that are logically possible are really possible and others are not. There are, in other words, only certain ways in which actual entities can change so as to bring about something

---

12. See the article "Contrary-to-Fact Conditionals" in *The Encyclopedia of Philosophy,* edited by P. Edwards (New York: Macmillan, 1967), vol. 2, pp. 212–15.

that was previously not the case. But if that is the case, and if our concepts of the objects in question reflect, among other things, these possibilities (and these possibilities *as* possibilities), then the prepossessions just described – the ones that say that what is merely possible and does not therefore exist could not be present or an element in what is present – need to be reexamined. More concretely, if the actual world contains within itself an element of possibility, then instead of being the antitype of all those cognitive apprehensions that address themselves to a world of actual objects, imagination would be more in the nature of a further exploitation of the reciprocal relationship between the actual and the possible. Generically, imagination might well be viewed not as a gratuitous association of an arbitrarily selected property with some otherwise familiar object – a horse that can fly, for example – but, rather, as the kind of counterfactual cantilevering of the possible off actual objects in the way suggested by the analysis of the causal relation.

There can be no doubt that the element of possibility built into actual entities is centrally involved in imagination in many of its typical manifestations. I can, for example, imagine what the city in which I live would look like after a nuclear weapon had been dropped on it. A hundred years ago, no one seriously believed that anything of that kind was possible; but we have learned, to our sorrow, that it is and that this is something that could happen to our cities. It is in fact not too much to say that this possibility has become an element in the way we perceive and think about our cities at the present time. When we imagine such a possibility, we are not taking leave of the real world for a realm of fantasy; we are envisaging our cities as they may possibly one day be.[13] Although no claim to actuality, whether past, present, or future, is implied by what I am imagining in such a case, the possibility I imagine is anchored in an actual entity and an actual situation. As a possibility associated with something actual, it can properly be said to be both absent and present. It is in fact, in its own distinctive way, present in its absence.

There is, of course, an obvious objection that could be made to this whole line of thought. Even if it is allowed that a place can be secured for possibility within the real world by such considerations as these, it will be asserted that imagination conceived as dealing with possibilities implicit in the causal relation is by no means coextensive with imagination as we ordinarily understand it. The reason is that the kind of possibility that has just been discussed lends itself to prediction – if not categorical, then hypothetical – much more naturally than it does to anything we would normally call "imagination." Typically, imagination does not remain within

---

13. An unusually powerful example of this use of the imagination is *Ridley Walker* by Russell Hoban (New York: Summit Books, 1980).

the domain of what could happen – that is, of what is contrafactually predictable on the basis of real-world causal relations. Precisely because the example of imagination I have given is anchored in the real world, it must, on this view, be a poor guide to imagination in its freer and more luxuriant manifestations.

To cite an example of imagination in its freely elaborative mode, there are novels in which none of the characters are real people. They may live on a nonexistent street in a real city like London or in a city and country that are wholly imaginary. In the one case as in the other, things may happen that could never happen in the real world. A house may turn into gingerbread, a horse may talk, or, as in science fiction, imaginary technologies may permit things like time travel and brain transplants. In none of these cases is it easy to see how the possibility entertained in imagination could be the possibility *of* an actual entity, as in the "realistic" cases of imagining. The kind of presence in absence of possibilities that was described earlier does not seem to fit such cases as these.

Although I have put off the discussion of human action until Chapter 5, it has to be pointed out here that imagination is not confined to things that we might observe happening without any active participation on our part. We also imagine what we or other people might do and what they might be able to create or discover or invent in circumstances very different from those that now prevail. On a deterministic view according to which there can be only one sequel to every state of the world, this fact would not make much, if any, difference; but as a practical matter, it greatly increases the number of possibilities that can be attributed to any given situation. Short of some miraculous feat of self-objectification by virtue of which we ourselves, as well as the mixture of knowledge and ignorance in which we live, could become elements in our own predictions, it is hard to see what grounds there could be for insisting that the situations in which we live can develop further in only one direction. Even if we could make ourselves and our actions part of such a reckoning, that very fact would create a new situation with its own spectrum of possibilities to which the preceding calculation would not be applicable.[14] Clearly, to commit ourselves in principle to Spinoza's view, which treats possibility as simply a function of our ignorance, would not only involve a strenuous abstraction from the circumstances of ordinary life but would do nothing to remove the actual ignorance in which we unavoidably live. The one and only thing that, on a view like Spinoza's, can and must happen in a given situation must, accordingly, remain an empty postulate. **But** if there is no way of eliminating the possibility that there are multiple possibilities – many things that could happen

14. I have discussed this matter in some detail in my *Principles and Persons: An Ethical Interpretation of Existentialism* (Baltimore: Johns Hopkins University Press, 1967), pp. 145–53.

– then it will make sense to envisage what *might* happen in a given situation even if we are not at all sure about the conditions that would bring about a particular result. For such an understanding of some actual situation, "imagination" seems exactly the right designation.

An example of imagination in this sense would be a book like Sinclair Lewis's *It Can't Happen Here*. In the face of confident claims that fascism could never become an element in American political life, Lewis imagined just such an eventuality. He did not predict that a political figure like the one he imagined would emerge, nor did he claim to have some scientific warrant for any such prediction. But the possibility he envisaged was not without a link to the actual world. It was a possibility attributable to this country in the twentieth century and to its political institutions; and Lewis drew extensively on his knowledge of both in telling the story of an American fascist. It was a plausible story, and at the very least, it may have shaken the complacency of some who had been certain that nothing like that could ever happen. As things turned out, fascism did not come to this country in the 1930s. Even so, the conclusion that a determinist would draw from this – namely, that fascism was never possible at all – does not seem much more convincing in retrospect than it did at the time.

This still leaves unaccounted for the many examples of imagination in which what is imagined is plainly impossible by any normal, real-world standard. People have imagined flying horses like Pegasus and talking horses like Mr. Ed, although neither flying nor talking is a possibility that can be sensibly attributed to any actual horse or to horses as a species. The Greeks, who first imagined Pegasus, may not have been completely clear on this point, but the people who conceived Mr. Ed surely must have been. It is true that one should be a little cautious about consigning all such imaginings to the category of the merely fantastic since the same Greeks who imagined Pegasus also imagined Icarus – a man who could fly – and it has turned out that human beings can indeed fly. It is not, however, my intention to suggest that imagination stands or falls by its ability to make lucky guesses of this kind. What I want to suggest instead is that imagination as the exploration of real-world possibilities provides the basis for a further development in connection with which the question of whether what is envisaged is really possible takes on a rather different aspect.

This further development is that of imagination as fantasy – the projection of events and situations that are *understood* to be impossible. Its distinctive feature is that it draws the causal powers of various kinds of entities into the circle of what could be otherwise. Carpets do not have the power to transport us through the air in the world as it is, but might this not have been otherwise? Clearly, the point of view from which we might conclude that it could would have to abstract in a radical way from the actual causal ordering of the world we know and would have to treat what are now viewed as being, at best, logical possibilities as real ones in another kind of world. It might be objected that a story told about things and events in such a very different world could have no relevance to our own, since objects with such different powers would not satisfy any meaningful criteria of identity with their ostensible counterparts in our own world. Perhaps this is why writers who develop fantasies of this kind are often at pains to make the exotic entities they describe as similar as possible in all other respects to those that are familiar to us. By doing so, they in effect try to reassure their readers by convincing them that a world in which things that are impossible in ours can occur is nevertheless one that in all other respects satisfies their sense of reality.

One purpose of such stories may be to relieve us of the constraints of our ordinary, sublunary existence, and the popularity of chivalric romances in the past and of science fiction in our own day shows that an interest in such fantasies is by no means limited to those who are too naive to be able to distinguish between what is really possible and what is not. Others find it harder and harder as they grow older to interest themselves in stories that violate too emphatically their sense of what is real and what is possible. There is a middle ground, however, that may be defined as a willingness to accept fantasy provided that the non–real-world possibilities it puts before us serve as metaphors for something else that is deeply interesting to us and that may be possible in the world as it is presently constituted. If, for example, we are invited to imagine Swift's Houyhnhnms or the Bible's lion that lies down with the lamb, what we imagine is, at the literal level, impossible. It may, nevertheless, express something that, although sharply at odds with conventional ideas of what can happen in human life, is being seriously proposed as a challenge to those conventional ideas of what is possible and deserves to be taken seriously.

The line of thought I have been developing suggests that just as the actual involves an element of possibility, so possibility, even in its more radical forms, remains dependent on actuality. If this is correct, then the difficulty of applying the concept of presence to what we imagine no longer seems so formidable. That difficulty was simply that because no such entities as the ones we imagine exist, there is therefore nothing that could be present to us. But if, as I have been arguing, what we imagine is always some transformation of actual entities or of the actual world, then what is present is a possibility that attaches to an actual entity – either to a particular entity like this horse, or to some indefinite but actual entity that we refer to simply as a "horse." We typically think of possibilities as abstract entities awaiting instantiation in some realm of their own outside the space and time of our world. On the view being proposed, however, their linkage with actual entities would be much closer than this picture suggests; and when they are understood as transformations of which actual entities are susceptible, the difficulty about their being present is substantially reduced. This is because it is associated with other transformations, like a caterpillar's becoming a butterfly, which we do not think of as requiring the postulation of subsistent entities, either in order that they may occur or in order that we should be able to think of them.

But if the presence of possibilities has become less of a mystery, it is still not clear *how* this presence is to be conceived. More specifically, is it a matter of images in the sense that images are somehow essentially involved in imagination even though they cannot, as has already been noted, constitute the substance of what we imagine? An image is supposed to be a kind of mental picture, and such pictures are supposed to be the stand-ins for whatever cannot be present *in propria persona* because it does not exist. In other words, the claim here would be that if something is now present to me that has the traits that would belong to the thing that I am imagining if it existed, that something can only be an image or picture of that thing. This image exists as the thing itself does not, and so the image must be what I am seeing since I cannot see what does not exist. The assumption here is evidently that imagination must have an actual object of some kind, and since that cannot be the object itself or the state of affairs that is imagined, it can only be an image or picture thereof. The effect of such an assumption is thus to reduce imagination to the status of a deviant case of perception.

It is not difficult to show how different imagining is from seeing a picture of something. Suppose, for example, that I am imagining a house that I would like to build. Let us say that it is a one-story white stucco house on a large wooded lot. In imagining such a house, do I see something white in anything like the way I see something white when I see a white house or see a picture of a white house? If a mental image were, as Hume declared it to be, simply a fainter replica of an earlier sensation, it would be comparable to an afterimage, and the answer to this question would have to be yes. In my example, I would, accordingly, have to say that imagining a white house is like having visual sensations of a white object. But if this were really the case, then I should be able to say in what part of my visual field this image is located, as I can in the case of afterimages. In fact, however, it makes no sense to locate something that is being imagined in this way. Again, if what is being imagined is something auditory, like a melody, it makes no sense to ask whether it is louder or softer than some background noise that I may be hearing at the time I am imagining it. It is true that I can imagine the melody as being played or sung loudly or softly, but I can't compare the one loudness with the other. If that were possible, then it might happen that the sound made by the radio playing in my room would be drowned out by the song I am imagining if I were to imagine it as being sung very loudly. More generally, if imagination had as its "content" an

image that was like a picture of whatever is being imagined, then just as
pictures can have a place in the same room, say, as the objects they are
pictures of, and can be *seen* in just as authentic a sense as the latter can, so
mental pictures would consort in the mind on a common footing with (the
perceptions of) the objects they are pictures of. But in fact, what we see
and what we imagine seeing, as well as what we hear and imagine hearing,
simply are not thrown together, hugger-mugger, in such a way as to make
it possible for them to compete with one another or to be compared and
located in relation to one another in such ways as these. What is imagined
is not present to me in the form of an image that counts as an item of
experience alongside all the rest. Instead, it is present to me in its own
distinctive manner as something possible, and its presence in absence is
not dependent on the actuality of an image that would be an occurrent
element in my experiential field.

These considerations suggest that we need to call into question the underlying assumption that imagination is a kind of seeing (or hearing or
whatever) that differs from normal seeing only in the way that seeing a
picture of the Taj Mahal differs from seeing the Taj Mahal itself. But in
order to do this successfully, one must first acknowledge the fact that imagination can unquestionably have a visual or an auditory character. I can,
for example, imagine how the house I am thinking of building would look
from the front. It would be a mistake, however, to conclude that on such
occasions there is something that I do in fact see – a something that is not,
of course, the still-to-be-constructed house itself but is a picture or an image
of it. When one says that it is *as though* one were seeing something, this
should not be taken to mean that one is in fact seeing something – an
image or a picture – and it is as though one were seeing something else –
a house. Instead, we have to understand this "as though" in such a way
that its contrafactuality applies not just to what is seen but to the seeing
itself. There is no house and I am not seeing it, nor am I seeing a picture
of it. When I imagine how something that is still merely possible would look
from a certain angle, the seeing in question is itself merely possible and
forms part of what is being imagined. One could say that in such a case I
am thinking of what a certain (possible) house would look like if I were
(possibly) to see it. The visual quality of such imagining is therefore to be
accounted for not by postulating the presence of an (actual) image but
simply by reference to the fact that it is the visual appearance of – in this
case – the house that is being imagined.

Is all imagining tied to possible seeing or hearing in this way? Suppose
that I were to imagine a peace conference that might be held to resolve
the Arab–Israeli conflict. To imagine such a thing is almost certainly to
imagine representatives of various countries coming together somewhere
and speechs being made and perhaps documents being signed; but pre-

cisely because it is indeterminate who these people would be and where they would meet and what they would say, I need not imagine seeing or hearing them speak in some way that would involve the much greater degree of specificity that would permit me to imagine how they would look or sound. I can, in other words, imagine such an event at a level of generality and indeterminacy to which any number of "scenes" would be appropriate, but without entertaining any one of these in a way that would give a specifically visual or auditory quality to my imagining of this conference. If I wished, I could always spell out what I am imagining in greater and greater detail; and if I were to do so, I would eventually reach a point at which I would be imagining some rather fully determinate scenes. One might even say that I must be capable in principle of proceeding in this way in the direction of fuller specificity and determinateness. In fact, much of our lives is made up of just this kind of mainly nonintuitive imagining of all kinds of things that might occur, although this fact gets little recognition from philosophers. Some of the latter even deny that they have "images" at all, but they can hardly deny that they *imagine* eventualities that might occur, and so they are left with the rather unattractive alternative of arguing that this imagining can only be a private verbal description of what is being anticipated.

Is this, in fact, the only alternative to an "image" view of imagination? If a linguistic account of imagination requires that when I imagine something like a peace conference I must be imagining hearing or seeing words – the words that stand for the kinds of things or events that are involved in a peace conference – rather than how these things would look or sound, then the suggestion is plainly mistaken. The actual sound or shape of words can play a role in imagination if what we are thinking of includes or is made up of words – for example, if I were imagining the first sentence in a novel that I hope to write. But just as surely as words are present to my thoughts on such occasions, they are *not* present on others. When I imagine what it would be like to walk on the moon, I am neither using words to tell myself a story about such a walk nor am I thinking of – as distinct from using – the words that stand for the things I would see and the things I would do there. I can, of course, imagine telling a story about such an experience, and in that case, depending on the degree of detail in which I imagine this storytelling, I would be imagining myself using specific words. It may well be that what I imagine in such a case consists of states of affairs that involve entities for which I do have words, and that in that sense there is a linkage between imagining and language. That would be quite a weak link, however, and it would certainly not imply that imagining is a kind of speaking.

It may be that this account of imagination can cast some much needed light on dreams and dreaming. It was noted earlier that dreams figure prominently in the skeptical case against the reliability of the senses and for the view that the status of the "external world" is somehow deeply problematic. They could hardly do so if it were not for the traditional philosophical assimilation of dreams to images or pictures of things that we perceive in normal waking life. Any such account of dreams runs directly counter to the view of the imagination that I have been developing; and although I cannot undertake a detailed discussion of this complex matter here, the preceding discussion does suggest another more fruitful approach to dreams. First of all, the idea that having a dream is like watching a movie in an ultraprivate screening room is profoundly inaccurate and misleading. The fragmentary and ambiguous character of the scenes that make up our dreams – in many cases, their marked indeterminacy – is so clear that the idea that they could constitute a kind of rival reality that contradicts everyday perception is hard to take seriously. It is true that we sometimes wake from dreams so much under their influence that it takes a moment to reorient ourselves in our actual environment, but this absorption in our dreams does not really pose any epistemic issue any more than a daydream that fully captures us for a moment does.

Daydreams, in fact, deserve far more attention than they normally receive in philosophical discussions of dreaming. They differ from dreams by virtue of occurring, as dreams do not, in the midst of ordinary perceptual life, but in other respects they are indistinguishable from dreams. Interestingly, however, although daydreams proceed very much in the way dreams do, no one seems to think that they give any support to skeptical theses about perception. I draw attention to them both because they can readily be characterized in the terms made available by my account of the imagination and because they can serve as the intermediate term in an assimilation of dreams to imagination as conceived in terms of possibility. Suppose, for example, that on a hot day a bored office worker lapses into reverie and has a daydream of being at the beach and meeting a pretty girl. The daydream can be strongly visual, right down to the color of the girl's hair or swimsuit; but all the considerations that were marshaled earlier against the claim that to imagine something is to see something apply here as well. The man having this daydream can also imagine speaking to the girl and her replying but without in fact hearing anything – either what he says or what she replies. All this may, moreover, take only a second or two of real time, as actual encounters and their accompanying speeches could hardly do. Everything, in other words, speaks in favor of a view of daydreams that treats them as imagined possibilities and not as quasi perceptions of some mysterious kind. But in that case, why should dreams not be viewed in the same way? They, of course, occur during sleep and thus in the absence of normal perceptual experience; and the lack of a simultaneous contrast with actual perceptions may have made it seem more plausible to claim that in dreams we see and hear things in something very close to the usual sense. But the very fact that in dreams we understand so much about the things we "see" – so much that we could not possibly learn from what we describe ourselves as having seen and heard – should make us very cautious about such claims. It is as though the visual and auditory elements in dreams were only fragments of the larger scene in which they are placed – a scene that is itself understood without being unpacked exhaustively into such "views." Altogether, there is, it seems, a strong case to be made for viewing dreaming as imagining, though in the sense of entertaining possibilities and not images.

4

INDIVIDUATION

I

The approach to the philosophy of mind that has been adopted in this book does not attempt to demarcate a special domain of mental phenomena. Instead, the fact of presence – the "There is . . ." – in its several dimensions has set the agenda for this inquiry, and the progressive differentiation of the concept of what there is – that is, of the world – has replaced the analysis of states of mind and internal representations. As a result, at the point that has now been reached, a picture has emerged that is rather like the one Wittgenstein discusses in the *Tractatus* – a picture of the world in which there is no place for "the subject," – or, rather, in which it is at best "the limit of the world." In this vein, Wittgenstein remarks that "from nothing in the field of sight can it be concluded that it is seen from the eye"; and he adds that "solipsism strictly carried out coincides with pure realism" because "the I in solipsism shrinks to an extensionless point and there remains the reality co-ordinated with it." Although Wittgenstein goes on to speak of what he calls a "metaphysical subject" that must be conceived in non-psychological terms – not as "a part of the world" and not as "the human body or the human soul of which psychology treats" – this seems to mean mainly that the only "subject" he is prepared to recognize is one conceived as "the limit of the world."[1]

In spite of the affinity just noted, the wider context of thought to which these passages from Wittgenstein belong is very different from the Heideg-

1. Ludwig Wittgenstein, *Tractatus Logico-philosophicus* (London: Routledge and Kegan Paul, 1922), pp. 151–3.

gerian framework of the present study. This is most evident in the absence of any acknowledgment by Wittgenstein of the plurality of subjects that corresponds to the plurality of human beings. It is just this question of the singular or plural character of the subject that is to be taken up in this chapter. The difficulty about this is that since the theory of presence I have been developing renders what we have hitherto thought of under the rubrics of "mind" and "consciousness" in terms of the "There is . . . ," it may seem to remove any justification for postulating a subject that is any less singular and unique than is the world that is so disclosed. Indeed, the idea of associating plurality and thus, by implication, particularity with the "There is . . ." might be thought to be as incongruous as that of a plurality of systems of truth. Even so, the fact of particularity cannot be simply dismissed, any more than could the fact of error in an account that aspires, as this one does, to replace the concepts of mind and representation. Whatever their other disadvantages, the latter lend themselves readily to pluralization; and if they are to be jettisoned and replaced by the "There is . . ." that announces a world that is singular and unique, there will be an obvious need to show convincingly that under these circumstances the conceivability of more than one "subject" has not been effectively negated. Up to this point, however, in the account that has been given of presence as the "There is . . . ," the world as it is ordered in terms of its several temporal and modal dimensions has been pretty much the whole story; and this is very similar to the situation that Wittgenstein describes in his own idiom.

In this chapter, I attempt to show that a theory that begins with the fact of presence has the conceptual resources that enable it to deal with the individuated and plural character of the entities to which things are present. In marked contrast to Wittgenstein's quasi solipsism, I have been assuming, on the strength of the familar logic of the term itself, not only that when something is present, it is always present *to* something, but also that that something is another entity in the same world as that which is present to it. A human being is such an entity; and unless we are prepared to give up the postulate adopted in Chapter 1 according to which there are many human beings, it is evident that there must also be many entities to which things are present. In these circumstances, it must be possible to refer to *this* human being and to *that* human being; and entities of which this is true are what we call "particulars." The issue is thus to determine how a human being as an entity to which something can be present – that is, as what I am calling an ek-sistent – can be conceived as a particular and as one particular among many. This is the general problem of individuation that I want to take up in this chapter.

From what has already been said about them, however, it is clear that by virtue of their ek-sistence, human beings must be particulars of a very special kind. That will indeed prove to be the case; and this distinctiveness is so marked that even if it is accepted that an ek-sistent can be a particular, many questions will remain about its character as such. One such question has to do with the unity of an entity that appears to incorporate within itself what would ordinarily be regarded as a *relation* to another entity or entities. In dealing with this matter, it will also become evident that the nature of this unity cannot be adequately characterized without bringing in the relation – once again, this is what we would ordinarily call it – in which such a particular stands to itself. This is the reflexivity that makes this kind of particular what we call a "self." Taken together, these three features – particularity, unity, and reflexivity or selfhood – yield the central elements of a radically revised concept of *a* human being that is congruent with its grounding in the primordial fact of presence. Even so, the characterization of human individuality that will emerge in the course of this chapter is necessarily a very abstract one. In the chapters that follow, however, further increments of characterization will be added, and these will issue in a fully concrete delineation of the mode of being of human beings.

II

In attempting to determine how the concept of particularity applies to an ek-sistent entity, it will be helpful to take as a cue another claim is made in the passage from the *Tractatus* quoted previously – the assertion that *the* world is also *my* world.[2] This notion of "my world" is one that we sometimes invoke in ordinary life even though we might be hard pressed to explain what it means. More often than not, the implication of the phrase appears to be subjectivistic in the sense of entailing that there may be as many worlds as there are people. But on the more reasonable assumption that there is only one world with many human beings in it, the question must be, What is it that makes that world "my world" for each of these human beings? One thing, at least, seems clear. If we human beings were in the world in the way tables and chairs are, the world we would be in would certainly not belong to each of us – would not, therefore, qualify as being "mine" – in any meaningful sense. But if the presence of things in the world to each of us is a necessary condition for the world's being my world or yours or anyone's, the fact of presence by itself does not seem to be the whole story. What the "my" in "my world" suggests is that there are differences among the ways the same things are present to different people –

2. *Tractatus*, p. 151. This could be taken to mean that the world is mine and no one else's; and because Wittgenstein does not address the status of other "metaphysical subjects," this possibility is not explicitly excluded. In stating as he does, however, that "I am my world," he also adds "(the microcosm)," and this presumably implies some restriction on how much "my world" takes in and thus suggests that there may be other "microcosms." Normally, of course, the use of "my" in "my world" presupposes a contrast with what is not mine and thus at least possibly someone else's.

differences, as we would ordinarily put it, in the way we "see" things. If that is the case, then the idea of individuating entities to which things are present by reference to these differences must suggest itself.

There has been at least one great effort in the history of philosophy to work out a concept of human being along these lines. It was Leibniz's view that monads – for present purposes, these can be effectively equated with minds – were differentiated from one another and thus individuated entirely by their internal states. That may not seem a very promising beginning, but Leibniz also held these states themselves to be perceptions – perceptions that represented the world from the perspective on it of a particular monad. Every monad represented the same world as every other monad, and each one also represented the whole world but with great differences in the degree of salience and distinctness with which its various parts were represented. Even when it lacks the powers of reflection and thus of self-consciousness, a monad is thus a unity in multiplicity and "a perpetual living mirror of the universe."[3]

Although his conception of the purely relational character of time and space moves in a direction quite different from that of Cartesian dualism, Leibniz's position remains in important respects a theory of representation. Indeed, the "windowless" self-sufficiency of these monads is such that they seem almost as much like so many closely similar worlds as they do like different perspectives on the same world. But what is most remarkable about this theory is the fact that the representational function now constitutes the being itself of the entity that Leibniz calls a monad. For just this reason, what Leibniz tells us about it may offer clues to the way particular entities conceived in this way can be individuated – clues that may be useful for a theory of presence even after the concept of representation has been dropped.[4] Thus, instead of speaking of perceptions as the internal states of a monad or soul, we could speak simply of the perceptual field of a particular human being and ask whether what this field includes and excludes would not offer an adequate criterion for differentiating one subject of presence from another.[5] But if we share a single world that is present to each of us – in part if not as a whole, as Leibniz supposes – there would

3. *Monadology and Other Philosophical Essays,* translated by P. Schrecker and A. M. Schrecker (Indianapolis: Bobbs Merrill/LLA, 1965), p. 157.
4. A very interesting discussion of Leibniz's representationalism and the limitations it entails can be found in J. Moreau, "Leibniz und das phänomenologische Denken," *Studia Leibniziana, Supplementa,* edited by K. Muller and W. Totok (Wiesbaden: Franz Steiner Verlag, 1968), vol. 1, pp. 22–33.
5. It seems best to individuate human beings by reference to what they perceive, and not to include what they remember or otherwise think of even though these matters themselves are to be conceived in terms of presence in absence. For one thing, the possibility that the whole world would have to be thought of as being uncovered if any part of it is uncovered would have to be taken more seriously if Thought were included and not just perception; and this might at least make it somewhat harder to distinguish one ek-sistent from another.

surely be differences in the way that world is present to each individual. Such differences in the relative prominence and articulation of the way the same things are present to different human beings would, according to Leibniz, be enough to distinguish one of them from another. If that is the case, then it would follow that even if the character of that to which what is present is present were not further specified, and even if it were conceived simply as something that is more or less passively "appeared to," it would be differentiated from all other such subjects either by the selection of objects in the world that makes up what is present to it or by the "angle" from which this representation is effected.

A question can be raised as to whether Leibniz is really entitled to make this assumption. This is because, in the course of his argument, he uses a concept of a perspective or point of view that may be at odds with other elements in his theory of monads. In its original sense, the notion of a point of view presupposes a spatial milieu in which different observers occupy different positions and, as a result, either do not see the same things or see them from different sides or angles. Because Leibniz treats space in relational terms that make it finally a construction out of perceptions, the monads that contain these perceptions cannot themselves be in space; and so, the ordinary notion of a point of view is not applicable to them. Nevertheless, according to Leibniz, monads are differentiated from one another in just the way one would expect them to be if they were in space. It is just as though one monad were closer to this object than to that one, and so, in its perceptions, the former will be more prominent and more distinct than the latter. The trouble is that, apart from an abstract interest in having a plurality of individual entities while at the same time avoiding difficulties that might arise out of the Principle of the Identity of Indiscernibles, Leibniz offers no real justification for this carryover to a transcendental level of a way of differentiating points of view (and thus monads) that is most at home in a conception of human beings as occupying positions in space.

It thus appears that by taking monads out of space, Leibniz denied himself the only basis on which his doctrine of a plurality of monads could have been founded. In the absence of the encompassing spatial milieu in which the diversity of points of view could be accounted for, there is no good reason why the "points of view" of monads should differ at all or why they should be distinguishable in terms of the representations they contain. These considerations might seem to show that this kind of spatial location must be the determining feature of monads or human beings for the purpose of identifying them, and this line is taken by P. F. Strawson in a similar criticism of Leibniz's theory.[6] He goes on to argue that there is an impor-

6. P. Strawson, *Individuals: An Essay in Descriptive Metaphysics* (London: Methuen, 1959), pp. 117–32.

tant implication here for the way we individuate human beings or, in his idiom, "persons" in what he calls "singular identifying reference." Since the experiential field of one person might conceivably be the same as that of another, he claims, only the coordinates that delimit the spatial envelope each of them occupies can satisfactorily distinguish one from the other.

This seems a fair criticism of Leibniz's position, since in the case of any two monads, neither one would turn up among the other's representations of the world, because neither one is in space; and so that difference between the two fields would not be available to differentiate them. What Strawson does not appear to notice, however, is that, according to the criterion he proposes, the ontological status of a person would be defined in terms of the perspective of an observer who sees a body occupying a certain space. This point may have been missed because the perspective from which identifying references would be made is described in a way that appears to make it at least as transcendental as the one Leibniz adopts. Or so it would appear to the extent that this perspective is not identified as that of a being situated in the same space as the one being identified, and that could be itself the object of such a reference by the one that is now its object. The difficulty here is that when the perspective of identifying reference is pluralized, and it is accepted that it is part of a system of reciprocal relations among like entities, it will follow that any limit it places on the human being who is being individuated in these terms must also accrue to the one who is so individuating him. For one thing, since both the one and the other are to be conceived, for ontological purposes, as spatial occupants, it would follow that they are susceptible of being fully characterized in terms of the functioning of the body that occupies that space; and this would presumably also mean that these would be the terms employed by physical science in something like its present way of conceiving such entities.

The question this raises is how a body conceived in this mode could transcend itself in such a way as to be able to refer to something that is other than itself.[7] But unless some provision is made for this capability in the makeup of the corporeal entities that so identify one another, it hardly seems appropriate to claim that they have been identified in a way that has anything to do with their being specifically human beings or persons. In Chapter 1, it was shown that the familiar ways in which this has been attempted lead to an impasse, and that such a conception of "persons" as bodies presupposes but does not itself provide for such a mode of functioning on the part of human beings. Nothing like the identifying reference that Strawson has in mind would be even imaginable unless the particulars that are to be identified by their spatial coordinates were or could be

7. This point is effectively made by John Mackie in his essay "The Problem of Intentionality" in *Phenomenology and Philosophical Understanding*, edited by Edo Pivecic (Cambridge: Cambridge University Press, 1975), pp. 37–52.

"there" for the entity that is to identify them in this way. It follows that *that* entity itself must be identified in a way that does not shut it up inside the spatial coordinates by which it is physically delimited, and yet this is just what Strawson proposes to do.

What has been said thus far in criticism of Leibniz and Strawson strongly suggests that a way must be found to combine the modes of individuation they propose. Only in this way will it be possible to do justice to the spatial locatedness of the entity to which what is present is present without confining it to the spatial envelope its body occupies in the manner just described. This is just another way of saying that this entity must be individuated not simply in the terms set by a unidirectional identifying reference by another like entity, but in a way that reflects the fact that it too stands in just such a relation to the latter. If this can be done, then both my criticism of Leibniz and Strawson's would be met – the former because monads would be in space and would thus be "points of view" in the normal sense of that term and the latter because the worry about identical experiential fields would be unnecessary. Those fields could not be exactly the same, because one of them would (or in principle could) contain the person who is being referred to and the other the person who is making the original identifying reference. It is, of course, possible that both the former and the latter might be perceived by the one and/or the other; but if they were, the way in which the one – the perceiver – would be present would be unalterably different from the way the other – the perceived – is present, as the discussion in Chapter 1 has showed.

There is good reason to think that individuation in the sense described can be achieved along lines already laid down in the discussions of the preceding chapters and, more specifically, in a feature of the concept of presence that was proposed there. That concept (and thus the concept of the "There is . . ." as well) is one that has been shown to be intimately linked to that of absence in its many modes. More specifically, there would be no place for absence in this sense if the subject of presence were single and unique and if its counterpart were simply the world as a totality. Nor would there be a place for absence if we had to deal entirely in representations – that is, in mental states – as Leibniz does because representations have no perduring reality when they are not before the mind and cannot therefore be absent in the way that something is of which we can *think* during its absence. This is because to think of a representation when it is not present to our minds is to make it ipso facto present. What *is* possible, however, and pervasively actual is the absence of some part of the world that has been present and may be again; and absence in this sense entails that the entity to which the part in question was present is not coextensive with the world to which it belongs. It is transcended by the world that is present to it; and this is to say that it is finite, and finite in a way that it cannot deny without thereby trying to shrink the world to its own size. It may be true, as some observers of our species have suggested, that we do our best to achieve this, but so far success has eluded us.

It is evident that in such a conception of individuation as this, the concept of limit would still have an important place, though not in Wittgenstein's sense. Each subject would delimit a part of the same world that would typically overlap with those delimited by others but would never coincide perfectly with them. If it were a matter of extramundane subjects, then such a perfect coincidence would not only be possible, there would be a strong presumption in its favor for the reasons that have already been stated. But when a particular is individuated by the varying patterns of the presence and absence of entities that are in the first instance a function of spatial location and orientation, this can hardly be the case. These perspectival variations may have to do with the way a line of sight is blocked by other objects, and this can happen only if a subject of presence under these constraints is itself in the same world as the one that is present to it. It has a locus in the space of that world, and this locus broadly coincides with the space occupied by the body I call mine. In Chapters 6 and 7, I shall examine the possibility that it may just *be* that body, though not in a sense that simply turns it over to physical science.

Commonsensical and even obvious as these conclusions may seem, they take on momentous import when set against the long tradition that denies to the subject of presence – conceived as a soul or a mind – this intra-worldly status while at the same time insisting on its particularity. It may be asked, however, whether in situating the subject of presence *in* the world that is present to it I have not given up the idea that it is individuated by what is present to it, inasmuch as I make this individuation derive from a prior individuation in terms of spatiotemporal location. This worry can be seen to be groundless, however, if we keep in mind the differences between the role of spatiotemporal location in the individuation of natural objects and of those beings to which entities are present. In the former case, we think of the entities in question as occupying a spatial envelope, the coordinates of which can be specified. This is the space that they are *in*; but if, *pace* Leibniz, human beings are in space, they are not in space in that way, although for certain limited purposes they can be envisaged by other human beings as though they were simply spatial occupants. The place that a human being is in is the place *from* which other entities are present to him; and a human being is individuated by that place, not as its spatial envelope but as the field of entities that are present to him from that place. To individuate another human being in the sense of making an identifying reference to him is thus not to enclose him within his spatial coordinates but to determine the point of origin for his disclosures of other entities. There is, therefore, no reason to think that spatiality, in the sense that applies to natural objects, is in any way prior for purposes of individuating human beings or that individuation by the field of presence is somehow irreconcilable with an appeal to spatial location.

Against this background, it should now be possible to determine whether or not the Leibnizian idea about individuation can, with the proper modifications, be adapted for use in a theory of presence. Let us suppose that I am sitting in my garden surrounded by familiar trees and banks of flowers and lawn – a visual scene that, according to Wittgenstein, gives no hint of the fact that it is seen from by my eyes. Perhaps this last claim would be true if the scene were static, as is a painting, in which nothing changes. But suppose that a breeze stirs the leaves of the tree and a nest becomes visible that was hidden a moment ago. The fact that the nest was hidden by a branch and revealed when the leaves moved can hardly be dealt with otherwise than by concluding not only that the previous scene was incomplete – that it did not include something that was nevertheless "there" – but that it was incomplete in a way that had to do with where I was sitting and thus with the position of my eyes. This certainly amounts to saying that my field of vision is limited and that, if I had been sitting somewhere else, the scene might have included at least one thing – the nest – that it did not include when I sat where I did. Seeing some things rather than others and always seeing less than there is to see thus appears to be unavoidable, and it gives a clear sense to the notion of the "I" as a limit.

The import of this notion of a limit can also be expressed in the language of presence and of absence. The point here is that in the temporal perspective set up by the later view – the one that includes the nest – it becomes evident that the nest lay altogether outside the original "There is. . . ." It was in fact "absent" from it in a more radical sense of the term than has been considered thus far. Up to this point, absence has been understood as presence in absence, and this is the status of an object that is familiar to me but is not being perceived at a given time. But the status of the nest at the time of the original view was quite different. It was not absent in the way that something I am thinking about is absent. If that had been the case, there would have been a sense in which it *was* comprised within the original "There is. . . ." What becomes evident after the nest is revealed is that it was absent the moment before in a way that rules out any such inclusion. At the same time, the nest revealed by the movement of the branch did not come into being at that moment, so there *was* something – this nest – that was not included in the original "There is . . . ." The latter was therefore finite and limited in this respect. It is true that its limited character comes to light only by virtue of a subsequent "There is . . ." that is not so limited, but the latter has been placed in a position in which it can understand itself as finite in the same way even though *ex hypothesi* it cannot specify the respect in which it is.

It is in some such way as this that a human being as an ek-sistent can be individuated. There is admittedly no established or especially natural way of referring to a particular of this kind. The Heideggerian language of place does seem suggestive, however, and it may be that to describe such a particular as a "locus of presence" would be appropriate. For one thing, it readily lends itself to pluralization. There would be as many such "loci" of presence as there are human beings, and the example used in the preceding discussion suggests how this plurality could be realized. If I perceive something – in my example, the nest – that I could not see a moment ago, this new situation is one that might find expression in some such statement as "There is a nest in the tree that was there a moment ago as well but was not then perceptually accessible to me." Having acknowledged the imperfect matchup of what was present and what there was in the tree a moment ago – this last determined, of course, by what is present to me now – I am able to say that if my position had been different or if the breeze had moved the branch a little sooner, the nest *would* have been present to me. What I am asserting here is a kind of virtual presence that contrasts with what was actually present to me and which, in some sense, splits me in two as the being that occupied one point of view but that might have occupied another at a given time. But to do this is to accept a discontinuity or break within presence, a presence that lies partly outside the particular presence that I am. Now this is the place where another *actual* being like me could be accommodated in "my" world – that is, in a place that emerges from the original presence in the temporal process I have been decribing. The criteria we might use to determine that that place is in fact occupied by a being like me in the relevant respects is another matter that need not be discussed here. Once that determination has been made, the locus of presence that is that being will also comprise much of what is also present to me and at the same time. We shall in this sense, share a world even though the perimeter of one locus of presence does not coincide exactly with that of another.

III

These reflections on the finitude of presence suggest another dimension in terms of which it can be individuated. Up to this point, the discussion of individuation has been dominated by considerations that in one way or another have to do with spatial location. But even if the space of a "point of view" (as contrasted with the space occupied by a body) is enough to individuate a human being in the sense of picking him out from among all other human beings at a given time, it is itself bounded in another way. I have in mind the *temporal* range and boundedness of a human life understood as a locus of presence. In the case of material objects, this omission might not raise any serious difficulty because time does not contribute much to the individuation of such objects beyond supplying the date at which they are in a certain spatial position. In the case of human beings, however, such a procedure would enclose a human being in his present in much the same way as he was enclosed in his spatial envelope by Strawson's method of individuation. What this would miss is the fact that presence is individuated as much by its temporal limits as by its spatial ones; and this means that the concept of a life must be brought into the discussion at this point. A human being, after all, *is* his life in a sense that is just as funda-mental as that in which he may be said to be his body, and thus his location and orientation in space; and whatever else it may be, a human life has a beginning and an end. Birth and death are the terminal points between which such a life "stretches itself out." An attempt must therefore be made to define the relation in which they stand to the presence that, on this view, they help to individuate.

There has been much controversy about the way these events – the be-ginning and the end of a human life – are to be identified. Questions are raised as to whether a human life begins with conception and whether "brain death" is the proper criterion for determining when a human life has ended. Typically, however, these questions are raised against a back-ground of assumptions – both physiological and psychological – that assim-ilate birth and death as the boundaries of life to our ordinary undifferen-tiated understanding of beginnings and endings, and thus to the corresponding ways of being in time. It is clear, however, that the line of thought developed in the earlier chapters points to a very different con-ception of the kind of time human beings are in and thus of the way a human life is bounded. One thing, at least, is clear: The beginning of this life is not like the turning on of a light, nor is its end like that light's being turned off. Instead, a human life emerges gradually out of another kind – that of the fetus or infant – in some way that we have great difficulty con-ceiving. And although death may come in an instant to someone in the prime of life, the normal curve of human life has a final phase in which it may gradually yield to and even disappear altogether in a life that in many respects is not unlike that out of which it emerged. It follows that if "ek-sistence" designates the kind of life that is made possible by presence, then it is continuous at both of its ends with another kind that we can think of only in privative terms like those we use in thinking about the lives of animals, that is, in terms that at once relate them to ek-sistence and are intended to mark the distance that separates this life from the one we use as our standard.

On the whole, it appears that although thinking about either birth or death in the first-personal mode is enormously difficult, it is easier to think about the latter than about the former. Death is out ahead of us when we are in the midst of life, whereas birth or conception lies behind us at a point at which we had no ability to understand or reflect on what had just occurred. In any case, it seems more feasible to use death rather than birth as a way of trying to understand the temporal boundedness of presence. To begin with, it is worth noting that our most familiar way of understanding death is one that compares it to sleep.[8] Sleep regularly interrupts our lives in a way that, dreams apart, we think of as being a kind of temporary death; and so it is natural for us to say, with Shakespeare, that "our little lives are rounded by a sleep." If we are pressed to think about sleep and death in any more specific way, we may say that in sleep the "portals of the mind" – the senses – are closed but that within the mind itself the imagination at least can still function and fill the mind with its fantastic products – our dreams. At the same time, however, we have the idea of a dreamless sleep as a true hiatus in the internal functioning of the mind, as well as in its sensory intake; and it is this suspension of all mental functioning, if it actually occurs, that we compare to death. There is, of course, a difference: In the case of sleep (and other episodes of unconsciousness as well), we live through the rupture so effected and awake or "return to consciousness" as the same persons we were before it occurred. But it seems to us that we might equally well *not* have awakened from such a sleep and one day will in fact not do so. Each time we successfully negotiate this passage, moreover, we have in effect passed through a state that, as far as mind and consciousness are concerned, is like a little death.

This whole way of thinking about sleep and death presupposes an idea of mind as consciousness and the whole inside–outside contrast that goes with it. The picture it offers is thus one of an inner theater in which suddenly everything goes dark – even, as in dreamless sleep, the house lights. Death is thus a darkness in which nothing can appear and into which we all must go. But even if one disregards the other sense modalities, there is an obvious difference between being in the dark and being dead. In the one case, although nothing is visible, this darkness itself is arguably what we see; in the other, not even this darkness can appear because there is no one to whom it could appear. More generally, there is no reason to think that even though we treat death as one term in a qualitative distinction between light and dark, it is really reducible to these terms. What is involved here is, I suggest, something much more radical – the difference between a state in which the world is my world and one in which it has ceased altogether to be that.

"My death" and "my world" are notions that are not commonly linked to one another. Especially if the latter is understood simply as the world that I am in, and "in" in the same way that everything else is in it, there

---

8. It would be important for my purposes to develop an adequate account of sleep as a part of our lives, but I cannot offer such an account here. It does seem to me that sleep is, in important respects, a return to a state like the one out of which we emerged at birth, but it is also significantly marked by features that derive from our normal waking lives.

will be little basis for an affinity between them. My death – any death – will then be just an event that takes place in one little corner of the world and is best understood in physiological or psychological terms – as "brain death," for example, or terminal loss of consciousness – and these are events that leave the world as such unaffected. This line of thought is in keeping with the fact that, after my death, the sun will still shine and the business of the world will go on pretty much as before. Other human beings will still be alive, and the world will still *be* whatever it is for each and all of them. All of this may well lead me to imagine my death as well as an event in the world of these people who will go on living when I am dead. When I think about it in this way, my death becomes an event in the one public world in which everything happens – a world that belongs to everyone but for precisely that reason does not really belong to anyone.

Even when I think of my own death in these terms, it is apparent that the undifferentiated publicity of this world that is neither mine nor yours is specious. At any rate, if there is anything that resists incorporation into it, it is surely my own death. It is one thing to think about things habitually in a way that blurs the distinction between the self and the other in the manner just described. This is an anonymous stance that is maintained through a delicate balancing off of the first-personal and third-personal points of view in which the claims of the former are not wholly surrendered, although they are presented in the guise of "what everyone knows."[9] What I come up against in the case of my own death is the disappearance of the very self that was abstracted from and thus occluded in this curious way. The fact that I will die forces my ek-sistence into a prominence that was denied to it under the regime of an anonymous publicity. It is pretty hard, after all, to get around the fact that in the case of my own death, there is a point beyond which I can neither observe nor imagine observing whatever processes may be involved in the termination of *my* life. If at that point I shift to the perspective of someone who survives me and in whose life my death is just another event, I have to recognize, as I previously did not, that this is what I am doing and that the view I thus vicariously adopt bypasses *my* death altogether. But to accept this is to acknowledge implicitly that death is not just another event in the world that enjoys the same uniform accessibility as everything else.

How, then, is my death to be more satisfactorily conceived? Not as an event taking place in the world but as the world's no longer being there.[10]

9. This is the view taken by Paul Edwards in his sharply deflationary account of Heidegger's conception of death in *Heidegger on Death: A Critical Evaluation* (La Salle, Ill.: Hegeler Institute, 1979). The idea that our commonsense understanding of death anticipates the whole of Heidegger's pioneering analysis of the kind of ending that death is somewhat hard to accept.

10. Clearly, this is true in the Heideggerian sense of world as a milieu of presence. It does not mean that entities (*das Seiende*) as such would have been annihilated.

What is thus raised into visibility is the fact of presence in its first-personal, individuated form, which ends without leaving any trace of itself when I die and obtains during my life in the kind of transparent implicitness that amounts to invisibility. But if presence ends in the death of a human being and if human beings die one by one, then presence itself must be individuated and each particular locus of presence is temporally bounded by what might best be called "nothingness." This is not "absence" in the sense in which that term has been used in this book and in which it is a modality of being as presence. That is the form of non-being that applies to entities that are or have been or might be present within the world. Absence so conceived presupposes an entity that is the locus of presence and thus of absence as well, and death is the end of that entity. What ends in death is thus presence itself, and so one may say that in death nothing *is* anything anymore. This is to say that the world that has been my world ceases to be mine, and the body that remains will be in the world only in the sense that is common to all objects. As such, it no longer *has* a world, and so the world can no longer be "my world" in the absence of an "I" to which it could belong.

All of this may sound paradoxical, because we feel so sure that little in the world changes just because someone dies. We, as those who live on, know that there is still a world and that everything in it continues in pretty much the same way even though the dead person is no longer in it. There is hence a great temptation to dissolve the paradox by treating the life of anyone who has died as simply a tract of "experience" that has now reached its end in the way a train completes its run by arriving at the last station. When viewed in this light, that life could not have anything to do with the individuated character of presence that is thus effectively denied; and if it called the world it was in "my world," that could only have been in some Pickwickian sense. Nor is there any need to invoke the concept of nothingness in order to explicate what that death amounts to. In this way, we refuse to acknowledge that the death of another entails the loss of a locus of presence for the same world that is also mine. But it is evident once again that I can do all this only if I claim some sort of implicitly transcendental status for myself as an entity for which entities are present in a way that does not involve the individuation of presence.

IV

In the preceding discussion the individuated character of presence was accounted for, and with it the plural and only partially overlapping character of the loci of presence that are constituted within the world by individual human beings. In order to understand more fully the kind of particular a human being is, however, it is necessary to do more than draw the outer boundaries of its field of presence. The internal unity of this field of presence must also be characterized; and it must be shown, at least in a preliminary way, how the unity of a human being as an ek-sistent entity – an entity to which other entities are present – derives from the unity of presence. This is not an easy task, especially since no account has yet been given of human action or of the body as these have to be understood in the context of ek-sistence. In advance of an account of the central role that action plays in the unity of a human being as well as of the human body, we are all too likely to conceive that unity in terms that are appropriate not to an ek-sistent as one particular among many but, rather, to things or substances. In that case, this unity will almost certainly be conceived as that of an entity that is self-contained and closed upon itself; it will thus, in Descartes's famous formulation, need nothing else in the world in order to be what it is. What I hope to achieve in this section, even in advance of any detailed discussion of the body or of action, is to show that the unity of an ek-sistent particular must be sought in a very different quarter. Paradoxically, it is as though the center of gravity of such an entity were outside itself as it is ordinarily conceived and were situated instead in the presence to it of the very entities that are other than it.

It will be helpful to begin by reviewing the conceptions of the unity of experience that have been most influential in modern Western philosophy. Among these, the position of Kant is of special importance because of the radically different approach to this whole topic that it opens up. Traditionally, the unity of the mind or soul was supposed to be guaranteed by the fact that it was one (immaterial) substance; and so, to Descartes, the "I" of his "I think" appeared to be self-authenticating. Locke, by contrast, did not think that the identity of this substance through time could be directly apprehended, and he argued that in practice the criterion of personal identity could only be what we are able to remember.[11] The skeptical view of these matters that Hume pioneered held that all we find when we search for "the self" is our impressions and ideas, and nothing like a perduring and identical substance. Any unity to be found in experience would, therefore, have to be constituted by the order in which the elements of experience – the representations that have been supposed to inhere in a mental substance – follow upon one another. This was the theory of the association of ideas, and it held that the order in which impressions as the original elements of mental life come to us is reproduced by the fainter copies of these impressions that are known as "ideas." This order in our ideas, as well as the resemblances we find among the units of experience, becomes so deeply habitual that we eventually suppose our ideas to be necessarily

---

11. See Locke's discussion of this in his *Essay Concerning Human Understanding*, Book II, Chapter 27 (Oxford: Clarendon Press, 1894).

connected to one another. In fact, however, the only connection for which there is any empirical warrant is psychological and is in principle distinct from any form of unity that may be supposed to hold in the world independently of our experience of it.

Although Kant appears to have accepted the doctrine of the association of ideas as a fairly accurate account of the way things go empirically, he rejected the idea of a purely psychological account of the unity of experience. This is implicit in the way he reinterpreted the contrast between inner and outer experience. Instead of being understood in the traditional dualistic manner – that is, in Kant's language, transcendentally – the inner–outer contrast was to be interpreted empirically; this meant that it was to be understood as a contrast within our experience rather than as one between that experience as a whole and a transempirical thing-in-itself. Even more significantly, since Kant takes space and time to be forms of sensibility rather than things in themselves, our outer experience – the experience we have of objects in space – cannot be a representation of a physical world as it exists in itself; and this is to say that our experience of the physical world must be immediate rather than inferential. It is no longer just a tissue of inner representations but "the existence of actual things that I perceive outside me."[12] Under these circumstances, and in the absence of any direct apprehension of a substantial self, the dualistic thesis of a priority of our apprehension of ourselves over whatever apprehension we may have of the existence of an external world becomes automatically suspect. Indeed, Kant argues that the priority runs the other way and that the continuity (and thus the unity) of my experience of myself is dependent on the permanence of the objects that I immediately experience as outside myself.

In these passages, Kant seems to come very close to a phenomenological as contrasted with a representational conception of human experience. Taken somewhat further, this line of thought might well make the unity of the phenomenal world of objects the basis of the unity of the entity to which they are present. Unfortunately, Kant's prior commitment to a representational theory of mind makes the ultimate import of all these theses more than a little ambiguous. After all, in spite of his talk of immediate and noninferential apprehensions, he does not finally conceive the phenomenal world in terms of presence, but rather as a manifold of representations on which various logical operations have been performed. Even so, I think it could be argued that in his account of the unity of experience, the noumenal–phenomenal distinction is of little significance, and his conception of the "I" as an "act" of synthesis makes the whole idea of a noumenal self superfluous. In any case, the view he sketches in these passages is so

12. *Immanuel Kant's Critique of Pure Reason*, translated by N. Kemp-Smith (London: Macmillan, 1958), p. 245.

powerfully suggestive that I propose to build on it without worrying too much about its ultimate consistency with his deepest philosophical commitments.

Since the argument I shall advance here is of Kantian derivation, in spite of the very different philosophical background from which it emerges, it should be pointed out that it does not incorporate the much stronger requirements that Kant attaches to his conception of the unity of experience. Kant wanted to prove that there could be synthetic a priori knowledge, and for that he had to show, against Hume, that the connections – most notably, causal connections – among phenomenal things and events were necessary ones. I make no such claim, and I understand connectedness rather as situatedness in the same space and time – what Kant calls the "forms of sensibility." Even the kind of unity of human being that I postulate, although it constitutes a necessary condition for ek-sistence, is susceptible of degrees; and it can suffer a good deal of erosion that may be manifested both in the difficulty we may experience in following out the various relevant continuities within our lives and in blockages and discontinuities due to resistance for which we ourselves may be responsible. More of this later.

The thesis I want to defend is that the unity of a human being is derived from the unity of his world. More specifically, the unity of experience, and thus of a particular locus of presence, is always a function of the connections among the objects that are present in it. In explicitly nonrepresentationalist language, this amounts to the thesis that the unity of an individuated locus of presence is the unity of the world as it shows itself in that locus, and that the unity of presence is the key to the unity of the self. Even Kant's conception of unity as mediated by an act can be retained in another form without any commitment to a *transcendental* "I" as the agent of this unification or to "representations" as the materials with which it works. This act would be conceived as the act of a human being and not of a mind or of a transcendental self, and it would effect not a synthesis of representations to form objects but a "mapping" of the world and a "tracking" of processes that occur in it. It is this conception that I want to develop further as a way of accounting for the internal unity of human being. In the next section, I set forth a nontranscendental conception of the "I" that is the agent of this act as an ek-sistent human being.

To speak of the unity of presence is to say that at any given time *many* things are present to each of us and to raise the question of what is involved in their being there together – their compresence or *syndosis*, as Heidegger calls it – for an individual human being. This question differs in at least one major respect from the one about particularity that was considered in the preceding section. Although the limits of a field of presence may change in the course of the actions undertaken by a given individual, those limits are not themselves set by anything the latter does. When it comes to the unity of that same field of presence, however, the case is different. That unity is not simply given, or perhaps one should say that its givenness to an individual human being is itself a matter of being able to work out the connectedness of the things that are given together. That ability takes many forms, but they all involve a distinctive element of temporality that is both anticipatory and retentive in character. Even when it is the unity of a set of perceptual objects that are there before us, so that we cannot help seeing them, their compresence is realized only to the extent that we pass from one to another and back. As I sit here in front of a word processor, for example, I notice the printer on one side of it and the closet door on the other side, and my ability to move back and forth between these objects without losing one as I turn to the other is a necessary condition of their being compresent to me.

These are casual and unmotivated shifts of perceptual attention, and the temporality involved in our understanding of the perceptual routes that link the objects in question together may seem to be so minimal as hardly to deserve such an impressive name. In any case, examples such as this are atypical, since it is not as though we spend our time running through the items in our fields of presence as though we were cataloging them. Our interest in them derives from the active interest we take in some project in which we are engaged – some outcome we are trying to bring about. Here, the criterion of relevance is not the adjacency of the objects before us but the functional role played in our project by objects that may be widely separated from one another. Since these projects differ from one individual to another, it might appear that the whole matter is in some vague sense "subjective" and that the unity of our experience must, after all, be conceived in psychological terms. It would be a mistake, however, to suppose that the differentiation that agency effects divorces us from the common order of objects and events in the world. What we think of as the "subjective" order of our experiences is primarily due to the fact that, by virtue of being agents, each one of us is coming at what is in the world – past, present, and future – in an idiosyncratic order that is dictated by our interest in certain outcomes rather than others and in the relevant instrumental relationships. As a result, each of us is dealing at any given moment with many different states of affairs that are connected with one another, in the first instance, through the places they occupy in some program of action. Superficially viewed, these may seem a hodgepodge of heterogeneous mental bric-a-brac that has little, if anything, to do with the order of things in the world and that, to the extent that it can be understood at all, can be understood only in psychological terms.

What I want to show here is that in the synergism of perception and expectation, as well as of memory and imagination, that characterizes these contexts of action there is an implicit acknowledgment of, and a reckoning with, the unity of the world in space and time as it is realized in the several modalities of presence. Then, in the next section and in the two chapters that follow, it will be shown that the unity of an ek-sistent particular as a whole is its unity as a locus of presence. This, moreover, is a unity that is realized in contexts of action, and is a function of its ability to spell out in terms of spatial and temporal continuity the relationships in which the entities and states of affairs with which it is conversant in its active capacity stand to one another.

It is worth noting, in this connection, that most accounts of the association of ideas appear to want to eliminate this context of action. A word is thrown out in some relatively contextless situation, and we are asked to respond to it with the first word it suggests to us. The word "pencil" may suggest "lead" or "smoke" may suggest "fire" and so on. If there is any meaningful psychological pattern in such responses, however, it seems likely that this would be because the subject of the experiment tacitly provides a context that would otherwise be lacking and moves with some at least vague intention from one feature to another of an imagined situation. Because the situations we imagine may differ, our responses will sound arbitrary even though, within each of those situations, they may be objective enough, especially if the situation is understood in terms of what is to be done in it. But because we are not able to work things out in enough detail to show what is really going on in such cases, we simply take what is available to us and treat some sequence of query and response as an "association" in a psychological sense. This produces, at best, a drastic abbreviation of a much more complex story in which the unity of the world has a essential place. Altogether, "association" would appear to be, at best, a misleading way of talking about the connections we make in our active commerce with the world; and the thesis that these connections have some purely psychological character that can be studied in abstraction from that involvement in the world is more than a little dubious.

In order to make my thesis more perspicuous, let me give an example and then contrast the ways in which it would be dealt with by an associationist approach and by a conception of unity of the kind I am developing. As I sit here in my study, I hear a number of familiar sounds from time to time. One such sound is that of the doorbell; and on this occasion, the time of day and the day of the week tell me that it is the milkman letting me know that he has left our order outside the door. Here, if you like, there is an association between the sound of a bell and a thought of the milkman – an "association" that may be peculiar to me. After all, someone else might very well hear the doorbell without any thought of the milkman; and there might even be someone who did not recognize the sound as that of a doorbell. What this talk of "association" misses, however, is the situation in which this sequence of sound and thought is embedded. What I hear is not so much the sound of a bell as it is a signal that the milk is outside the door. And because the milk needs to be brought in before it begins to warm up, I get up and go to the front door, and I bring the milk in and place it in the refrigerator. This is the situation from which what I hear and the thought that follows it have been abstracted; and it does not seem that, as so abstracted, they tell us very much, and certainly not that I associate bells with milkmen in any more general way.

It is, of course, true that not all the situations for which it might be thought that special psychological explanations are needed are as straight-forward as this one. My association with the sound of the doorbell might have been a wholly private one that found no expression in overt action – as private, say, as Proust's memories of Combray that came to him when he tasted the madeleine dipped in tea. Those memories were, as he so often insists, of a special kind that had to do not so much with specific facts that he might recall from that time as with what it was like to be in his aunt's house in Combray as a little boy. But even if my associations with the sound of the bell were memories of this kind, they would be memories of something from an earlier time in my life and they would, therefore, be connected to it by sequences of events that I can more or less reconstruct. The crucial point here is that in both the simple case – that of the bell and the milkman – and the more complex one, there is a connectedness in space and time between the two terms that are said to be associated; and it is a condition of the unity of the kind of particular that a human being is that he be able to make that connection.

Even my simple example readily illustrates the character of such con-nections. They are effected by the familiar "routes" through time and space that run from where I am sitting in my study to the front door and the milk cartons and then to the refrigerator. All these objects have a po-sition in space, and all the events – the ringing of the doorbell and my going to the door – have a position in a single time. As I move to bring in the milk, there are sequences of events and an order in the way different objects – the bookcase in the hall and the front door, say – come into view. In my actual movement to the front door, I have to take into account the positions of such things as doors and walls, and extraneous events like the ringing of the telephone; and in doing so, I reckon with the order of all these objects and events and thus with the unity of the small patch of the world through which I am moving. Of course, in a more general way, most of this was (or could have been) present in absence to me before I set about this task; and it will be so still when it is complete, as will the sequence of actions I have just completed.

It is along such lines as these that the unity of my experience as an active being, and as one that has a past and a future, has to be understood. It is apparent that at every point this unity presupposes the unity of the world in space and time, as well as the interdependence of the objects and events that make it up. If there were no such unity, then it would be impossible to arrange the various elements in our active lives along routes of the kind that has just been described; and in that case, the unity of my life would be called into question. Of course, if we were to insist on some severely diminished sense for "the world" – one that allows things to be in the world only under some neutral scientific description that effectively obscures the functional role they play in our lives – then the idea of our being able, in principle, to trace the routes of which I have spoken would become highly problemetic. A great deal of what has a place in the world as a milieu of presence would have to be removed from it, and someplace else would have to be found to accommodate what could not be fitted into such a world. The price to be paid for such a decision would be high, however, especially in terms of the gratuitous subjectivization of a great part of our lives and the resultant proliferation of psychological explanations that it would entail. It is surely preferable to avoid this result by accepting at face value the fact that our lives come to a focus in our commerce with the world. Each of us has a good working familiarity with the way things go in the world and with what can be expected to happen if I or someone else does not intervene; and these facts, together with our strong commitment to certain outcomes rather than others, set the context in which our lives form a whole.

It may be hoped that the sense in which the unity of the world subtends the unity of presence is now reasonably clear. What I have tried to show is that in our active commerce with the world, we refer to things in the past and in the future, as well as things and events in the present that are at a great distance from us; and it is only through a form of mediation that is peculiar to an ek-sistent particular that all these things can form a part of our lives. What is required is simply that it be possible to spell out, in the medium of presence in absence, some form of spatiotemporal continuity between whatever it is that we refer to and where we are in space and time. Since our knowledge of the things and events that intervene between the one and the other is usually quite limited, this mediation may amount to little more than a direction in space and time. Even so, as putatively supplemented by information available in the public domain, it can be enough to establish a link to whatever is in question and to make it a part of our lives. Although the patterns of the referential commerce of each human being with the world and with the past, present, and future are distinctively different, the linkages and continuities we depend on in our active lives represent a selection from a common stock; and in that sense, the unity of presence presupposes the unity of the world.

Earlier in this chapter, it was stated that the unity of an ek-sistent entity cannot appropriately be conceived on the model of the unity of an object or thing; and what has been said should have made this claim somewhat more concrete. The real point here is that the unity of a human being is the unity of a life. That unity is in no sense a given and must instead be understood in terms of a functional process that constantly and cumulatively re-capitulates itself. It might even be described as a performative unity in the sense that it is progressively constituted by the connections that each of us is able to make, both among things in the natural world and among events and stages in our own careers. But in speaking of the unity of the world in this way as in effect mediated by the mapping and tracking functions of the human beings – the ek-sistents – to whom the entities in question are present, I may seem to have laid myself open to a serious objection. Have I not presupposed the unity of the human being who performs these functions while at the same time claiming that his unity derives from the unity of the world and is therefore in some sense a resultant of these same functions? Even if everything that has been said about the way the unity of the world is implicit in the mapping and tracking involved in any form of life in the world, is it not possible that someone who would be identified by others as a single human being is carrying out these functions in radically discrete ways – so different and so separate from one another that they would have to be assigned to distinct loci of presence? If that were the case, there might be, for each person, a number of different forms of life continuity – different story lines, as it were – rather than a single network of references within which everything in our lives would be potentially linked to everything else.

The trouble with this objection is that it postulates a plurality of loci of presence for a single individual, but it does not make clear whether the resulting discontinuities would be detectable in the overt conduct of that human being. If they need not be so detectable, this hypothesis would seem to presuppose an effective split between mind and body, as though the discontinuities being postulated had a purely mental character. In that case, the hypothesis would be hard – perhaps impossible – to refute, but it would also have a gratuitous character since there would be no empirical reason to suppose that something of this kind is going on. On the other hand, if this is not the case and there are discontinuities in the conduct of the persons affected, as well as in their mental lives, there would be good reason to try to understand what is going on by analogy with actual cases in which there are empirical grounds for concluding that the unity of a human life is somehow breaking up. There are cases of people with schizoid tendencies or multiple personalities; but it is important to note that in such cases, a prior unity is typically giving way under the pressure of traumatic events in the lives of these human beings. There are also clear indications that the discontinuities among the fragmentary personalities into which such a life has fallen apart are not total and automatic but have to be maintained and even insisted on in a manner that testifies to a certain residual unity even though it expresses itself only negatively. It is also worth bearing in mind that such tendencies are latent in all of us, and that even without splitting ourselves in these drastic ways, we may effectively sever our relation to whole tracts of our own past lives, typically because they are too painful to be acknowledged. Here, too, the care with which we avoid these parts of our lives strongly suggests that we retain a certain tacit understanding of what we are keeping at this distance from ourselves and thus, once again, that we maintain a kind of unity in what might be called its "deficient" mode. But even when this separation becomes much more pronounced than it is in most people, to claim that each of the personae generated in this process should be counted as a distinct human being goes well beyond anything that these alternations in the life of a given individual would justify us in postulating. It seems better to say that they are so many radically incompatible styles in which the life of that individual finds expression and that because they have not been reconciled with one another, they are kept as separate as possible; and the separateness so maintained is the form of unity that presides over that life. So viewed, they are fragments of a life that has not been able to establish itself securely in some positive form; but they do not require more than one locus of presence for what others would identify as a single human being.

What has just been said responds to the suggestion that there may be more than one "self" for each human being, but this still leaves the point about a circularity in my account of the unity of a human being unanswered. The next section should cast some light on this matter, but I want to point out again that it is the unity of a life that is at issue here. Such a unity requires that the person in question be able to connect incidents in that life with others by following the routes through space and time that lead from one to another; and in that sense, the unity of a life is a function of the unity of the world it has been lived in. The entity itself that is able to recapitulate its life is one that ek-sists – that is, one that has a world and that is itself in the first instance the being of the entities that make up that world. The latter mostly do not ek-sist, and their unity must accordingly be understood on a quite different model from that of the entity to which they are present. Having a past and a future and the ability to follow out the linkages among, for example, past pasts and past futures *is* a given in my account, though with the understanding that it is subject to considerable erosion and obstruction. The unity of a particular life, however, is realized pari passu with the actual exercise of that ability; and so there is no basis for the charge that this unity has been presupposed and that, as a result, the account that has been given of it here is circular.

V

Now that the particularity and unity that characterize a human being have been described, it is time to take up the third feature noted earlier: "self-hood," or "reflexivity." I have borrowed the latter term from logical theory as a relatively neutral designation for something that is usually referred to in psychological language as "self-consciousness" or "self-knowledge." The use I make of it, however, is quite different from standard accounts of reflexivity as a relation in which something stands to itself. In its philo-sophical affinities, my account of it is much closer, as I will show, to the Hegelian concept of reflection. First, however, it will be useful to consider briefly a more familiar sense of the word "reflection" that has largely shaped the traditional philosophical understanding of self-consciousness. In this sense, self-consciousness is a special "reflective" act of the mind; and it is this conception that I shall initially be arguing against.

When human beings are thought of as compounds of body and mind, and when the mind is supposed to be the locus of perceptual and intellec-tual activity, it is generally assumed that its concern is principally with the "external world" of which it contains representations within itself. This absorption of the mind in the task of coming to know what is other than itself naturally induces, so the story goes, a certain obliviousness of itself and of its own "inner" functions that typically goes hand in hand with a dogmatic realism about the natural world. Even in this habitual, extraverted mode, however, the mind is supposed to be capable of turning its attention "inward" rather than "outward." This capability has traditionally been called "inner sense" and, more recently, "introspection." In looking into itself, the mind is said to detach itself from external objects (or the repre-sentations thereof) and to attend to its own internal functions, of which it is otherwise largely oblivious. Although introspection is often described in a way that seems to imply that it is a looking into the mind from outside, that can hardly be the case since it is the mind itself that does the looking; and it is not easy to see how it could be outside itself and looking in and, at the same time, the inside that is being looked into from without. It is more as though someone who normally spends most of his time looking out the window were to turn around and observe what is going on in the room from which he has been looking out. Even this way of construing introspection is somewhat misleading, however, because among the con-tents of the mind that are to be inventoried are the very acts directed to external objects; and so it is not as though the mind were simply turning away from the latter to something else. Instead, in introspection the mind must be thought of as turning in (or around) on itself; and in this reflective posture one mental act or content becomes the object of another.

What is puzzling about the way mental acts are envisaged by the doctrine of inner sense is that it apparently implies that, in the absence of such a supervening mental act, the prior act of perceiving or remembering (or whatever) that is its object would lack any awareness of itself. What this comes to as a thesis in the philosophy of mind is the requirement that anything that involves a reference to or description of a given mental act must be assigned to *another* mental act. This would entail that an act of remembering, for example, could carry with it no awareness that its object is being remembered and not perceived (or the other way around), and thus no awareness of its own character as an act of remembering. This, in turn, would require that in such a case it must be possible to separate the pastness of the state of affairs that is remembered from the fact that it is being remembered or recalled, and it is hard to see how this could be done. The underlying picture here seems to be one in which a mental act is something like a ray of light that can illumine only the object to which it is directed and not the source from which it itself emanates or, indeed, itself *as* a ray of light. Consistently with this picture, another ray of light would be needed to illuminate the first one.

When a picture of this kind is applied to our mental life, it might be questioned at the outset whether or not this life obligingly divides itself up into distinct countable acts that could take one another as their objects in the manner this theory requires. But even if this were not disputed, there are other serious difficulties about this way of conceiving self-consciousness. For one thing, although more than one mental act can occur at any given time – I can feel a pain and watch the car ahead of me at the same time – it is not so clear that this is possible when one act takes another as its object. Can I, for example, imagine something and at the same time "introspect" this act of imagining? It would seem that a supervening act of introspection would replace the act it is supposed to examine and thereby make it un- available for examination. But suppose the mind were to turn on itself very quickly; might it not then be able to catch a glimpse of itself in that prior act before it goes off the screen? Tempting as this idea may be, there is also a strong flavor of absurdity about it that must raise serious doubts about the whole picture from which it derives. There is, moreover, good reason to think that this picture is borrowed from contexts that are very different from any such supposed relation of the mind to itself. I can, for example, turn around quickly and catch my clerk with his hand in the till, but it is not clear that I can do anything comparable when I am the only one in- volved. What, after all, is it that I could be supposed to come upon in such a case? It has already been suggested that I could hardly *discover*, through a supervening act of reflection, that I was perceiving something and not remembering it; and the same conclusion seems to hold for the other fea- tures that mental acts are supposed to have. It is conceivable that we are misled into thinking that there must be a two-stage process of this kind by an analogy with the contrast between seeing some object and saying, either to ourselves or to others, that we see it. In such a case, the saying does appear to supervene on a previously mute seeing, and this at least seems like what the doctrine of inner sense describes. There is no reason to think, however, that I regularly give myself reports of this kind or that without them I would remain oblivious to the character of the mental acts I silently perform.

All of this gives good grounds for doubting the assumption that every episode of perception or memory is constitutionally lacking in self-awareness and that this deficiency can be made up only by another act that supervenes upon it. Because the whole topic of self-consciousness has been so dominated by the idea of inner sense, it might seem as though this adverse conclusion about the latter would effectively remove the whole concept of self-consciousness from the agenda of a study in the philosophy of mind. That is not the case, however, because even if self-consciousness is not a matter of performing second-order mental acts, each individual human being is still an "I" and understands himself as such. There is a need, therefore, for an alternative conception of what is involved in this form of self-reference. What I will try to show in this section is that reflexivity is a feature of human being as such and not a feat of contortionism that the mind performs. It is also one that can only be understood in the context of a theory of presence; and it accordingly presupposes the particularity and the unity of presence that have already been discussed. One could even say that it pulls these together in the form of an "I" – that is, of an entity that is, by virtue of this reflexivity, a "self."

Up to this point, the idea of presence has been implicitly understood as presence to something, but little has been said about what having something present to oneself is like. Nor is this a topic about which philosophers generally have had much to say, presumably because all such questions were rendered moot by the notion of the mind and of perception as having a representational proxy of some external object in the mind. Under these auspices, presence is exclusively intramental in character, and it is simply a matter of the mind's having something inside itself. But when this apparatus is set aside, as it has been in this book, this question of what having something present to oneself is like becomes pertinent.

The account of perception in Chapter 2 has already prepared the ground for a further discussion of these issues. What became clear there was the fact that the presence of an object in perception has an indexical character and that the arrow of indexicality runs both ways. The object that is present is "there," and the manner in which it is present indicates the locus of the entity to which it is present, at least within certain limits. In its simplest terms, this means that since objects are transcendent and can be viewed from indefinitely many points of view, the side or aspect of such an object that *is* visible shows at least roughly where the viewer stands. Again, the fact that a remembered event carries with it a certain approximate location in time thereby locates the person who remembers it in a certain temporal relation to it.

If we try to characterize further what this business of being "appeared to" is like, we encounter a serious difficulty. It springs from the fact that it is natural to begin by asking what the entity in question is and then trying to determine how an entity of that type might be conceived as having something present to it. When we proceed in this way, however, we are almost certain to go wrong. The reason is that presence-to is being treated as though it were some sort of problematic further increment to an object that has been conceived independently of it. The presumption is thus that we already have a concept of ourselves as human beings – whether as body or as mind makes little difference – and that this concept is to serve as the stock onto which that of presence-to is to be grafted. Since the prior concept has typically been designed in a way that rules out the very possibility of presence-to, the prospects for such a graft are not exactly bright. There is an alternative to this way of proceeding. That would be to argue that the ways of conceiving ourselves that we already have on hand presuppose another deeper, though inarticulate, understanding that we have of ourselves as ek-sistents, and that it is not possible, without serious distortion, to reverse this order of priority in the manner just described and attach presence-to to something that has already been conceived in abstraction from it. If this suggestion has merit, as I believe it does, then it is that prior understanding of what we are as human beings that needs to be explicated; and the theory of presence that has been set forth in this book is an attempt to provide just such an explication. Although the account that has been given up to this point of human being still needs to be amplified in many respects, it has already been shown that it can provide a framework for the understanding of the particularity and unity of human being. What I want to show now is that the same holds true for that feature of human being that we have traditionally thought of under the rubric of "self-consciousness."

If we simply think in terms of an entity to which another is present without trying to specify further the character of the former at this point, certain things become clear. One of these is something to which Hegel first drew attention when he spoke of the subject as being "reflected back into itself" from its object.[13] What this somewhat cryptic phrase expresses is a reversal of the kind of directionality that the traditional theory of mental acts attributes to them. As has already been noted, these acts have been

---

13. For Hegel's concept of reflection, see Hermann Glockner, *Hegel-Lexikon* (Stuttgart: Fr. Frommans Verlag, 1957), vol. 2, pp. 199–200.

thought of as being like rays of light that issue from the subject and illumine some object out there in the world. Unfortunately, as has also been pointed out, these same acts that are supposed to pluck an external object out of the darkness also terminate in that object in a way that leaves *them* in the dark. But even in the terms set by this picture, in which object consciousness is conceived as an intentional act, there has to be some place for the fact that the object of such an act is made present *to* something. Normally, we would probably say that it is present to the mind that performs this act; but if this mind, in turn, is treated as a sequence of acts, it seems that being present to a mind will be equivalent to being present to or in a mental act of some kind. Because each such act is supposed to be oblivious to itself, there will be no place in it for the reflexive reference to itself that would be implicit in the fact of the presence to *it* of something else. There is thus a real difficulty about how there can be any such fact.

The best that can be managed when these assumptions about mental acts are in force is to invoke another mental act to do what the first one cannot, and in this way the picture of one act taking another as its object is introduced. Clearly, however, the original fact of presence-to cannot be captured by these methods. For one thing, the deficiencies of the first act would be reproduced at the level of this second-order act (and its successors), which would necessarily be oblivious of itself. But for this very reason, it is hard to see how the supervening act could offer any insight into what the original object's being present to the prior act involves since it is supposed to be oblivious to just this aspect of itself. At best, it would represent a purely formal grasp of a "relation" between the prior act and its object that could not be more concretely understood.

This is where the notion of reflection, as Hegel uses it, comes in, and it has a quite different sense from the one that requires the mind to catch itself "in the act." Nor is it necessary, for Hegel's purposes, that any raylike acts should be thought of as issuing from that to which an object is present. All that is needed for reflection in the sense with which he is concerned is the fact of something's presence *to* something else, without any special implication of agency or transmission of any kind. This sense of "reflection" is borrowed from the specifically optical one in which it signifies the bending back of a ray of light from a mirror to its source. In Hegel's phenomenological use of this picture, however, it is some ordinary object that serves as the "mirror," and what is "reflected" is not an image, in any ordinary sense, of the "subject" that views that object. It is, rather, the fact that that object is present to *it*. One could put this another way by saying that through this reflection, that to which something is present is drawn into this same fact of presence, and in such a way that there can no longer be any question of its being oblivious to itself. What this means is that instead of coming at these matters as though one were talking about something or someone other than oneself – an x to which a y is present – one makes it explicit that presence is always first-personal, and thus reflexive, in the sense that nothing can be present to an entity unless the latter is present to itself.

Even when this point is accepted, there is still another way in which we may revert to what really amounts to a third-person account of the connection between selfhood and presence. This is what happens when we begin to speak as though the "self" to which presence points were some sort of object or entity that is in principle independent of and prior to this fact. But when we hypostatize the self in this way, not only do unanswerable questions arise about just what this entity may be, this hypostatized self may also begin to take on a relation to itself. When this happens, for example, when it is claimed that the self constitutes itself through self-interpretation, the paradoxical consequence is that the reflexivity of which "the self" is just a rather imprudent nominalization accrues to this new substantive in an iterative redundancy that is decidedly peculiar.[14] Generally, unless we decline the gambit of hypostatization at the outset, matters can only get more and more impenetrably confused. The only real alternative is to insist on the equivalence of reflexivity and being a self, and to construe the former in terms of the impossibility for an entity, however characterized, to be drawn into the fact of presence as that to which something is present while remaining oblivious to itself in the way that mental acts have been supposed to be. Viewed in this light, "the self" would simply be the entity – the human being – to which something else is present and which is thereby present to itself as that to which something else is present. The claim this involves is that presence makes an entity a self, that is, an entity into which its relation to something else is reflected back and that thereby is for itself in this special way.

There is a long tradition of thought that opposes any such conclusion as this. Although it may insist, in good Cartesian fashion, that the truth of consciousness is to be found in self-consciousness, it also seeks to disjoin the latter from the former, often in the belief that this is the way a distinction between animal and human consciousness has to be made.[15] Animals would, on such a view, have only consciousness and not self-consciousness, whereas humans would have both. One suspects that this way of contrasting animal consciousness with human self-consciousness gives too much weight to the fact that animals do not talk and therefore do not say "I," whereas

14. An example of this conception of the "self" can be found in Charles Taylor, *Sources of the Self: The Making of the Modern Identity* (Cambridge, Mass.: Harvard University Press, 1989), Chapter 2.
15. The applicability of the concept of presence and its cognates to animals is barely touched on by Heidegger. References to such comments as he does make can be found in my *Heidegger and the Philosophy of Mind* (New Haven, Conn.: Yale University Press, 1989), pp. 236–7 and 241–2.

human beings do both. That fact certainly has its special importance in certain contexts, but it will not do to identify selfhood with being able to say "I". After all, in other respects, animal behavior gives ample evidence of reflexivity, for example, when a bird sees that a hawk is about to attack *it*. The bird that is thus understood to be under attack is certainly not identified by its position or its properties; in seeing the hawk coming its way, it understands that it is *itself* the hawk's target. This would hardly be possible unless the presence of the hawk to the bird were at the same time the presence of the bird to itself as that to which the hawk is present.

What distinguishes the human from the animal case is not reflexivity but, rather, the differences between the temporality of the one and the other. Everything suggests that, as a self, an animal is confined within its present and its immediate future in a way that stands in marked contrast with the extended availability of its own past (and, in another sense, its future) to a human being. To the degree that this is the case, only a very thin form of selfhood can be attributed to an animal, not because it lacks a relation to itself but because the range and hence the content of that relation are so severely restricted. The sense that human beings have of themselves is not only much richer and more highly differentiated; it is such that we are able to attend to episodes in our own lives out of an interest that is relatively independent of the requirements of action. But if, as I am arguing, "self-consciousness" is not, in either the human or the animal case, something that gratuitously supervenes on a consciousness that in no way requires its services, it would surely be better to stop talking about it in language that inevitably suggests that it does just that. Conceivably, one could try to fit it out anew along the lines Sartre proposed as an implicit or "non-thetic" self-consciousness that accompanies every act of consciousness, as the occasional "thetic" acts of reflective self-consciousness do not.[16] Even though this is an emendation of a theory of mental acts that Sartre would have been better advised to abandon outright, it is certainly a move in the right direction. In a suitably dementalized version, it would replace the nonthetic character of these mental acts with the indexical character of presence as presence-to. In that way, the element of self-consciousness would not be a feature of an act – something that is hard to conceive in any case – but of an entity that is conceived in terms of the presence of something to it, and that is thereby always a self in the sense just indicated, although there would be no single or mandatory way in which this fact would be manifested.

This line of thought can be developed further in such a way as to cast light on the notion of the "I," although once again, the fact that human

16. See J.-P. Sartre, *Being and Nothingness: An Essay in Phenomenological Ontology,* translated by Hazel Barnes (New York: Philosophical Library, 1958), Introduction, pp. lii–lviii.

agency has yet to be brought into the discussion means that a major dimension of selfhood can only be roughly indicated; and the same might
be said of the body. The first point that needs to be made is that it is the
human being as a whole to whom something is present. For all the undoubted importance of specific, spatially demarcated organs like the eyes
and the brain in such transactions, it is not possible to treat them as the
entities to which what is present is present. At least under the mode of
conceptualization that mediates the scientific understanding of the functions of these organs, it is no more possible to conceive of something as
being present to these organs than it would be to do so in the case of a
chair and a wall. Clearly, this would be the case for the human being as a
whole as well if his wholeness were conceived simply as the aggregate of
his physical parts. Nor would it be of much help to include the relations
in which these parts stand to one another. The reason is that, as relations
are usually understood, there is an implied contrast between them and
what something is – its properties. The effect of this contrast is to make
relations something "external" – something that may or may not supervene
on something else in the manner that has already been discussed in connection with self-consciousness and consciousness. In the standard interpretations of reflexivity as a relation, moreover, there is the further disadvantage that this relation is supposed to apply to everything since everything
is identical with itself. This assumption will be discussed in detail in Chapter
7, but it is clear even now that it would make the concept of reflexivity
useless for the purpose it serves here – that of making a contrast between
human beings and things.

     What has just been said about relations – external and otherwise – sug-
gests a more general point that is often missed, I suspect, precisely because
it is so patent. This is the fact that in presence – most notably in perception
– things are *together* before they are apart. By "apart" I mean logically separate from one another in the Humean sense or in the manner of substances as Descartes conceived them. This logical separateness pervasively
characterizes the ways in which we think and talk about almost everything,
and it has the effect of making invisible to us the fact of presence from
which we perforce begin, and which we also clearly presuppose in everything we think and do. This is the fact that, for all its separateness and
"otherness," this table, for example, is present to me and I am that to
which it is present. This is the togetherness that a conception of the world
as made of separate objects cannot find a place for and for which peculiar
locutions must be found when, willy-nilly, it proves impossible to leave it
completely out of account. If it is to be thought of as a relation at all, it
certainly cannot be an *external* relation in the sense that separates what a
thing is from the relations in which it stands. This is not because there is
some unbreakable logical nexus between this table and me, as critics of the

doctrine of internal relations have construed it to mean. The assumption implicit in such interpretations is that internal relations are the starting point for a "flower-in-the-crannied-wall" metaphysic and that if relations are internal in the sense of being essentially embedded in their terms, it should be possible, at least in principle, to spin out the whole content of the world from any one of its constituent parts. But even if the doctrine of internal relations in this version has been discredited, there are still good grounds for the much more limited claim I have been making that the relation between a human being and his world is not an external one. This thesis is compatible with its being the case that the relations between the things that make up that world can be, and typically are, construed as being external.

The further claim advanced in this section is that the same holds for the relation of a human being to himself. It may be worth noting here that this claim is not primarily concerned with the language in which we describe ourselves. There is a strong disposition these days to construe all such claims in this way, usually with the implication that since there are many such modes of description, no one of them can be regarded as being in any way obligatory. But if this is supposed to mean that reflexivity as such is somehow optional, then that would plainly be a mistake since reflexivity is presupposed in all the options we are supposed to have in this regard, including the option of never using the first person in describing the person that I am. Indeed, reflexivity is so far from being arbitrary that in it both the particularity and the unity of human being are subsumed and fully realized. As so subsumed, they define a particular of a very distinctive kind in which every aspect of its being and its agency presupposes the presence of the world it is in. Now it is just such an entity as this that says "I," and this saying of "I" is the purest and most concentrated expression of its special character. The "I" has in fact a patent and self-declaratory character that almost all philosophical accounts miss because they invariably turn into a search for some special kind of object that they think "I" must denote. It has already been pointed out that this search is a peculiar one since it can only be described in language that presupposes the very "I" that is supposedly being sought. The supposed mystery about the "I" that inspires this search is in fact wholly specious; and so far from being the putative object of such a search, what the "I" expresses is the reflexive posture of a finite ek-sistent that is implicit in even the idea of such a search. Any entity that stands in the relation to itself that makes the idea of such a search possible is a self, and "I" is the word that declares its presence and its character as such.

There is another question about the *way* in which a human being is present to himself that can only be noted here in anticipation of a much fuller attempt to answer it in the chapters that follow. What can be said now is that although self-presence is the presence to itself of a human being as a whole, this does not mean that every feature of a human being must enjoy an equal prominence within it or that these features are given in some ideally neutral and objective manner. That is plainly not the case. When the active character of human being and of the human body come into the discussion, not only will the sharply selective character of self-presence be fully evident, but the kind of selection it involves will be shown to be closely bound up with the active orientation and practical agenda of the human being in question. This point will take on a special importance in the discussion of the body in Chapter 6.

5

POLARITY AND AGENCY

I

In the preceding chapter, a first step was taken to move beyond the concept of presence toward an explicit account of the kind of entity to which what is present is present. Instead of devising a special name for such entities, I have been referring to them simply as "human beings"; but, following Heidegger, I have chosen to call their mode of being "ek-sistence." The concept of ek-sistence presupposes that of presence; and at every point, an account of ek-sistence is an account of the presence of entities to the entity that ek-sists. At the same time, however, ek-sistence is a concept richer than that of presence as such, and it subsumes under itself a number of features of human being of which this is also true.

Some of these features progressively made their appearance in the preceding chapters, which were mainly devoted to giving an account of presence as such; but with the exception of a fairly detailed discussion of error, their special status vis-à-vis presence has been only briefly acknowledged. With the account of particularity, unity, and reflexivity in Chapter 4, however, a discussion of the features of human being that are central to its ek-sistence was begun. Even so, perhaps because these three features have a somewhat static character, it may not have been fully apparent that the discussion was crossing a watershed from presence to ek-sistence. If that was the case, then the present chapter should remove any uncertainty on this point. It introduces another, quite different side of ek-sistence that has nothing static about it at all and that finds its fullest expression in human agency. With this account of the active side of human being, a new and important dimension of concreteness accrues to the concept of an entity that ek-sists, and a further increment will be added by the account of the body given in the next chapter.

Before taking up the topic of agency, however, it will be necessary to examine certain matters that are intimately connected with it and in fact set the context in which action is undertaken. Although I have been trying to avoid psychological terminology for the purposes of this account of human being, that may not be altogether feasible in the case of all the concepts I want to take up now. This is not because these concepts are unincorporable into the ontological theory of human being I am proposing but, rather, because the English language does not afford a satisfactory way of expressing their ontological character. Ideally, I should have been able to follow the example of Heidegger and find acceptable ways of adapting to my purposes the words that English makes available for talking about "feeling" and "desire."[1] In fact, however, I have not been able to devise a non-psychological idiom for these concepts. The best I have been able to do is to bring them together under the common heading of "polarity." What I want to convey by means of this – in intention, at least – nonpsychological term is the fact that, to put it as flatfootedly as possible, things *matter*, and that their mode of presence accordingly takes the form of contrasts between possible outcomes of various kinds – contrasts in which the occurrence of one of these outcomes is less or more welcome than that of the other.

Although it is widely held that the ultimate source of such differences has to be understood in psychological terms, I am not primarily concerned here with showing that that is not the case, although I am convinced that it is not. I am using the term "polarity" to mark the difference between a world in which nothing matters at all, one way or the other, and a world in which, for whatever reason, such contrasts obtain. Polarity is precisely the ordering of the field of presence of a given individual human being in terms of pairings of actual and possible states of affairs. It matters greatly, for example, whether the injury someone has sustained in a car accident turns out to be a concussion and not a skull fracture. My argument will be that such orderings are constituted first passively in feeling and then actively in desire. It will also be shown that the wider context in which polarity, as so conceived, orders presence is one of agency – agency understood as a power of the entity that ek-sists to (try to) bring about one outcome rather

---

1. The words Heidegger uses are *Befindlichkeit* and *Entwurf*. The latter is more or less captured by the usual translation of it as "project" since this word has a Latin root meaning "throw" and thus reproduces the *-wurf* part of *Entwurf*, which also means "throw." By contrast, *"Befindlichkeit"* is untranslatable into English in any way that preserves the connotations of the verb that serves as its base: *sich befinden*, to feel or fare – well or ill – in the sense of finding oneself in a certain place in one's life. The Macquarrie–Robinson translation renders it as "state of mind," which is uniquely inappropriate in light of the fact that Heidegger is talking not about "minds" but about *Dasein*.

than another in such situations. Accordingly, polarity and agency are deeply implicated in each other – polarity as the condition under which alone action could have any point and agency as the power to intervene in a world in which something has been constituted in feeling and desire as preferable to something else.

Although words like "feeling" and "desire" figure prominently in this brief preview of the line of argument I will be developing, it should be evident even now that their role is not the one typically assigned to them in the usual psychological story that is told about them. That story reflects an assumption that the field of objects we encounter in perception and otherwise must be conceived in terms of pure actuality. On this view, presence as such would be a matter of objects simply being there in a way that involves no essential element of modality or of axiological contrast. The attitudes and preferences we unquestionably have, would, on these assumptions, derive from some source that is prior to and independent of presence; and they would then attach themselves selectively to elements within the field of presence, and thus produce our familiar patterns of preference and desire.

The trouble with such an account is simply that the feelings and desires that are superadded to presence in this way would themselves have to be conceived in a reified manner; and it can be shown that any such conception places serious difficulties in the way of an understanding of the relationship in which they stand to the objects on which they are supposedly "projected."[2] In a general way, one can say that the effect of so conceiving feelings in particular is to give them the status of somewhat exotic *objects* – "exotic" because of their lack of physical properties but "objects" nevertheless because this is the only status available for them. If, in spite of their peculiarities – which, not surprisingly, have aroused strong prepossessions against them on the part of many philosophers – feelings are accepted as discrete elements in the array of objects that are present to consciousness, then the latter can be thought of, as before, as standing in a spectator relationship to what passes before it. In the case of feeling, this mode of treatment may seem defensible because of the "sensuous content" it is supposed to have – content that is held to be anomalous and yet must be accommodated somehow. But it can also be extended to desire and then to action itself, which typically lacks any such exotic content, and with even more peculiar results. The outcome in this case is that we become the spectators of our own actions, and this consequence has an incongruity

---

2. This psychological conception of projection is widely used and is utterly different from what Heidegger has in mind when he speaks of an *Entwurf*. Indeed, the conception of a project as something like a transfer of a feeling (or whatever) from one thinglike entity to another can be viewed as an attempt to make up for the absence of a working concept of ek-sistence and of the transcendence that characterizes it.

about it that may help us to detect what went wrong at the outset in the treatment of feeling and desire.

II

Few concepts have suffered more from the application to them of fixed philosophical prepossessions than has that of feeling. The inventory of the contents of the human mind – its "ideas," as they were called – that philosophers made in the seventeenth and eighteenth centuries presupposed a distinction between the ideas or mental contents that had counterparts in the extramental objects they were thought to represent and those that resided only in the mind. The former were the so-called primary, or physical, qualities – size, shape, and motion – and the latter were the secondary, or nonphysical, qualities like color and sound, which appeared to inhere in external objects but could be shown by further analysis not to do so. In all this, it was accepted, as a matter that only a child or a naive person could be deceived about, that feelings like pleasure and pain do not really belong to the objects that might produce them in us. Because their purely internal and subjective status was thus effectively uncontested, such feelings were in one sense the paradigmatic case of secondary qualities; but because they did not even *seem* to be the properties of anything in the world, they did not receive as much attention as did those that seemed to be so, and they have sometimes even been reclassified as "tertiary" qualities. The trouble with all this was that the notion of something's being "in us" and, to make things worse, *only* in us was not at all clear and needed careful scrutiny it did not receive.

If feelings are in us because they are not properties of objects, it is clear that they can have no epistemic value. Not only do they tell us nothing about the way things are in the world; they often interfere with our efforts to discover the nature of those things by inclining us improperly to some view of the matter in hand for which there may be no supporting evidence. It follows that the only epistemic value that feelings can possibly have, on this view, is in self-knowledge – that is, in our apprehensions of our own inner state. By the terms of this whole approach, however, such knowledge is confined to the one individual who is both its object and its subject. Feelings are thus necessarily private and inaccessible to others; and any report of one's feelings must finally rest entirely on the say-so of the individual who gives it. It cannot be verified or confirmed by anyone else. The status of feelings is thus doubly problematic: They are deviant objects that have no place in the world, and their existence in the mind is sealed off from independent inspection.

This was bad enough, but there was worse to come. If this peculiar status derives from the dualistic assumptions of seventeenth-century philosophy, as has been suggested, one might expect that it would have been revised when these assumptions were abandoned. It is worth noting, therefore, that in the present phase of the philosophy of mind these assumptions have been widely challenged; yet the status of feeling can hardly be said to have improved. Feelings have, in fact, become even more troublesome because there is now little willingness to grant them a domicile in the mind (and thus outside the natural world), and to do so on terms that would at least keep them from causing trouble for the serious business of scientific knowledge. To those familiar with the history of philosophy and the desperate expedients to which partisans of some deeply implausible theory can be driven, it cannot come as a surprise that severe measures have been proposed to deal with the anomalies that feelings generate. Typically, these would simply deny any reality whatever – that is, any status as objects – to feelings insofar as they prove unassimilable to the ontological categories of physicalism. Pains, for example, are now often declared to be simply identical with the stimulation of "C-fibers," with the implication that everything that needs to be said about them can be said in the language of neurophysiology. Some aspects of this line of thought will be taken up and examined critically in the next two chapters. Even in advance of this scrutiny, however, the extreme character of an abolitionist position of this kind surely justifies an effort to determine whether there are more attractive alternatives to the original assumptions about feeling that result in its being assigned first a marginal ontological status and then no status at all.

One such alternative would be to question the initial assumption that classifies feelings as objects. This assumption says, in effect, that, in addition to the more or less standard material objects that we perceive, we also encounter others that are abnormal because they lack the physical properties that would make it possible to assign them a place in the world. But suppose that feelings were treated not as marginal (because mutilated) members of the class of objects that are so encountered but, rather, as the encountering itself, that is, as themselves a modality in which objects can be present. In order to test this line of thought, we may take a familiar bodily feeling as our example – a stomachache, say. This example has the advantage that we are not usually aware of our stomachs through any other sense, and it is only when something goes wrong that our attention is called to this part of our body at all. Significantly, when we have a stomachache, we tend to say that the ache itself is what we notice or become aware of; but it is just this way of conceiving the matter that I want to challenge. Why should we not say, instead, that the ache is my awareness of my stomach or of that part of my body? In the language of presence, this would be to say that on such an occasion my stomach is present to me in the modality of a feeling of a certain kind – in this example, a feeling of discomfort.

There is at least one potent reason why we may not find this suggestion persuasive. Often, the parts of our body in which we feel a pain, say, are parts that are readily accessible to another sense like vision. My hands, for example, are almost constantly in view; so if I suddenly feel a pain in one of my hands, it seems natural to think of this pain as a new element in a situation that was already present. The hand was already there, and now there is also a pain, and the pain is somehow in the hand. Thought of in this way, the presence of the hand is a given and one that is attributable to another sense; and so it seems less natural to conceive the pain as the way in which the hand itself is present. In the example of the stomach, however, no other sense is involved, and so it would seem strange to try to set up a conjunctive relation between the feeling and the affected part of the body in this way, not to speak of going on, as philosophers are wont to do, to ask puzzling questions about how something nonspatial (a pain) can be *in* something (a stomach) that occupies space.

But even in the case of a conspicuous body part like the hand, it can be shown that such an approach would be inappropriate. Even though we are accustomed to seeing (and touching) our hands, a feeling of pain in one of our hand is independent of their visibility, and there is no reason to think that a part of our body cannot be present in more than one way. If on a cold night I wake up in the dark because I left one hand outside the bed covers and it has become chilled, that hand is just as authentically present in the feeling of cold that wakes me up as it would be in a visual perception of it. Independently of any other sense, the feeling itself presents my hand as a part of me that is uncomfortably exposed; and it does so in a way that bypasses the puzzles that may arise when the hand is conceived primarily in visual terms as a spatial occupant.

It may be suggested that in such cases the feeling of cold or of pain can nevertheless be distinguished from the hand it presents and that, as so distinguished, it constitutes an object of a special kind – an object that, for one thing, cannot be a physical part of that hand. There is at least some truth in this suggestion, since the reflexive character of presence-to, as set forth in the preceding chapter, ensures that the feeling of cold or of pain will form part of the presence to itself of the human being whose hand feels cold. The strategy of the argument I am examining is to extract such a feeling from this context of reflexivity and then to treat it as though it were simply a given. It is surprising that the same philosophers who concentrate exclusively on the quality that is so made present in abstraction from the whole context of reflexivity in which it occurs then go on to make a great fuss about the anomalous status of the very feelings they have isolated by this procedure. It is also clear that once a feeling has been separated in this way from the part of the body that it has been described as presenting, it is not at all clear how it could present the latter at all. We would, in effect, be saying that there is the feeling that would be quite opaque in itself, and there is the hand, and then there is also a relation between them that we express by saying that the feeling is in the hand; but the way in which that relation is present and the way in which the hand is present would have to be attributed to something other than the feeling itself. What that might be remains a mystery, but it seems much like a reversion to the notion of a consciousness before which both the feeling and the hand would independently appear together with a relation between them. It seems much simpler and more accurate to hold that the feeling itself is the way in which the hand is present, and that the distinction between the presence of the hand and the feeling – this inevitably becomes the presence of the feeling – is one that cannot be maintained.

This whole way of separating out feelings qua feelings is very different from the way we ordinarily treat them on those occasions when we say "My hand (or my stomach) hurts." Statements like this are not reports of sensations; they express a way in which a human being is there for himself, and it is a way that reveals how he is doing – how things stand for him – and where he is along some axis of polarity. In the examples given thus far, some part of the body presents itself as affected in one way or another; and this is surely the primordial form of polarity, since whatever else it may be, a human being is certainly a body, though in a sense that will not be made plain until the next chapter. The mark of bodily feelings is their localization – the stomachache "in" the stomach and the pain "in" the hand – and it is the anomalous character of this localization that is at once a standing puzzle for the physicalist and a clue to the quite different status for feelings that is being proposed here.

Feeling is not tied to this sort of localization, however. There is another set of feelings – the ones that are often called "intentional" – that have no definite locus in the body even though they may be expressed in bodily gestures and postures. Thus, we are happy and sad about things that have no connection with the state of our bodies, and even pain and pleasure have analogues that are not localized in our bodies in the way that an ache or a tickle is. I can be sad because a friend has died, although I am in the pink of health; and such a feeling is both non–self-regarding, in the sense that it is the death of my friend that makes me sad, and an index of how things are for me. Similarly, such an event does not affect my physical person, as when I fall and break my leg. But, of course, in another sense, the death of my friend *is* something that happens to me, and it is this fact that my feeling of sadness takes in. We may speak of a feeling like sadness at the death of a friend as the effect this event has had on us, and there is no harm in such locutions as long as they do not fall into the hands of philosophers. Unfortunately, when that happens, a style of analysis tends to be introduced that turns such an event into a causal sequence in which an event – in this case, my friend's death – produces in me a generic feeling of sadness. A feeling, whether of sadness or whatever, that is conceived in this way is much harder to recognize as the modality in which what has happened is disclosed to and registered by me. If anything, such attempts to treat such feelings in this pseudoconcrete way as "effects" produced in me that are in principle independent of their "causes" are even more implausible than they are in the case of bodily feelings. The latter at least have a bodily location that is indeed "in me" in a certain sense, and this makes it easier, though no less mistaken, to assign them the status of objects that was discussed earlier. There is, by contrast, a patent absurdity in according the same sort of treatment to feelings like sadness or joy, as though they were *Gegenstände* – something set over against us and available for our puzzled inspection.

What this really amounts to is an attempt to establish a distinction between our feelings and ourselves that is not possible in these cases. Instead, these feelings have to be understood as the way the events in question present themselves to us, and this is at the same time the way we are – the way it is with us – in the presence of these events. Thus, in my example, with the news of the death of a friend, my prospect becomes one of living in a world that no longer contains the person who died, and it is that prospect that my feeling of sadness registers. Someone else may, of course, read of this death in the newspaper and not care much one way or the other. In a limited sense, moreover, the fact that people who did not know the deceased learn of in the newspaper is the same fact that brings grief into the lives of those who did. But absence of feeling here does not signify superior objectivity, but rather a detachment from the consequences of this death for any life connected with that of the person who died; and it is those consequences that are disclosed – that are present – precisely in the sadness felt by those who are not so detached.[3]

Feelings, it now appears, are not side effects or by-products of the knowledge we gain of certain facts or events that are in themselves quite neutral. They are rather the way in which these facts themselves are present in the dimensions in which they form a part of our own lives. This may sound like an epistemic interpretation of feelings – and so, in a way, it is, but only with important qualifications that need to be understood. There is, to begin with, an element of passivity in feelings of any kind. We do not decide or choose to feel sad or happy or angry; and although we can resist these

---

3. It seems clear that indifference – the *ataraxia* that was so highly praised by the Stoics – is itself what Heidegger called a *Stimmung* and thus a modality of feeling. Heidegger's most famous analysis of a state of feeling is the one devoted to anxiety in *Being and Time*; but there is another in his lectures that is devoted to boredom. See his *Die Grundbegriffe der Metaphysik: Welt – Endlichkeit – Einsamkeit*, vol. 29/30 of the *Gesamtausgabe* (Frankfurt am Main: V. Klostermann, 1983), pp. 89–198.

feelings, we cannot eliminate them at will, although we can try to do so, usually with bad results. Instead, things happen, often as a result – whether intended or unintended – of other things we have done, and they make us angry or happy, joyous or sad. In light of these facts, it is natural to think of these feelings as the effects such events produce in us, and there would be a corresponding bit of knowledge that registers this fact. But, of course, if feelings themselves have something like an epistemic function, *this* cannot be the knowledge that they yield. There is, after all, nothing sad about the fact that certain kinds of events make me sad, and it would certainly be incongruous (and circular) to suggest that I am sad *because* such events make me sad. If sadness can properly be thought of as "saying" something about anything at all (as it must if it is to have an epistemic aspect), then *what* it says must concern the events that take place themselves and not their effect on me, which is, of course, just my sadness itself. In that case, however, *what* can these feelings possibly say about these events if it is not that they have a certain effect on me? This, of course, is just another way of asking what there can be in the world to feel happy or sad about other than the fact that certain things make us happy or sad. And the implied answer to this question is that there is nothing.

There is, plainly, something strange about such a question. It seems as though it were being asked by someone who always stands at a considerable distance from any feelings that may come his way and observes them as effects that are being produced in him.[4] It seems to be assumed, moreover, that this way of speaking about feelings is the only appropriate one once it is understood that feelings are effects and are produced in us without our having to give our approval. But in that case, it would also follow that, like all effects of causal action of whatever kind, they must stand on their own once they have been produced; and this means that what a feeling is in itself will be quite different from what produced it – so different, in fact, that the only link between the two will be an external causal one. But how are we to reconcile this with the fact that we are *pleased that* someone accepted our invitation or *angry at* someone who did not? What such locutions express is clearly an internal relation between the feeling in question and what we call its "object"; and this is a relation that is not only inseparable from the feeling itself but also runs in the opposite direction from the causal one. It is, we may say, the feeling that gives the import of the fact in question, and in that sense the feeling is a modality of presence – the fact in its polar relation to its relevant contrasting term and thus an index of how things are with us.

---

4. A good characterization of this objectifying treatment of the life of feeling can be found in P. F. Strawson, "Freedom and Resentment," in *Studies in the Philosophy of Thought and Action*, edited by P. F. Strawson (New York: Oxford University Press, 1968), pp. 71–76.

The trouble with the conception of feelings as effects is that it treats the fact that we do not ourselves voluntarily produce our feelings as implying that they are something that happens to us in the way that a bruise is produced by bumping into a piece of furniture. This acknowledges an important truth: that there is a primary element of passivity in all feeling in that it registers what happens *to* us – the outcomes that actually occur. Moreover, it certainly appears that at least the feelings localized in the body, such as the pain that often accompanies a bruise, are as independent of everything except the physical constitution of our bodies as are the physical changes in the body that occur when we are bruised. At any rate, we suffer pain in a way that appears to be independent of our beliefs or our attitudes or our other personal characteristics. I have already tried to show that, even in such cases as these, treating feelings as effects unavoidably produces puzzles that can only be resolved by understanding them as modalities of presence. But in the case of feelings that are more diffuse – emotions like anger or moods like depression – the element of passivity (or, if one likes, of vulnerability) is still present, but it is not dependent on any facts about the body. Whether we feel joy or anger when something happens depends, rather, on what we had hoped for or cared about in connection with this event. Even if hoping and caring are not necessarily under our voluntary control, they are certainly closely linked with the choices and preferences that are at the core of our active natures. In this sense, we as individuals are vulnerable to certain feelings because we are actively engaged in behalf of goals that can be adversely or favorably affected by the course of events; and for people who are not so engaged, such events may be indifferent. We say that we are "affected" by what happens, and that locution expresses this quasi passivity of ours but not the context of active engagement by which it is mediated. It will become apparent, as we examine the way context itself is constituted by desire and action, that both are involved in the kind of polarity that characterizes presence at the level of feeling.

A conception of feeling along the lines I am proposing may be misunderstood in any number of ways, but one in particular requires attention. It may be thought that what I am getting at is some notion of feeling as a signal that we use as the basis for inferences we draw about whatever concerns us. Such an interpretation would assimilate what has been said about feeling as a modality of presence to a familiar epistemological paradigm, but if that proves reassuring to some, it also has a far more serious disadvantage because it presupposes the very conception of feeling as an object that has been rejected. On this view, feelings turn up in our experiential fields and prove to be useful as indicators that can be employed for purposes of prediction by a consciousness for which they are objects and which is itself detached from them. But the point about feeling that needs to be made here once again is that it is not the contingent excrescence on the epistemic self that this interpretation treats it as being. If it were that, then a feeling of anger, say, would be something from which that self has always in principle detached itself; and the polarities by which our worlds and our lives are ordered would be, in the first instance, the subject of epistemic determination by a subject that could be characterized independently of them. Although the extent of the difference between any such conception and the one presented here cannot yet be fully explained, it is already clear that, on my view, knowledge of any kind, but scientific knowledge in particular, is not a central redoubt to which each of can withdraw by consigning other elements in our nature to the status of "externalities." As such, they would have the status of objects of some kind to which a nuclear epistemic self could then address itself, free from entanglement in the partisan concerns they represent. Instead, feeling pervades our being in a way that cannot be contained within some delimited area of givenness. It is not just *how* we are in the sense of how things are with us, but also *where* we are within the interlocking networks of polarities in terms of which our worlds, and we ourselves as entities that have worlds, are constituted.

If feeling is a modality of presence, a question arises about its scope and its degree of independence from – possibly even its priority to – other modalities of presence like language. We certainly speak on occasion of feelings as "interpreting" the world for us; and although this way of putting things does not quite accord with the conception of feelings as modalities of presence, it may be useful to ask what such interpretation involves and what it presupposes in the way of other modalities of presence, among them our linguistic capabilities. Is it possible, for example, to be afraid of something simply in the modality of feeling, without having either the concept or the word for "fear" or its cognates? Once we have these concepts and use them regularly to describe episodes in our lives in which we are afraid of something or someone, it is as though the understanding of such situations laid down in our talk about them displaced the feeling of fear itself or transformed it into a psychological accompaniment of an understanding that is primarily conceptual and linguistic. This can even reach the point where it becomes difficult for us to imagine that fear itself (or any other feeling) could be separated from a language-mediated grasp of a situation.

We know, however, that children (and animals) show fear in a way that is independent of any ability they may have to describe the situation in language that would express what is fearsome in it. Typically, such fear is directed to something that they perceive – a person they have not seen before or an unfamiliar animal – and they do not have to have a word for that object or a descriptive adjective in order to be afraid of it. Later in life, when most of the objects we perceive have acquired names, and when our powers of memory and imagination are more highly developed, feeling still seems to retain much of its autonomous character. If, for example, we watch on television some event like a mass shooting or a gas explosion in a city, the feelings of sorrow or dismay that greet such events do not appear to be mediated by any linguistic formulation of the import of what is taking place before our eyes. It does not, accordingly, seem farfetched to speak, as Heidegger spoke, of our feelings as the primary mode in which the polarities that constitute that import are disclosed, both before and after we have acquired mature linguistic competence.

This line of thought suggests another observation about feeling that might, if further developed, have important implications in a number of areas. What I have in mind is the possibility that feeling may not only be independent of language in the ways just discussed but may also be at variance with the explicit accounts we give of ourselves and may disclose in its own way aspects of our condition to which, for whatever reason, we deny recognition in those accounts. What this comes to is the possibility that a more strongly developed conception of feeling as a central element in ek-sistence might also render superfluous theories of the "unconscious" as a part of the mind to which we do not have access. What has not been noted often enough is the peculiar dependence of this concept of the unconscious on that of consciousness, and thus on that of the mind. But if the concept of the mind is vulnerable to criticism along the lines that have been developed in this book, then that of the unconscious as a kind of subbasement to which what cannot find a place "in consciousness" is consigned must be equally so. This is not to suggest that the kinds of facts the concept of the unconscious was designed to deal with are simply to be dismissed. What might be proposed, however, is that in the transition to the conception of a human being as an ek-sistent, they might be more suitably accommodated under the heading of *Befindlichkeit* as Heidegger conceives it. The task, then, would be not to show how the unconscious influences our conscious lives *ab extra* but, rather, how we are able to hide from ourselves the way things are with us. It is surely relevant here that, like the unconscious, feeling as the disclosure of how things are with us is mute; and so it cannot offer any articulate resistance to the descriptions we give of it – among them, many that are designed to hide rather than to reveal the truth about how and where we are. But if it does not overtly contradict our descriptions – which, by the way, are the counterpart of consciousness in the old picture – feeling is certainly not controlled by them either and maintains its own stubborn independence of our attempts to reconcile them with our official versions of what is going on in our lives.[5]

---

5. It is certainly true that feelings can be repressed, but I would argue that this can never be done without consequences in the modality of feeling itself, which in their own distinctive way express what is going on in the life in question. It is one thing to say – to others and to ourselves – that we are happy when we in fact are not, and this is probably the form that repression most often takes. But we are certainly not able to make the state of feeling in

It is true that as we grow up we learn to control our feelings so that they do not altogether dominate our responses to events that affect us strongly. Valuable as it is, our ability to do this – and thus, in some sense, to discount our own feelings – may contribute to a sense of their marginality, as well as of the privileged character of a form of presence in which they are at least nominally discounted. This is another route leading to the objectified conception of feeling discussed earlier; and it converges, in a somewhat paradoxical way, with the requirements imposed by the "scientific image" of human nature. In the early "naive" stages of this process, it is easy to miss the degree to which this new objectivity is itself saturated with "affective content" that is exceptional only because the polarities it involves are now defined in terms of the exclusion of feeling itself. Indeed, the mentality so formed can on occasion take on a disagreeable element of compulsiveness that is not improved by its being invisible to those who are affected by it, perhaps as a result of the very theory to which they give their allegiance. *Naturam expellas furca, tamen usque recurrit* is an adage that applies with great force to all such attempts to deny to feeling its constitutive role in the ordering of our lives, and this means in the ordering of our way of being in the world.

The distorting element in most philosophical analyses of feeling appears to be the fact that feeling is regularly conceived as a type of mental content. For the purposes of philosophical analysis, sentences like "I feel a pain in my tooth" or "I am depressed by the news from China" replace sentences like "My tooth hurts" and "After Tiananmen Square the situation in China is hopeless." The latter would ordinarily be characterized as expressive statements and the former as self-descriptive; but it may be that even the term "expressive" is too closely linked by its etymology to the same assumptions that are explicit in the other usage. What is being assumed is that we must not speak as though feelings of whatever kind could be domiciled in any part of the natural world; and the only alternative to such a view is taken to be the thesis that feelings are adjectival to the mind and that reference to them must therefore be cast in the self-ascriptive mode. But to conceive the available alternatives in this way is, of course, to adopt a substance theory of the mind, with all the familiar difficulties that entails. If, instead, the primitive notion for a philosophy of mind were to be that of presence, then the way would be open to a conception of feeling as neither an internal state of the self nor a peculiar denizen of the external world, but the original way in which the polarities inherent in the presence of an active entity to its world are disclosed.

To this it might be replied that although the self-ascriptive mode may indeed be open to criticism along the lines just suggested, it nevertheless

which we actually live a happy one, and so the tension between our descriptions and our actual affective life remains.

remains a fact that on occasion we become aware of pains as pains and of other feelings as feelings; and it can hardly be illegitimate to ask what kinds of entities these are, apart from the functions they may be supposed to have in the life of the person to whom they "belong." For example, one would like to know whether they are immaterial since it makes no sense to talk of them as occupying space in any normal sense. This appears reasonable enough, and yet one wonders whether the reference to feelings as "entities" about whose status a very proper question is being asked is as innocent as it seems. It is not possible to throw much light on this matter before the unitary concept of a human being is presented in Chapter 7; but an "entity" can seem surprisingly like an "object" in these contexts, and the choice between "material" and "immaterial" as the master description for this entity is not an inviting one. It seems too much as though "immaterial" were supposed to name something in the way that "material" does when all it conveys here is the fact that adjectives of location, size, and shape are no more informative when applied to feelings than they would be in the case of numbers. But if "immaterial" is uninformative, its antonym, "material," is far too restrictive as it is ordinarily construed. A human being certainly has location, size, and shape, but to conclude from this that all of his attributes must therefore be material in the sense of occupying space in some measurable way would be unjustified – most notably so in the case of feeling. It will be shown in the next two chapers how the "materiality" of the human body can be reconciled with the possession by a human being of features that are not material in the sense of taking up space.

III

In the account just given of feeling, the broad outlines of the concept of polarity were also delineated; but there is at least one major respect in which that account needs to be amplified. It was shown that feeling expresses the way things are with us, that it incorporates a strong element of passivity – that is, of being subject to a situation that in some way affects our interests, and that we may or may not be able to change it but in any case cannot just wish it away. At the same time, it is clear that this passivity is not the whole story even of feeling as such. We are active beings even when there is almost nothing we can do about a given situation; and the situations in which we find ourselves are typically ones that we do not merely suffer or enjoy but that we want to terminate, modify, or maintain. It is this active response to such life situations that I am calling "desire," and as has already been indicated, desire in this sense is intermediate between feeling and action. It is the complement of feeling in that it takes sides for or against the situation in which we find ourselves and in which we feel pain or pleasure, sadness or joy, as well as its likely sequels. In doing so, it anticipates action by looking to certain outcomes of change that are more attractive than others. Although there is a point at which desire becomes mere wish because there is no connection between these outcomes and anything one can do oneself, agency is, at least in a very broad sense, a presupposition of desire, as desire is of feeling. Like feeling, desire discloses the world in terms of polarities or contrasting possibilities, but it is much closer to action than feeling is because it is explicitly directed to something that can then, in one way or another, become the object of action. In desiring such an object – a state of affairs, really – we may feel pleasure or have some other feeling about it, and to that extent desire is certainly not divorced from feeling. What I am imagining on such occasions, however, is the actualization of a state of affairs that is merely possible; and it is as possible rather than as actualized that it is the object of desire.

This section will give a brief account of desire as occupying this intermediate position between feeling and agency; and it will show that desire, like feeling, is a disclosive modality of ek-sistence and thus presupposes presence. Such a conception of desire as a modality of ek-sistence encounters resistance similar to that described in the case of feeling. In the former case as in the latter, we tend to simplify the character of the relation to objects that desire constitutes by assimilating it to more familiar paradigms; but in so doing, we miss what is most distinctive, from an ontological point of view, about desire. Although it is not as plausible as it was in the case of feeling to take desire "neat" – that is, as a self-contained state of the self that is of philosophical interest mainly because of certain somewhat anomalous properties it possesses – this does not mean that no attempts have been made to assimilate desire to an ontology of self-contained things and properties. When so regarded, desire becomes a "state" in which a human being finds himself – more specifically, a "dispositional" state. This means that even though there may be, at any given moment, nothing that shows a person to be in this state, there are nevertheless definable circumstances that will call forth conduct of a kind that is what one would expect of a person with such a desire.

This concept of a dispositional property makes it possible to treat desire as a property that something either has or does not have at any given time in as unambiguous a sense as it has a color or a size. It is true that little is said about what difference having such a property makes to the present state of the human being who has it. It is as though the import of the fact that this desire is a desire *for* something were being treated as being entirely predictive in character. In that case, it would entail nothing specific or concrete about the present state of the human being in question beyond its being such that conduct can issue from it that will somehow engage the object of the desire it is supposed to be. This strongly suggests that in this account the connection between the one and the other – the present state and the object of desire – is being conceived in terms of an observational model like the one described in Chapter 1. Implicit in this picture is an observer who makes the connection between the present state of the person in question and the eventual conduct that is supposed to be implicit in that (dispositional) state. This is, of course, quite different from the understanding that the person who has the desire would have of it. It is hardly likely that that understanding would be cast in this peculiarly distanced, predictive mode, the effect of which is precisely to transfer the nexus of desire with the world from the human being who has the desire to the one who is postulated as observing the latter over time.

The introduction of this intermediary term has the effect of severing the connection of desire with the world, at least for as long as no questions are raised about what is implicit in the conception of such an observer. Because that observer is a human being, and one who is assumed to be neutral in respect of the desire qua desire, he can take over the disclosive function of desire in its first-personal form while making it appear that his relation to what is so disclosed is a purely predictive one. A desire, of course, is not a prediction; but in a dispositional account, it is as though a prediction had been substituted for a desire's transcendence of the immediate circumstances in the life of the person who has it toward the possibility that is what the latter desires. Predictions at least have the virtue of being familiar and unproblematic in the eyes of those to whom this dispositional account appeals; and so this substitution has the advantage of accommodating within a thing-ontology a nexus that would otherwise have to be assigned to desire itself as a modality of ek-sistence.

There is not much in the philosophical literature that offers a promising alternative to this picture. Beyond the fact that desire is – supposedly – the principal source within us of resistance to the directives of reason, philosophers have had little to say about it, especially about the character of the relation to the world it involves. One great exception to this lack of interest is Hegel, who speaks directly to this matter of the role of desire in our relation to the world. There is a famous (and famously difficult) passage in *The Phenomenology of Spirit* that comes in the course of a demonstration that our consciousness of external objects is really a form of self-consciousness and that these objects have no reality apart from this self-consciousness. In an earlier comment that anticipates this passage, Hegel remarked that animals appear to have understood this fact long before human beings did. The proof of this is, he says, that animals "do not stand idly in front of sensuous things as if they possessed intrinsic being"; instead, "they fall to without ceremony and eat them up."[6] There is a wonderfully surrealistic quality to

6. G. W. F. Hegel, *The Phenomenology of Spirit*, translated by A. V. Miller (New York: Oxford University Press, 1977), p. 65.

this passage; and one would like to think that it was not wholly unintentional on its author's part, although he certainly gave few signs of possessing an advanced sense of humor. However that may be, the analysis of desire that follows in the section on self-consciousness shows that he was also making a serious philosophical point.

That point is not so much that the objects around us, both animate and inanimate, have no "intrinsic being" as it is that in desire and in the "consumption" that follows it, objects are envisaged in a way that is quite different from that of theoretical knowledge. This is a fact that can be easily missed if we suppose that the object of desire simply *is* some free-standing object, like an automobile or a steak, and if we do not make explicit the modification of such an object that is always implicit in a desire for it. I do not necessarily have to consume that object in the literal manner of Hegel's example and thereby make it part of my flesh, although this certainly conveys graphically the new relation to me that the object takes on in desire. My desire for something like an automobile may only require that it be moved from a showroom to my garage, with a concurrent change in legal ownership; the automobile can remain otherwise – that is, physically – unchanged. The minimal character of these modifications, by comparison with those involved in being eaten, does not alter the fact that, in the one case as in the other, the "object" of my desire is quite different from the one I would have if I were simply to look at this automobile and feel pleasure at its beauty or if I were to study it in the way an engineer might. To desire it is to project a change for it as a result of which the object will come to stand in a new relation to *me*; and so, as Hegel points out, the desire for an object has a reflexive or self-referential character. In other words, what I desire is, among all the possible modifications of which any given object is susceptible, the one that brings it into a relation to a use that I can make of it or to an intention or purpose that is mine. As Hegel puts it, "consciousness, as self-consciousness, henceforth has a double object: one is the immediate object, that of sense-certainty and perception which however *for self-consciousness* has the character of a negative; and the second, viz. *itself*, which is the true essence and is present in the first instance only as opposed to the first object."[7]

In Hegel's account of it, this analysis of the reflexive character of desire is only the beginning of a dialectic of self-consciousness that leads to still more comprehensive modes of self-understanding. Although I am principally concerned with desire as a modality of ek-sistence, this further development has definite relevance to my theme. Specifically, Hegel's point about the reflexive character of desire amplifies the account of reflexivity given in the preceding chapter. It was argued there that what Hegel calls

---

7. *Phenomenology*, p. 105.

"self-consciousness" is a necessary condition of presence-to, that is, of something's being there for me. In the case of desire, as Hegel points out, there is not just this kind of reflexivity but also another, more active kind as well, in which I envisage the object of my desire in a pairing with myself and as becoming in some sense part of me. It follows from this that in desiring something, I am also desiring myself as I would be if I were to get what I now desire. For Hegel, desire is like sense experience in that it generates a dialectic of subject and object in which the finite self is always being drawn further, by the very desires and beliefs it thinks of as having stable and self-contained objects, into a more and more comprehensive form of selfhood – that is, into understanding itself in terms that are far more inclusive than those with which it begins. A crucial juncture in this dialectic of desire as self-consciousness is the encounter with other like beings who encounter me in the same way I do them and in the same context of desire. Here again, Hegel tries to show that the only consistent resolution of the conflict arising out of this plurality of sources of desire would have to be one that modifies our understanding of selfhood by making the element of intersubjectivity – of what he calls, not very happily, *Geist* – essential to it.

Although it is not the purpose of this section to explore further these aspects of desire, they have been noted here as a way of offsetting the established assumption that, like feelings as understood through an analogy with sense qualities, the desires of an individual human being simply are, opaquely, what they are in a way that makes them impervious to the wider natural and social context of the lives in which they are in fact embedded. Indeed, it would hardly be too much to say that in the course of the process Hegel describes, the separateness of self and world, and of the desires of one self from those of others, becomes more and more difficult to maintain. What is certain is that as our desires come to be addressed, more and more, to the fundamental determinants of our well-being rather than to some passing advantage or acquisition, they will have to be mediated by understandings with other human beings who have desires of their own and will have to satisfy conditions that are general in character. In this sense, it can truly be said that other human beings are the ultimate objects of desire, and that it is in our relations with them that the eventual definition of the self that is implicit in our desires will be achieved.

What has been said so far, especially about the reflexive character of desire, might well seem to invite a different conclusion, namely, that there must be something necessarily egocentric and even selfish about it. One effective way of meeting this objection would be to go through Bishop Butler's argument showing that the fact that what *I* desire must necessarily be *my* good in no way entails a restriction on what can count as my good. What *I* desire may very well have to do with the well-being of other people

– people who may even be unknown to me – and thus meet every meaningful criterion of disinterested benevolence while remaining as much *my* desire as it would if it involved self-enrichment at the expense of others. Similarly, when things go well or ill for us and this is registered in the modality of feeling, the "well" and the "ill" for me may be closely bound up with how things are for other people. In any case, there is no a priori restriction implied in the way either desire or feeling is being conceived here to some conception of the self that abstracts from such concern for others.

But if desire is not necessarily egocentric in some ethically objectionable sense, it does not follow that the fact that the good I desire is ipso facto my good is no more than a grammatical implication. It is not always easy to distinguish between the proprietary attitude that goes with first-personal acquisition and consumption – this is what we ordinarily call "selfish" – and the way in which even the most disinterested beneficence realizes the aspirations of its sponsor and thus has a place in his or her life. The broader and narrower forms of selfhood that correspond to these contrasting modes of self-realization are certainly very different from one another, but not so different that there is not an ever-present possibility – even a likelihood – that the interest I take in some undertaking in behalf of others may impart a proprietary quality to it. This need not make my desire to help others a selfish one, but it may well mean that it is not exactly selfless either. Even so, there is no need to be alarmed. After all, if the criteria for a selfless desire are so stringently defined as to permit no return of any kind to me – even one that does not affect the benefits this desire envisages for others – then there might be good reasons for doubting whether such a desire is possible at all. In that event, we could hardly blame ourselves for having desires that are disinterested although not immaculate in this impossibly demanding sense.

A still more important point is implicit in the way selfhood enters into the constitution of an object of desire. This is that although desire is neither necessarily selfish nor – possibly and ideally – selfless, it is properly characterized by what one might call "selfness" in a sense of that term that is intended to be neutral.[8] Once the distinction between an inside and an outside is called into question and a human being is understood as one that *has* a world, it becomes evident that what I am cannot be defined as what is contained within me or what I can manage in one way or another to incorporate into myself by "consuming" it. It is instead to be understood in terms of the kind of world I have and, more specifically, in terms of what I do that makes it one kind of world rather than another. I cannot act in any way without thereby making myself the corresponding kind of person,

---

8. This word translates Heidegger's expression *Selbstheit*, which serves the same purpose.

and so what desire projects is at once and indivisibly a state of the world and a modality of selfhood. What this means is that desire is not only reflexive in the sense that has been explained but a vehicle of transcendence as well and thus a disclosure of possibilities.

Before developing this last suggestion further, it is worthwhile to note a thesis some philosophers have proposed about desire. This thesis would make all the particular desires we have for particular outcomes throughout our lives so many expressions or specifications of a kind of master desire or *conatus vivendi* of which the object is, for each human being, some character that would accrue to his or her own life as a whole. This would be an implausible claim if it implied that the life of each one of us is perfectly integrated under some such master desire, for this is certainly not the case, even apart from the way our lives are affected by events over which we have no control. What cannot be denied, however, is that to the extent that we are able to shape our lives at all, we want our lives as wholes to have some overall character. We typically want them to run their normal course – that is, not to be cut short by accidents or disease – and we want them to be happy or fulfilled in some special way. We may also despair of any such possibility and give our lives over to chance impulse and self-destructive habits; but such lives, too, bear the mark of disappointed hopes that have to do with one's life as a whole. What all of this shows is that desire is not purely local and commensurate with its immediate object but is, instead, reflexive in a more complex way than at first appears. It is not just that in wanting something I also want myself, as Hegel points out, but that, to varying degrees that presumably reflect my control over what happens to me, I also want myself as a whole, and this means as having a life that as a whole has a certain character. And since the kind of life I can have depends on the kind of world I have, to desire my life as a whole turns out once again to involve a desire for a world that makes it possible.

In what has just been said about the reflexivity of desire, I have begun to touch on another important feature about desire as a modality of eksistence. Desire refers beyond the situation in which we find ourselves to some as yet unrealized possibility. Its object is thus not actual but possible, and as such it falls into the province of the imagination discussed in Chapter 3. It was shown there that it makes sense to speak of possibilities as being present in absence, but now it is necessary to show how this is accomplished in the context of everyday life. My contention is that desire as the imagining of possible goods orders the world of everyday life in terms of polarities. Suppose, for example, that I am in prison and, to make things worse, I have no prospect of being released. Being free is still something I dream of and long for, and it is still a possibility, if only in the sense that an earthquake or a revolution might bring it about. There are other possibilities as well, among them that I will end my days in this cell. Of these two possibilities that thus polarize each other, one is associated with hope and the other with dread and despair. There are people who, over time, are so broken by prison life that it becomes the only life they can imagine. But for those who have not been broken in this way and are still able to project another future for themselves, freedom is the possible future for which they live and, to the degree that it is feasible, prepare themselves. It is safe to say that such persons *desire* to be free; and to say this is to say that they live for – one might even say "toward" – this possible outcome of their present situation, even though there may be little or nothing they can do to make it more likely. This is, admittedly, a very dramatic example of desire, and there are many more humdrum objects of desire, like the next meal or the end of a work shift, that are so certain to come along in due course that we do not even think of them as possibilities and do not normally build up a great head of steam in anticipation of them. But one can easily imagine circumstances in which they might be indefinitely postponed; and then all the urgency of our underlying desire for them would be restored, and they would polarize our lives in much the same way that the possibility of freedom does that of the prisoner.

To desire something is thus to live for or toward it in the sense that it is the possibility – the possible state of the world – that interests us and that we would, if given the opportunity, do whatever we could to bring about. Is this enough to justify speaking of desire as the *disclosing* of that possibility and as the modality in which it becomes present in absence? Against this, it might be suggested that someone might entertain any or all of these possibilities, apart from any desire one way or another that that person might have. Possibilities would, on this view, be intrinsically neutral and accessible to all in much the same way as the domain of fact is supposed to be. Desire might still be defined in terms of the possibility it postulates, but it would not *as desire* make it present in absence as a possible future. Against this view, I want to argue that the connection between possibility and agency, and thus derivatively desire, is a much stronger one and that desire is always implicated, directly or indirectly, in the presence in absence to an individual human being of one possibility rather than another.

One peculiarity of the view I want to refute is its assumption that possibilities as such are somehow divorced from the life of the human being who envisages or entertains them. It is as though the element of the nonactual (and thus of transcendence) were being bracketed in a way that would prevent it from destabilizing, in an ontological sense, the life in which, in one way or another, it figures. It may be that this view becomes plausible once we are so familiar with the idea of alternative possible futures for ourselves that we can begin to speak about them as though they were like the succession of patterns unrolled before us in a wallpaper store, and with much the same alternation of indifference and interest on our part.

But the effect, once again, of such a view is to cast us in the role of spectators of our own lives, and in this case of our relation to the future. Such a view is plausible only as long as we tell some story or adopt some metaphor – the wallpaper example is one such – that assigns the responsibility for one possibility's being before us to someone or something else. Such stories have a way of breaking down if one presses them too hard, however, and at that point it invariably turns out that an interest – a desire – is at work and that it is our own. If one considers the unlimited variety of possibilities that might be present in absence to any given individual human being at a given time, it becomes evident that only a desire or an interest deriving from a desire can account for the fact that one thing is present in absence rather than something else. Indeed, in the absence of a desire that picks out one possibility rather than another, our whole active relation to the future, as well to possibilities as such, would become deeply problematic.[9]

The conclusion to which all this points is that if anything can be said to orient us toward the future – any future – and thus to possibility as such, it is surely desire. This is also to say that it is desire that discloses such possibilities, and the polarities among them, to us in a primordial way, whatever sophisticated disengagement from that original projection of our lives into such a future we may later learn to simulate. The idea of a future that is projected ahead of us as a set of possibilities, independently of any interest we have in it one way or another, and thus of anything that we can do to make it take one shape rather than another, is surely too obviously a product of an intellectualistic philosophy to be taken seriously. To divorce the one from the other can only result in a psychological conception of desire as some mix of representations and feelings and an equally unsatisfactory account of possibility in which its relation to those who have some commerce with it remains permanently obscure.

What has just been said may also serve to clarify the intention with which this account of feeling and desire has been put forward. Most signally, it is not being proposed as a theory of motivation or as a psychological substitute for a theory of justification. But the strong reaction against past attempts to use feeling and desire for such purposes should not, I think, be pushed to the point of wholly obscuring the role of feeling in our lives, as has sometimes happened of late. Philosophical hedonism, with its attempt to objectify and even quantify pleasure and pain, was undoubtedly a perversion of that role; but it would be equally misleading to fail to do justice to the fact that, in the absence of feeling, there would be no occasion for the elaborate exercises in discursive casuistry to which morality now often seems to be reduced.

9. In spite of the role I am assigning to desire in this matter, it would still not be the case that I summon things out of absence into presence in absence. The idea is rather that a desire brings with it a whole context of matters that have a bearing on its satisfaction or frustration.

IV

It was stated at the beginning of this chapter that agency is the context in which both feeling and desire have to be situated and understood; and it is time now to take up agency in its own right and to make good this claim. Although I shall not offer a proof that feeling and desire could not occur otherwise than as functions of an entity that is also able to act, it does seem clear that in the absence of any ability to change one's own situation, desire would not be distinguishable from hope; and although feeling might still involve contrasts between what is better and what is worse, these contrasts themselves would be disconnected from their normal significance for action in a way that is hard to imagine. But even though no strict proof of the dependence of feeling and desire on agency is to be offered, it must be evident that agency comes under the same heading of ek-sistence as do the other two. Not only is it attributable to the entity to which what is present is present, as is the case with feeling and desire; actions also make changes in the world that is so present as feeling and desire by themselves do not. In action, accordingly, we not only ek-sist in the sense of "standing out" in the world by virtue of its presence to us; we intervene in that world and thereby make it different from what it otherwise would have been. In this sense, action is the fullest expression of ek-sistence as the counterpart of presence.

The way the production of these changes in the world is to be conceived and described has been the object of a great deal of attention of late. The work philosophers have done on human action has emphatically under-scored its intentional character, and it is now widely accepted that action cannot be conceived simply as a sequence of physical movements together with the changes that these may produce. An action can, after all, end in failure, as a series of physical movements cannot, and yet we cannot say in what respects it failed unless we know what the agent was trying to do. For that, we must have the agent's "description" of the action in question so that we can gather from it what the goal of the action was and perhaps what kinds of reasons may have motivated it. Welcome as this acknowledg-ment of the intentional character of action is, it will not amount to much as long as the concept of human being that presides over these analyses has not been brought into the discussion. Specifically, the idea of the agent's description on which so much depends needs to be better under-stood than it typically is. All too often, it is interpreted in a literal manner that effectively equates it with a bit of verbal behavior – what the agent says or would say about what he is doing. When this happens, the intentionality of an action is readily assimilated to the status of a feature of such an utterance, and action itself comes to be viewed as the sequence of events in the world that is described in this way. Neither the utterance nor the action is thought to have any special ontological status that needs to be better understood, and a side-by-side coexistence of action and description is accordingly viewed as unproblematic. The unnoticed consequence of proceeding in this way is that the role of ek-sistence and of presence in human action is obscured to the point of invisibility. As a result, the fact that, apart from any verbal behavior that may or may not occur, an action orients itself within the situation in which it occurs has to remain implicit – something that everyone understands but that there is no way of formulating explicitly in the terms made available by the object ontology that governs the way both speech and action are conceived.

In this section, an attempt will be made to show that, as a fundamental modality of ek-sistence, action is coordinate with possibility as an element in presence. The preceding sections of this chapter, as well as the account of imagination in Chapter 4, have already shown the centrality of possibility in our commerce with the world. In the discussion of desire, for example, strong emphasis was placed on the fact that what one desires is something that is possible. We may, of course, never have an opportunity to act on that desire; and if and when we do, we may fail to make actual the possiblity in question. What needs to be added to this account is the fact that the possibilities implicit in presence are not confined to those that are projected by desire. If, as has been argued here, entities are present only as elements in states of affairs, and if the being of something is to be understood as what brings it into presence as the domain of truth, then, as was noted in Chapter 3, entities can present themselves as being what they are only in a pairing with what, alternatively, could have been or could be the case. When we seek to determine why things happen one way rather than another, it is obvious that there are many things or events that *could* bring about the change from something's being the case to its not being the case. What I want to suggest now is that, among these, human agency occupies a distinctive place, and that there corresponds to this "could" of presence a "can" of human agency that expresses a fundamentally important feature of ek-sistence.

The distinctive thing about this "can" of ek-sistence is not a claim that the agent to whom it applies will successfully bring about an intended result if he tries. Whether some action will be successfully completed depends on so many features of the situation that no assurance of success can be given in advance. The "can" that is relevant here is one that has to do with trying rather than succeeding; and what I want to argue is that when something is present as something that could be otherwise, then the entity to which it is so present can either leave it as it is or try to alter it. It is true that there are criteria for even trying to do something, and that one can seriously be said to be trying to bring about a change of whatever kind only if there is at least some reason, however slight, to think that this *can* be done – that is, brought successfully to completion – with the means available. Even so, the point still stands that within these limits, action presupposes that we can either try to do something or not try at all. When we act, we are doing one thing rather than another – going to New York rather than not going there, say – and the latter is just as possible as the former in the sense of being something we can try to do or to bring about. To put this in the idiom I have been using, to ek-sist is to have a world in which things could in principle be otherwise than they are, and it is also to have a dual ability to intervene – whether effectively or not – either to keep things as they are or to change them. If feeling discloses that something matters, and if desire discloses that something is preferable to the way things are now, then what action discloses is that I *can* either intervene to bring something about or not do so.

When we reflect on such facts as these, the claim that one can do this rather than that or that rather than this may give us pause, and we may wonder how this can be compatible with various general beliefs we have about the way the world works. There are even those who conclude that there is incompatibility here, and that our beliefs about being able to do either this or that have to be given up. Whether they *can* be given up in any real sense is another question that would have to be asked if this line of thought were taken farther. What seems certain is that if they *can* be given up, and if we *were* to give them up, drastic changes would be entailed in our understanding of what it is to act. For one thing, possibility would then figure in the account we give of human action in these new circumstances only as the name for an illusion that our ignorance makes unavoidable. Some think this would make no real difference in the lives of those who have to accept the illusory character of much that it previously never occurred to them to question. Still, it is hard to imagine human beings going through all the rigmarole of deliberation and decision making that leads up to action while letting it be understood, perhaps in a dramatic aside, that they understand all this to be simply a causal precondition for the one thing they can and will do. The assurance that this just happens to be the form that causality takes in human life is not likely to help them play their parts with anything like normal conviction in what they would now, with this new scientific understanding, have to perceive as a kind of play, and one that they are playing a part in but are not writing. The script would already have been written; and so, even when they first read it through without knowing how everything comes out – that is, what they will actually do and what will happen to them in the role they are to play – they will know that in the script all these things are already determinately fixed. Once again, this would be, in the most emphatic sense imaginable, a spectator's view of the life that is unrolling before his eyes.

Only in the last chapter of this book will it be possible to explain what really goes wrong when we think we have to adopt this extraordinarily strange perspective on our own lives. It is clear, though, that in doing so we are responding to a sense that we must willy-nilly accommodate everything in our lives – everything that we *are* – to the requirements of a conception of scientific knowledge from which the notion of alternative possibilities has been rigorously excluded. In fact, however, the compulsion we are under is far more philosophical than scientific, and the philosophy driving it is that of actualism – the thesis that something is real only if it can be known in a manner that at no point requires one to accept that there are possibilities that are not actual. But since action in any form that has not been antecedently distanced in the paradoxical fashion just described is essentially bound up with possibilities, the form in which it can be acknowledged under such auspices as these is at best a severely mutilated one that has to be supplemented, tacitly and illegally, by a less constrained version. In what follows, I want to show what action involves when it is not subjected to these constraints; in this way, its relation to feeling and desire will also be made clear. Both feeling and desire presuppose possibilities that stand in contrast to some actual situation; and it is in action, our ability to do something or not do it, that possibilities have a place in our world and in our lives.

John Austin showed that if a human being is able to act in the full usual sense of that word, then the notion of "can" that is used to express this fact has to be taken in a categorical sense and not just a conditional one.[10] If "cans" were constitutionally "iffy," as Austin puts it, their use would always presuppose some condition under which the person to whom the "can" applies would perform the action in question. But if being able to do something is inherently counterfactual, as it must be on this view, then to say that I can do something would be to predict that in certain circumstances I would do it. As Austin points out, the trouble with this is that being able to do something is typically predicated only on some such condition as "if I like," which does not yield any genuine counterfactual. But in that case, to say "I can" is not in fact to predict anything; it is to say that my present state is such that in it either a given action or its opposite – not doing it – is possible.

It is perhaps not so well understood that if there is even one being of whom this is true, then the world must be such as to admit of such a fact. That is, there will be something in it – the object of the action x that I can either perform or not perform – that admits of being x-ed or not x-ed. It is this modal character of any world in which there is even one being who

10. J. L. Austin, "Ifs and Cans," in *Philosophical Papers*, edited by J. Urmson and G. Warnock (London: Oxford University Press, 1970), pp. 153–80.

can either do or not do something that figures so prominently in Heidegger's early writings. In the account he gives there, things are present to us as *pragmata* – that is, as things in use or manipulanda, and not simply as *res*. A hammer is something to hammer with, something that I can grasp and wield in a certain way so as to drive in nails. This is the way I perceive a hammer and all sorts of other tools, and this is the way I understand them long before I learn to objectify them as things with certain properties, such as size and shape. In this sense, the hammer and the hand go together in the sense that the former *is* what the latter can *do* with it. Clearly, what applies to tools applies to all artifacts, whether they be houses or watches or atom smashers, but artifacts are by no means the only manipulanda in our world. A hill is something to be climbed, a tide is something to catch, and a stream can be made to turn a mill wheel. Indeed, Santayana's observation that human technology is "nature caught in its own traces" seems to apply generally to the fixtures of the human world in their relation to the natural processes they exploit.

What these examples show is that at a fundamental level, the things we encounter in the world have a gerundive character, and that it is as something to be used or taken advantage of in some way or other that they are present to us. They could not be what they are, in other words, unless they were part of the world of an active being, of one who *can* do the kinds of things that they lend themselves to, whether by design or not. Heidegger argues that even when we come up against things that are just there, and are apparently unincorporable into any functional network of the kind to which hammers, say, belong, it is precisely as *non*functional entities that they are understood, and this means privatively and by derivation from what does have a use. In our usual way of conceiving these matters, however, we are accustomed to making all these distinctions in psychological terms that postulate a completely nonfunctional *res* in every case, and then making the distinction between functional and nonfunctional by reference to thoughts and perceptions evoked in us in the one case and not in the other. By contrast, the Heideggerian treatment of these matters asks what kind of a world (or, as we might now say, what kind of a "space") these things are in, and answers that it is an actional space of which possibilities of use constitute essential coordinates. What this means is that every object we encounter is understood not as the blank presence of a self-contained something that simply wears its identity on its face but, rather, as embedded in a network of possibilities. Generally, the way things in the world are present to an active being involves a context of possibility. The ability to orient ourselves within that network is essential to our survival, and it turns on our grasp of the possibilities implicit in our situation – possibilities that often remain just that because we have learned how to detour around them.

This modal character of the entities in the world of an active being is at the heart of the relationship of action and presence. Comprehensively, things in the world have a character that is expressed when we say that they could be moved or changed or preserved in one way or another. When we so describe them, the state in which these things presently are is contrasted (and thus paired) with another that would be the result of the action in question. Their being what they are at this moment is thus conditional on that action's not having been undertaken or on its not having succeeded, and the same kind of condition obtains prospectively in the case of the thing's remaining as it now is. It thus appears that in the first instance the modal character that attaches to a thing's being as it is is a function of my – someone's – not doing (or having done) anything to change it. Of course, few things are effectively controlled by *my* agency; but the point here is that, however narrow its scope, the conditionality of a thing's being as it is – a conditionality that is attributable to that agency – is highly distinctive.

The argument in this section is intended to show that the difference between agency and the other conditions for a thing's changing or re- maining as it is is a radical one, and that it cannot be explained away by reference to the limitations inherent in the first-personal point of view of the agent. Unquestionably, there are many other conditions for a thing's being or remaining in its present state. Among these are the various natural events that might change that state; but the actions of persons other than ourselves – actions in which we do not participate – could have the same effect. This last is an especially complex situation inasmuch as it involves agency but not our own, and discussion of it will be deferred for the mo- ment. The case that involves natural events is difficult enough, but if we can work out the differences between first-personal agency and natural events as conditions for a thing's changing or not changing, that may sim- plify the task of dealing with the agency of others.

We often speak in a way that implies that modality is a feature of natural events independent of their relation to us as active beings. We say, for example, that a certain house *could* be washed away if the river overflows in the spring. In saying this, we may imagine ourselves watching the spread- ing waters bring this about; and the less we can do about it, the purer the spectator relation in which we stand to this possible event. Typically, we do not know whether it will take place or not, and so we say that it *could* have a certain consequence rather than that it *will*. If we know enough about whatever determines whether the river will overflow and whether, if it does, the house will hold or not, we say simply that these events will happen – unless, of course, there is some way in which, on the strength of this knowl- edge, we could intervene and thereby affect the outcome we otherwise merely foresee. But if, for example, a large comet were headed toward the Earth and we wanted to change its course so as to avoid a collision, the present state of our technology would probably not permit us to do so. If in such circumstances we therefore go on saying "would" instead of "will," this can only mean that we are less than certain about what is going to occur. Possibility in this sense would be epistemic in character and would reflect our uncertainty and not any element of modality in the situation itself. There can also be an element of indecision, as well as of uncertainty, in such cases, for example, if there is something I could do about some prospective event of an untoward character but I have not made up my mind to do it. In these circumstances, I might say something like "I may have the river diverted from my land." This use of "may" expresses not ignorance but indecision. "I may" in this use also implies "I can," as it would not if this were a case of epistemic uncertainty. In the latter kind of case, the use of "may" means only that the event in question is not precluded by anything we know about – in this case – the house and the river. The point here is that if I *can* do this, then I can also *not* do it or have it done; and there is no analogue to this kind of duality in the case of natural causes.

It appears that there is only a superficial similarity between the way we speak about our own actions and what we say when we are unsure or ignorant about what some natural event will bring about or even whether it will occur at all. The possibility that is just a cover for our ignorance is different from the possibility that derives from my being able to do something or not do it. G. H. von Wright has suggested that we are able to understand the kind of possibility that ostensibly applies to natural events and finds expression in counterfactual statements of various kinds only because we ourselves are able to alter the state of the world in such a way as to make the protases of these conditionals true in circumstances in which there is every reason to think that they would otherwise not have been.[11] If this is the case, then the appearance of possibility in the natural domain created by the truth of such counterfactual statements as "If a large comet were to strike New York City, many people would be killed" depends on our ability to interfere in the course of events in ways that can then serve as the template for imagining such a possibility.

Our imagining does not, of course, make a counterfactual true, and there are plenty of false contrafactuals. But if the *actual* course of the world is the only source we have for determining which counterfactual statements are true and which false, then the course of the world must be understood as including the experimental variations that we introduce into it. The question that then arises is why the events that occur in connection with these "interventions" should not count as simply "more actuality" – that

11. G. H. von Wright, *Explanation and Understanding* (Ithaca, N.Y.: Cornell University Press, 1971), Chapter 2.

is, as supplying information about how the entities in question behave in actual fact – rather than how they *would* behave if some merely possible event were to occur. On such an actualistic interpretation, moreover, the idea that our actions "intervene" in the course of nature would have to be abandoned, and these actions would count simply as natural events of a special kind on a dead level with the events they prevent and those they bring about. In that case, we, as those who interest ourselves in questions of this kind, would have to learn to think of such actions, including our own, in a new and unfamiliar way. We would have to view them as if they were natural events for which we, as the beings who so regard them, bear no responsibility and that pass before us simply as so many elements in the movement of the one actual and nothing-but-actual world.

It has to be understood that this is not just a question of our being able to carry out an esoteric psychological stunt – that of identifying ourselves with our actions, on the one hand and, on the other, detaching ourselves from them so that we can in some sense watch ourselves acting. That would suggest that what we have to do is to perform an unusual mental feat – that of being alternately conscious of ourselves as agents (and thus as the locus of possibility and modality) and then oblivious to this fact about ourselves so that our theoretical view of things will not be disturbed by it. This seems difficult enough, especially since it is unclear how we could be sure that we had succeeded in staying on one side or the other of this line at any given time. But it is not some implausible stunt of this kind that is in question here. Even if we were to suppose that something like this could be done, the real issue would remain. That issue concerns the character of the world in which we live, and it cannot be dealt with by simply acting as though that world did not possess certain features that we otherwise attribute to it. Thus, if it is indeed the case that I can either do something or not do it, then it must follow that the world I am in is a world of possibilities and not just of actualities. I can, if I like, try to withhold attention from them, but any such attempt presupposes what I am trying to avoid acknowledging – the fact, namely, that there are such possibilities.

What would be required, if possibilities are to be denied the status that action appears to entail for them, would be something quite different from the on-again, off-again alternation of mental states just described. It would be something like a demonstration that the one view subsumes the other and that human actions can be conceived satisfactorily in terms deriving from the perspective of the actualism set forth previously. It is sometimes suggested that, for these purposes, it is better not to think in terms of the first-personal case and to consider instead the actions of other people. Superficially, at least, the case of other human beings and their agency might seem to be intermediate between my own first-personal case and that of natural entities. I can hardly deny that they act in the full sense of that expression, but at the same time, I am able to observe the actions of other people. Accordingly, it might be thought that here, at least, something like an equivalence of actions and natural events is realized; and this, in turn, suggests that since others can watch me act in just the way that I do them, it is this "third-person" point of view on the actions of both the other and the self that may enable us to avoid the paradoxes that ensue when a privileged status is accorded to the latter in these matters.

In Chapter 1, attention was drawn to certain peculiarities of this notion of a third-person point of view; and the assertions made there must put in doubt the whole idea that other human beings can be conceived in some way that is radically different from the way each of us understands himself and that does not commit us to possibility or any of the other concepts that make up the notion of ek-sistence. But in other respects as well, the whole objectifying approach to other human beings and their actions is manifestly defective. Because we can trace the contours of their physical being in perception, the embeddedness of other human beings in the natural world seems to be guaranteed in a way that leaves no more place for anything as insubstantial as possibility in any account of what we so observe than it does in an account of a natural event. But even at this level of observation, there is a great deal in the actions of other human beings that eludes this encapsulation. The speech of such persons is a conspicuous example of something that cannot be treated in such a way. It has already been shown that speech presupposes presence, and there is no way in which words can be equated with physical objects or events. And once what someone says becomes an element in the picture we form of him, his actions will inevitably be drawn into the kind of understanding that bases itself, in one way or another, on what is said. In this way, every feature of ek-sistence can be shown to be implicit in what we take in when we listen to someone speak. All of this effectively blocks the attempt to treat other human beings in a way that excludes possibility from the context of their actions; and with the failure of that attempt, the whole effort to build a concept of action on such a contrast with the first-personal cast must also be given up.

It might be objected that the connection made here between action and possibility as a constitutive feature of our actual world is circular because it makes perfectly good sense to say that action itself is possible. It is true that one can meaningfully say "I can act"; but it is very doubtful that "can" functions in such a sentence in the way it does in "I can go to New York." The difference is that in the latter case I can also not go to New York, but I cannot *not* act – at least, not if "act" is to be understood as doing anything that would count as an action. The reason is that not going to New York would count as an action in any situation in which going there had been considered. Being able to act is thus not a special psychological capacity that we might or might not have independently of anything that has to do with the ontological constitution of the world. Possibilities and the active character of human being are thus strictly coordinate facts that cannot be disjoined in the way a psychological interpretation of the latter would entail. To this it might be added that it is in terms of this unavoidable character of action that human freedom is best conceived. As long as there is something that can either be done or not done in the world that a human being inhabits, that individual will not be incorporable into a closed deterministic system. Possibility is what stands in the way of all the attempts that have been made to achieve that end; and it would not be hard to show that the authors of such systems always stand outside them in ways that they are powerless to alter.

In what has been said so far about human action, it has been assumed that the agent is always a human being and not some part thereof. Consistently with this view, a case has also been made for the thesis that there are no mental acts, or at least no acts that are acts of the mind but not of the body. Even if this thesis is accepted, however, we are left with a number of words that, at least grammatically, denote actions of which we are the subjects, but for which we do not have any readily available rubric of classification once the idea of intramental goings-on has been ruled out. Notable among these words are such epistemic terms as "think" and "believe" and "know" – indeed, almost all the words that were subsumed under "think" by Descartes in his famous list together with a number of more modern ones like "experience." Descartes was so impressed by the purely mental character of these acts that he argued that one would be able to think and doubt even if one did not have a body or a personal history at all. But if this is not the case, then there is a pressing need to show how the items on Descartes's list can be brought under the holistic conception of action that has just been outlined.

Fortunately, such an interpretation of these acts is possible, and it is based on two facts about human beings. One of these is our susceptibility to error, and the other is the fact that there are not only many of us but that in this manyness we are able to communicate with one another and to engage in what might be called "epistemic cooperation." A good deal has already been said about our liability to error as part of an attempt to show that the paradigm of error need not be allowed to control the terms in which we think about knowledge and the mind, as it has during much of the modern period. It has been stressed that it is we – the same people who make these errors – who are able to detect and correct them. What is more, we typically do so in concert with our fellow human beings, with whom we negotiate the best account we can of whatever we are trying to get right. There is, accordingly, a clear need for a language in which such cooperation can be carried on. What is more, the language of presence does not readily lend itself to that purpose because it offers only the two alternatives of something's being present or not.

I want to suggest that although the terminology of mental acts is an unhappy one, at least in the way it has been used by philosophers, the words traditionally construed as denoting mental acts serve an important purpose. In everyday life, they function as the pragmatic communicative idiom needed if epistemic cooperation is to be possible. In this use of the words I have in mind, they express a kind of second-order evaluation of some prima facie characterization of what is present to the speaker, as well as a rough assessment of the possibilities of error that past experience with comparable situations suggests there may be in the current one. For example, to use "know" in such a context is to stand by the adequacy of what has been said about what is there; and the use of other verbs like "believe" and "think" implicitly accepts the possibility of revisions in that characterization and appeals to other observers – that is, to other "loci of presence" – for a fuller account of the matter at issue. The underlying idea here, which once again owes a great deal to the work of John Austin, is that, as instruments of epistemic cooperation, mental-act words indicate the degree of reliance that the person addressed is to place on the information being imparted.[12] Clearly, however, these words can serve this purpose only in overt speech acts. As such, they are actions of the human being whose utterance they are and of that human being as a whole, rather than of the mind as only one part of that human being.

12. J. L. Austin, "Other Minds," in *Philosophical Papers*, pp. 42–84.

6

BODIES

I

In books dealing with themes in the philosophy of mind, the concept of the body is normally assumed to be on hand at the outset, and so, in one way or another, it implicitly sets the context in which a concept of mind is to be introduced. Since the aim of this book is to present a unitary concept of human being, however, it would have been self-defeating to begin with an unexamined concept of the body and then try to determine how many other features of human being can be associated with it. If there is to be a unitary concept of human being at all, then "the body" cannot be the free-standing concept it is usually taken to be. Instead, it must be an element within the more complex concept of a human being as an ek-sistent. The latter is the concept that I have been gradually assembling; and the point has now been reached at which the fact that human beings are or have bodies must be given explicit acknowledgment in that concept.

Although this hardly needs justification, it is worth noting at least one specific consideration that makes it necessary. This is the fact that the account of action in the preceding chapter would be radically incomplete unless the body is brought into the story. To say that something acts is to say that it makes a change in the world, and that is possible only for an entity that is itself in that world and in it in a way that permits acting on it. We know of no way in which that can be done in a world of material things like ours unless the entity in question is or, as we also say, has a body. But if that is so, then the entity that acts must be conceived in a way that makes its being or having a body intelligible.

That is not an easy task. The difficulty is that because human bodies are material and matter is, famously, "opaque," bodies have been thought to be the very antithesis of presence and to be properly conceived only as part of the object domain, that is, as what is present rather than as that to which something in that domain – a tree, say, or a planet – could be present. Philosophers have even gone so far as to declare our bodies to be just so many material objects that are different from other such objects mainly because they regularly keep bobbing up in more or less the same parts of our perceptual fields. As has just been noted, it has also been recognized that they stand in a special relation to the active side of our natures, and this has been interpreted to mean that our bodies are the "instruments" that enable us to use still other objects in the course of our actions. But even as an instrument or tool, a body would remain an object – a *Gegenstand*, something that stands over against me – and as such, it has seemed radically unincorporable into any idea that we might form of ourselves as beings that perceive and think.

It is impossible to persevere in this way of conceiving the body in the face of the conclusions reached in the preceding chapters. The reason is simply that the view of the body as a physical object presupposes the conception of a mind that serves as a repository for every feature of human being that cannot be treated as a property of such an object; and it is just such a conception of the mind that has been shown to be in deep trouble. But if that is the case and the mind can no longer serve as the *alibi* – the elsewhere – in which everything that has had to be eliminated from our concept of the body can be accommodated, then we must try to conceive the body again in a new and more inclusive way. In place of the dualities that have marked our thinking about our bodies, what is plainly needed is a conception of a single entity that is at once a self and a body. Admittedly, this is not easy to come by, and our established conceptual habits do not make it any easier. For example, it has been noted that we tend to say that we *have* bodies. Unfortunately, this can make it sound as though these bodies of ours were like other things that we are said to have and that can, in principle at least, be either associated with or detached from some nuclear self that each of us would be said to be rather than to have. But if I try to overcome this duality by saying that I simply *am* my body, this is likely to be confused with an endorsement of the thesis that the sciences of the body must have the last word about what I am as a human being.

It hardly needs saying that no such endorsement is intended here. What I do want to show in this chapter and the next is that the idea that I am my body is capable of being construed in ways that are very different from (and far more plausible than) the account that such naturalistic theories propose. In order to do this, however, it is first necessary to explore the preconceptions about the body that appear to place such formidable ob-

stacles in the way of any account that associates it with presence otherwise
than as an object that is present to something else. What I will try to show
is that these conceptions of the body are in one way or another dualistic
and remain so even after dualism itself has been rejected. I shall then show
that when these preconceptions are set aside, a much richer concept of the
body and of its unity comes into view. Finally, a way of integrating the
concept of the body with that of ek-sistence, and thus of presence, will be
proposed. The general thesis of physicalism itself about the body and its
identity with the mind will be taken up in the next chapter.

There is a residual difficulty in the approach I am adopting; and although in one respect it is merely terminological, it can become quite
serious and should therefore be noted before going any farther. This difficulty consists in the fact that even when one conceives the human body
– the body that is always someone's body – in a way that embeds it in the
concept of a human being, a strong pull is exerted on this embedded concept of the body by its nonembedded cousin – body in the sense of "physical object." But when this concept of body reasserts itself at the expense
of the embedded one, the effect is to turn the claim that I am my body into
something very like its opposite – that is, into the physicalistic identity thesis
that I reject. Unfortunately, there seems to be no way, linguistic or otherwise, of forestalling this interference with what I am trying to do in this
chapter. That can be described as an attempt to show how a human body
differs from a physical object without reintroducing any of the dualistic
apparatus that has dominated our thought about the body for so long. In
this way, I hope to develop the concept of the human body to the point at
which what "it" does is more appropriately described as what "I" do and,
in so doing, to give a defensible import to the thesis that *my* body is what *I*
am. Until that point is reached, however, I will be talking about "the body";
and this will tend to make it sound as though "it" were some sort of object,
and thus create confusion about what I am trying to do. Since I have not
found a way of detouring around this source of confusion, I can only hope
that by pointing it out here, at the beginning of this chapter, I can help
the reader to understand my true intentions.

II

The idea that the human body is an object among objects developed pari
passu with a dualistic conception of the mind well before a thoroughgoing
physicalistic ontology was founded upon it. Once the mind was conceived
as knowing itself and affirming its own existence independently of any
knowledge it might eventually achieve of the existence of a physical world,
the distinction between what is in the mind and what is in the natural world
underwent a fundamental change. Every predicate except those in which

the physical sciences deal was withdrawn from natural objects and assigned to the mind; and in this way, the abstractive procedures of the new mathematical science of nature were justified by corresponding ontological theses. Most significantly, this new concept of matter was applied to the human body, just as it was to inanimate objects; and as a result, the status of our bodies came to be equated with that of all the other objects that make up the natural world. The only exception to this assimilation of the human body to its new status took the form of an acknowledgment that each such body has a special connection with a particular mind, by virtue of which it produces sensations in that mind and can itself respond to the volitional acts of the latter by moving in the appropriate ways. Although this postulated interaction gave rise to serious philosophical anomalies, it is important to see that the body was originally constituted as an object in this dualistic context.[1]

With time, the specifically dualistic character of this scheme became more and more unacceptable; but the gradual erosion of the conception of a mind that acts on the body from without did not seem to render problematic the status of its erstwhile partner – the dualistically conceived human body. Instead, it was the anomalous status of mind as an intruder in the natural world that was held to be at fault, and the purely physical or "mechanical" character of what took place in the human body was typically not called into question. One reason for this may have been the great popularity in the modern period of a metaphor that seemed to take care of whatever difficulties there might be in conceiving the body as a physical object. This was the idea of the body as a machine. One reason for the attractiveness of this metaphor is the fact that it softened the otherwise stark contrast between material objects as such and our familiar, everyday understanding of our bodies without abandoning the assimilation of the latter to the former. After all, machines are undeniably material objects and operate in accordance with the purely physical principles that inform their manufacture, but they also have a *function,* as most material objects do not, and can therefore be fitted into the purposive economy of the human beings who design and use them. The underlying thought is thus that human bodies differ from other material objects only in the way machines do; and it was evidently supposed that this difference did not alter the ontological status of our bodies. There was, of course, the fact that, when the human body is described as a machine, we cannot claim to have designed it or produced it ourselves; and so, under the older dualistic dispensation, a nonhuman artificer – God – had to be postulated. More recently, the place of God has been taken by the evolutionary process, and the idea of the body as having been designed and made by

1. It is worth pointing out that the notion of the body as an object takes on its problematic character, at least in part, as a result of the philosophical connotations of the word "object" itself. On this point see footnote 5 in Chapter 1.

anyone at all has been largely abandoned. Even so, it is still common to conceive the body as a machine – more specifically, to conceive a part of the body, the central nervous system, as a computing machine. Indeed, in the contemporary philosophy of mind, the so-called functional states of this body/machine are sometimes proposed as plausible equivalents of what were once called the "mental" states of the human beings whose bodies these are.

It is this conception of a human being as the user of his body – the body that is conceived as a machine – that needs attention. It may be that we have become so accustomed to this way of speaking of the body that we hardly notice the strained character of the metaphor we are using and the multiple incongruities it entails. It is not difficult, however, to show that our bodies are not really comparable to the tools and instruments we use. For one thing, after we have used an instrument, we lay it aside until the next occasion on which it is needed, but this is not true of our bodies. They cannot be laid aside by their "users" unless we are prepared to think of ourselves as souls that "put on" their bodies at conception and take them off when we die. In the same vein, although an instrument like a cane serves as an extension of my limbs when it is in use, it can on other occasions be observed in the way any other object can. If my body were an instrument and thus an object, it ought to be possible to observe it, too, in the way I do a cane or a hammer or any other instrument outside their contexts of use; and yet, this is possible only within quite definite limits. If I am observing an object, whether it be a house or a mountain, it is normal to move around it so as to be able to view it from all sides. Clearly, however, I cannot walk around my own body, and I cannot see certain parts of it at all without resort to mirrors or photographs. This fact is usually dismissed as a mere consequence of the contingent fact that my eyes are placed in my head in the way they are; and, of course, it is a fact that I can walk around other human beings and thus observe them from all sides. Still, simply to transfer to my own body the same status of being an object that accrues to others as they figure in *my* perceptual field seems to miss the relevant point here, which has to do with my relationship with myself and not my relationship with other people. Other people, it may also be noted, are like me in this respect since their observation of their own bodies is limited in the same way mine is. In each case, moreover, the fact that our bodies are involved, by virtue of the walking around they do as well as in other ways, in what we ordinarily have in mind in speaking of observation might equally well suggest that the reason each of us can observe his own body only to a limited degree is that my body is not as separate from me, as an observer, as one would expect it to be when it is described as an instrument and an object.

This conclusion is strongly supported by the fact that, for many purposes, I do not *need* to observe my body in anything like the way I do objects

around me. Whether I am sitting or standing is not a matter I have to
determine by looking, and the same is true of other matters, such as
whether my eyes, which I cannot see, are open or closed. There are, of
course, many other questions about the state of my body that can be settled
only by observation – often by other people – and among these are such
matters as whether I have a stomach ulcer. But especially in matters that
have a bearing on what I am doing or am about to do, I do not have to
proceed in the way I would if I were gathering information about something
other than myself. For these purposes, there is no gap between my body
and "myself," that is, between my body and whatever it is supposed to be
that acts and, when necessary, observes. But if that is the case, then the
whole picture of the body as one object among many seems misconceived.
Instead of thinking of the incompleteness of our perception of our own
bodies as a mere empirical contingency, perhaps it would be better to think
of their observability in this way. Thus, although I can hold my hands before
my face and observe them, just as I could someone else's hands or, for that
matter, the hands of a clock, this is not the way I "know" where my hands
are, and I can grasp things with my hands without first locating my hands
by observation.

It is sometimes suggested that the only difference between the observation of one's own body and the observation of physical objects is one of
point of view. It is simply a difference in the placement of the observer in
relation to the object of observation. This sounds reasonable, but when one
tries to specify further what the point of view is from which I observe my
own body, things become a good deal less straightfoward. Generally, one's
"point of view" is where one stands while observing something, but in this
instance, the difference in question cannot be accounted for in these terms.
After all, where one stands is where one's body is; and I, as the observer,
cannot be anywhere except where my body is – the same body that I am
supposed to be observing. What, then, is the difference supposed to be
between where I am when I observe other objects and where I am when I
observe my own body? One might try to answer this question by suggesting
that in the one case – that of observing something other than myself – the
point of view is external and in the other – observing myself – it is internal.
This will not get us far, however, unless the problematic character of this
contrast can be alleviated by more precise indications of just what kind of
"inside" is being postulated here and what the "inner" position or locus
is from which we supposedly carry out these observations of our own bodies.

The conclusions reached in Chapter 1 about the inner–outer contrast
do not suggest that any informative answer to these questions will be readily
forthcoming. The plain fact is that to the extent that we can be said to
observe our own bodies at all, the position from which we do so appears to
be the same one from which we observe everything, and that is the place

where our bodies are. It is true that the parts of our bodies that we can observe are closer to us than most other objects; but it seems doubtful that this amounts to a significant difference in point of view. Indeed, this talk of a special point of view on our bodies appears to be a confused acknowledgment of the fact that "my body" is not something I come upon in my world, as it would be if it were an object. Instead, it is a condition of my coming upon anything at all.

The difficulty of applying the concept of observation to one's own body is by no means the only obstacle to objectification of the body. If the body were a self-contained physical system in the manner described and everything having to do with feeling or thought or choice were in the mind, it would not only be possible to observe it in the same way we do other objects; there would also have to be some way of setting it in motion from without. In the original dualistic picture, certain mental events like decisions were supposed to have this effect on the body. They corresponded to flipping the switch that starts a machine. Unfortunately, even if one accepts this dualistic picture of the body in its relation to the mind, at least two facts are hard to reconcile with this version of the way the body is activated. One of these is that, in the case of many of the voluntary actions that the body performs, we have no idea of the instructions that would have to be given by the mind to the body. These are things that, as has already been pointed out, we know how to do without being able to explain how we do them. They are skills for which we have no mental formula, and they are instead laid down in our hands and eyes and in our bodies generally. If it is indeed *we* who have this knowledge, then it clearly follows that we cannot be distinct from our bodies in the way we are from the tools we use.

The other fact that speaks against the separateness of the body as an object we have to steer is that no such initiating mental events are discoverable. The events that we usually call decisions are typically prospective in character – "I will do so-and-so when the time comes" – and these produce no effect on the body at all. The only way one can actually bring about such an "effect" is by moving one's arm or hand or tongue in the appropriate way; and this movement is basic in the sense that there is nothing else we do in order to bring it about. I may say that my arm moved because I had commanded it to do so just before it in fact moved, but this is an assertion without any discoverable empirical content. No one can isolate that decision from the bodily event, and it seems clear that describing the latter as the "effect" of another (mental) event is simply an inference from a priori assumptions incorporated into the dualistic language we use in talking about such matters. Once again, it turns out that there is no distance of the kind postulated between the movements of my body and what I am doing; and this is hardly what the conception of the body as an object would have led one to expect.

There are other ways of showing that what we think of as the action of the mind on the body is not analyzable in the terms afforded by the "body as object" thesis. If I am amused and laugh heartily or am sad and weep, it is not as though some inner feeling had *caused* my eyes to shed tears or my larynx to emit a peal of laughter. I may in fact do my best to keep from laughing or crying but fail in the attempt. But how is such a failure itself to be understood? If the body were an object that is distinct from me, then it would presumably do things that express my grief only if weeping and laughing were in its repertory of competences as a machine and if I directed it to do one or the other. If I laugh or weep, then on this view I must have mentally pushed the appropriate buttons and caused my body to behave in these ways. But when I do not want to show my feelings by either laughing or weeping, I cannot have performed the mental act that set off these performances. Or if I did, it must have been inadvertently; and yet this presents difficulties since I typically have no awareness of having performed any mental act, much less the wrong one, whatever that might mean. The only natural way of dealing with these matters is to abandon the notion of my body's being an object that I somehow have to steer through its routines, as though it were an automobile I am driving, and simply acknowledge that my laughter and my weeping express my feelings because my body is not something distinct from me.[2]

But what about the "anonymous" functioning of the body at the level of the cell and of organs like the liver or the brain? Surely, an objector might insist, there is every reason to retain the metaphor of the machine in describing what goes on in our bodies without any awareness on our part of the complexity of these biochemical processes or even of the fact that they are occurring at all. This opens up the whole question of the relations between the macrobody – the body of action and perception – and the microbody – the subterranean life of biological systems and processes of which we are only now beginning to form some halfway accurate idea. Although I reserve most of my discussion of this for the next section, it is worth pointing out, first, that the line that separates one from the other – the macrobody from the microbody – is anything but well defined, and it is possible for the two to interact in surprising ways, as the examples of biofeedback and yoga demonstrate. At an even more fundamental level, the transfer of functions from one part of the brain to another in cases of severe trauma is certainly not something that conforms in any readily per-

---

2. A study in which the role of the body in laughter and weeping is insightfully described is Helmut Plessner, *Laughing and Crying,* translated by James Churchill and Marjorie Grene (Evanston, Ill.: Northwestern University Press, 1970). The chapter in Merleau-Ponty's *Phenomenology of Perception,* translated by Colin Smith (London: Routledge and Kegan Paul, 1962), devoted to the sexual character of the human body is also worthy of more attention than it has received.

spicuous way to the paradigm of the machine. In such cases, the continuity of some function like speech that is associated with the macrobody is achieved by changes at a level of brain process that are remote from anything we can either directly affect or are normally aware of. We can, if we like, imagine these transfers as being effected by some super program for the nervous system in which the traumas in question and the appropriate corrective measures are all anticipated. In this way, the brain and the body as a whole would once again assume the aspect of a very advanced machine in which everything is "hard-wired" and backup systems abound. In espousing this picture we are, of course, attempting to save the machine model itself by postulating a designer-programmer of well-nigh infinite ingenuity who takes the place of the watchmaker God; and we may even, in a speculative flight, go so far as to identify this programmer with the evolutionary process.

Since this picture is the mainstay of the view of the human body as an object and a machine at the present time, it may be appropriate to give it closer attention. It has already been pointed out that this conception of the human body is a lineal descendant of dualistic interactionism, and that it is alive and well, although its parent has been largely discredited. To use Ryle's phrase, one could say that although the "Ghost in the Machine" has taken some hard knocks of late, the Machine it haunted is still quite popular. What is even more remarkable, however, is the fact that it has not lost its dualistic character. What I have in mind here is that because the functions of machines are built into them by the human beings who make these machines to serve the purposes of those who will use them, machines are what they are only in a dependency relation to their makers and users. The best proof of this is that it is regularly assumed that the machine to which the body is compared is one that is functioning properly. If a machine were to break down or malfunction, deterministic physical explanations might still be given for what occurred, but the machine would no longer be performing its function. Strictly speaking, this does not mean that it would no longer be a machine, but its identity as such would be "on loan" from its former condition as a properly functioning machine or its future one after it will have been repaired. The point here is that nothing could count as a machine unless the notions of purpose and function were somehow applicable to it. The dualistic character of machines is, accordingly, not confined to the case in which they are placed in relation to a mind that is explicitly conceived in terms of some radical contrast to the body; it can also derive from the functional design of the machine and the relation this entails to something or someone who makes the machine in such a way that it will serve the purpose implicit in that design.

It is true that in popular discussions of very sophisticated machines like computers this dependence on its human designers and users is often held to be somehow precarious. People seem to be afraid, because of the speed and efficiency of the calculations that such machines perform, that one day they will break out of their servile role in our lives and establish their supremacy over us. Impressive as the feats they perform may be, however, the fact remains that even machines that can design other machines will have been designed by human beings to do just the kind of thing they do; and they will function in a way that serves the purpose that guided their design. To that extent, even the most advanced machines would still owe their character as machines to their human designers and users.

But if the concept of a human being as the designer and user of these machines is an element in the concept of a machine, it is equally significant that this concept is an unanalyzed concept of commonsense provenience and is not itself the concept of a machine. It is instead the concept of a being that understands how something can be done and has either *made* a machine as a means of doing it with less effort, and perhaps more rapidly and accurately as well, or *uses* the machine that has been so made. But if a machine is made by a human being (or by something that is similar to a human being in the relevant respects), and if a machine qua machine must do what it has been designed to do, then there will be something unavoidably circular and redundant about any attempt by a human being to understand itself or its body by analogy with a machine.

The only way a machine could be really comparable to a human being would be if it could break out of the dependency relation that has been described; and to do that, it would have to take off on its own and function in ways that its designers had not intended it should and had no idea it could. But at least in the case of computing machines, there would be the difficulty that we would not know what to make of the products of its operations. Conceivably, the designers might be able to determine that they had unwittingly built more capacity into this machine than they had known or intended; and in that case, the machine character of this computer would be confirmed, and presumably the validity of the results it had achieved would be established at the same time. But if that could not be done, then the designers would have to choose between concluding that there had been a breakdown or that this "machine" was not really a machine. The latter conclusion would be almost unavoidable if there were some independent way of confirming the results achieved by this machine and if these results regularly proved to be valid. In such a case, this "computer" would have transcended the limits that define a machine as a machine. By reaching a valid conclusion in a way that is not merely accidental and yet is not reconstructable in terms of the way the machine was built to operate, it would in effect have placed itself on the same level as human invention and discovery. But for that very reason – namely, that for these purposes it would be indistinguishable from human beings as we know them without the benefit of this machine metaphor – such a "machine" could no longer be simply identified with a piece of hardware operating in accordance with familiar physical principles. Instead, its status as an "object" would have become just as problematic as that of the very human beings who use the machine analogy for purposes of self-description.

It increasingly seems clear that the whole conception of the body as an object is mired in a set of contrasts from which it cannot be extracted. These contrasts – the original dualistic ones, as well as the unavowed contrasts on which contemporary functionalism rests – fatally undercut the philosophical purposes that motivate the objectification of the human body. More specifically, the machine model itself presupposes a contrast between the machine and its maker or user; but when it is applied to the human body, one must either identify this maker and user with a mind that is independent of the body or the two – the machine and its user – will be one and the same, with the result that the contrast is wiped out and the concept of a machine subverted.

The inapplicability in principle of this whole picture to human beings can be made more perspicuous by the following considerations. If my body were an object I could observe and manipulate in the way I do other objects, it ought to be possible for me to refrain from any such intervention and to view my body as simply the physical system that it is supposed to be. It is extremely doubtful, however, that this is possible; and the reason is not just the psychological fact that we are so accustomed to understanding our bodies in functional terms, that is, in terms of the purposes they can serve. If that were the case, it would suggest that our relation to our bodies is at bottom a matter of the way we conceive and describe them, and that we describe them, for the most part, in functional language for the same reason we do a thermostat, even though we know that a purely physical description is also available. But it is clear that to view the body as simply the neutral x that can be conceptualized in one way or another would simply underscore its "otherness" and its character as an object. Such an approach cannot help us understand how I, as the one who describes my body in these ways, can also be the one who is responsible for, say, its being in a sitting rather than a standing position. No shift to a purely objective way of viewing my body can cancel out this fact that "I," the observer, however I may be conceived, am implicated in the state of my body in a far more direct and intimate way than I am in that of the thermostat or than I could be if it were simply an object that I can perceive and think about in various ways but always remain quite distinct from.[3]

3. The idea that understanding something in this way is an optional "intentional stance" is developed by Daniel Dennett in the book *The Intentional Stance* (Cambridge, Mass.: MIT Press, 1987). This view has some affinities with the conception of teleology as a regulative idea that Kant presents in the *Critique of Judgment*. Both clearly envisage the body as an

III

Not many philosophers have offered constructive alternatives to the concept of the body as an object. Indeed, it is arguable that there is only one: Maurice Merleau-Ponty.[4] In any case, it is his conception of the human body that will principally inform the discussion that follows. It is a conception of the macrobody and of its unity, and Merleau-Ponty's main thesis is that that unity cannot be understood by the characteristic methods of the natural sciences. It is the unity of an entity that has a world – something for which no place is made in those sciences – and as such it is inseparable from the unity of that world itself. But if this conception of the body is thus bound up with an ontological thesis about human being, it is also inspired by considerations deriving from the psychology and even the physiology of perception; and it is with this empirical side of his "phenomenology of perception" that I will begin my account of the macrobody.

In the preceding section, it was argued that, far from being in the first instance something observed – an object among objects – the human body has to be understood in a way that places it on the hither side of the contrast between that which perceives and that which is perceived. In more concrete terms, the way the objects we perceive are present to us is intimately bound up with the active stance of our bodies. By "stance" here, I mean anything from the direction in which my eyes are turned to the body's being in motion or at rest. Such a stance typically can be changed at will, though only within whatever range of adjustments our bodily constitution permits. One example of an active stance would be the position of my hand as I reach for a doorknob and prepare to turn it as a preliminary to opening the door and leaving the room. Even if I only perceive a doorknob without grasping or turning it, it figures in my perceptual life as something to grasp and turn with my hand long before it is understood in terms of its objective physical properties. But if I may be said to perceive something like a doorknob with my hand (and not just my eyes) even when I do not touch it, the same is true of my perception of another human being in some char-

object about which judgments have to be made; the only real issue is what kinds of judgments can validly be made about it. It hardly needs to be said that the conception of the body I am proposing requires a much stronger form of teleology than Kant allows.

4. Although Merleau-Ponty was very familiar with, and argued powerfully against, a physicalistic treatment of the body, he always assumed that the latter was associated with some conception of the mind – either empiricistic or intellectualistic – that was not itself physicalistic. In my opinion, he was right about this; and although his discussions are carried on in terms drawn from French philosophy that are often unfamiliar to us, a closer look at his characterization of "intellectualism" will reveal strong family resemblances to what I have been calling the "transcendental" side of physicalism. Merleau-Ponty's posthumous *The Visible and the Invisible,* translated by Alphonse Lingis (Evanston, Ill.: Northwestern University Press, 1968), is also rich in suggestive insights, although the book is incomplete and the argument is often hard to follow.

acteristic posture of grief or joy – an expressive stance of the body with which I am familiar and which I bring to what I see.

Countless other objects as well are perceived as things one does something or other with, and this means in terms of the way they lend themselves to operations included in the repertory of skills of our bodies. It is true that the physical structure of our bodies and the level of development of our brains and nervous systems set limits on the functions that our bodies can perform – what we are *able* to do. We could, however, study the anatomy and neurophysiology of the relevant parts of the body indefinitely without getting any sense of this functional dimension otherwise than by drawing on our own extrascientific experience of grasping and manipulating the objects in question. This active role that the body plays in perception blocks its being treated as itself, in any primary way, an *object* of perception.

In order to focus on a certain object in my vicinity, my body and sense organs must assume a certain orientation; and that orientation of my body is not something I observe or can treat as simply a certain disposition of the relevant parts as so many objects in space. Instead, it is normally understood by me entirely in terms of what *I* have to do and where *I* have to be in order to perceive the object in which I am interested. To understand the body in this way is precisely *not* to perceive it as an object, because an object is what is set over against me as a perceiver and there simply is no distance between me and my body, in this perceptual stance, that would make it possible for the latter to figure as an object in my perceptual field at the same time as it makes it possible for the objects in that field to confront me in the way they do. Even if I were somehow to catch a glimpse of myself – my body – in a mirror while assuming whatever stance is required, the effect would simply be to interrupt the perception in progress and substitute for it another in which my body would play a somewhat different but still nonobjectifiable role.

This active stance of the body in perception would not be possible if it were not for another feature of the macrobody: its unity. In performing the functions of perceiving, thinking, and acting in which the presence of the world is presupposed, parts of the body work together in a highly distinctive way, and so a question necessarily arises about the way the rapport among them is to be conceived. Suppose, for example, that I am changing a tire on my car. I find the nuts that hold the wheel in place hard to turn, and I try one way after another of using the wrench to turn them. When my right arm gets tired, I use my left; and I may even try to use my legs to bring weight to bear. All these different parts of my body thus converge on the same object, and they are all engaged in the same task. It is the identity of this task that makes everything that my hands and the other parts of my body are doing part of the same action of my body as a whole.

The fundamental issue raised by such examples is whether the unity of the body's functioning can be understood in terms of local neural trans-actions that cumulatively constitute human behavior or whether the body as a whole is implicated in these local transactions in a different, holistic way. The latter suggestion typically arouses the suspicion that some sort of mystical flummery is afoot, and so the idea that it might deserve serious evaluation does not find many takers. This attitude, in turn, stems from the conviction that all such holistic conceptions are radically inconsistent with the requirements of scientific inquiry. Not only are the objects constituted in such inquiries physical in an unprecedentedly rigorous sense; there has also been a determined effort to conceive their relations to one another in a way that extracts them from the web of implication that our ordinary ways of talking weave around them. The language we use much of the time is rich in suggestions of implicit sympathies and affinities among things and generally in a kind of dramatic unity pervading the events that are of in-terest to us. Against what is apparently a powerful inclination of our natures to live within a world over which this kind of spell has been cast, natural science insists on Bishop Butler's maxim that "everything is what it is and no other thing." Every object, and every part of every object, is held to be a self-sufficient plenum of being; and it is thus supposed to be opaque in a way that precludes its being a whole in any sense other than as an aggre-gate of parts that are themselves opaque in this same sense.

This conception of the body and of its parts as being defined by their opacity bears closer inspection. In its standard use, the word "opaque" denotes anything that does not let light through. In the sense in which I am using it, to call something "opaque" is not to deny that it is transparent in the ordinary sense of that term.[5] Glass, after all, is transparent, but it, too, is opaque in the sense that both a sheet of glass as a whole and the parts into which it can be divided in thought are just what they are, in complete logical independence of everything else. Being opaque in this sense is thus a state of impermeability and closure that seems to make it impossible to attribute to something so characterized any relational prop-erty that is not itself purely external. As a result, the relation that can hold among the internal parts of such objects will necessarily be of the type expressed by the phrase *partes extra partes*. This signifies, in the first instance, the divisibility in principle of all material objects as objects in space, and it applies to all human bodies – yours, mine, everyone's – simply as material objects. But the externality of each part of an object to every other such part must not be understood exclusively in spatial terms; nor, of course, should it be understood as some sort of causal independence, as though

---

5. The sense in which I am using this word is also different from the one current in the philosophy of language.

the actual removal of an adjacent section of such an object would leave its
neighbors unaffected. "Opaque" should be interpreted instead as implying
that every part of a spatial whole is separable in thought from every other
part and that, as so separated, it has a definite character that can be described without reference to any other such part, or indeed to anything
else at all.

But are human bodies really opaque in this sense? If they are, then the
only way we will be able to think of their functional unity will be in terms
of preestablished programs and messages being sent out from some general
headquarters in the mind or in the brain that is implicitly assumed not to
be limited by any opacity of this kind. There are, however, quite substantial
considerations that speak against the application to the human body of
these ways of thought and even against the view that natural science is
pervasively committed to them. For one thing, even in the most rigorous
neurophysiological research, the human body is conceived of as having
certain functions, and this means as acting in various ways in response to
certain features of its situation. But to say that someone – some body – acts
in a given way is not just to describe a movement or a series of movements
of one or more of its parts. It is true that some forms of reflex behavior –
invariant patterns of motor response to a given stimulus – appear to be
"hard wired" in a way that can be captured by a purely physical description
of a local neural transaction. There are, however, far more cases in which
more than one possible response might be appropriate to the situation of
an organism; and which of these responses is in fact executed will depend
on other matters with which that organism may be concerned.[6] Because of
this multiplicity of possible responses, one can speak of an equivalence
among them that permits a given movement to be supplemented or replaced by another that effects the same outcome. This equivalence is reflected in the way such movements are described, that is, in terms of what
they bring about rather than just in terms of their own observable properties. And because the essential element in these responses is what gets
done, and not the specific movement by which it gets done, such a description is functional in character.

What is most important here is the fact that an action that is performed
in the context of this interchangeability is clearly the action of the whole
body, not just some part of it. Because the organism is not locked into a
single pattern of response to a given stimulus, the explanation that must
be given for the response – the movement or lack thereof – that does take
place has to answer the question, "Why *this* response rather than *that* one?"
– it being understood that both are in the repertory of this organism. This

6. This thesis is developed with a wealth of detail in Kurt Goldstein, *The Organism* (Boston:
Beacon Press, 1963). This is a book on which Merleau-Ponty drew extensively in his *Phenomenology of Perception*.

question cannot be answered by tracing the physical process that links the stimulus to the response that actually takes place, any more than it could be for some alternative response that may occur instead. The only appropriate answer would be one that treats it as a unitary response of the organism as a whole to all the discriminable elements in the situation. We typically think of such a response as requiring the intervention of an act of the mind in the affairs of the body or, alternately, the kind of direction provided by a program that was itself devised by a "mind" that had anticipated just such a "choice" as this. The alternative to these dualistic approaches would be to conclude that the body itself makes this response, and not just as an instrument in the service of something or someone else. But if that is the case, then the body as a whole would have to be conceived in terms of function, and not simply as an aggregate of neural events that can be separately explained.

There is, of course, another, quite different way of reacting to the discovery that the movements we make in response to a certain stimulus vary with the wider situation in which the body is placed. This would be to argue that all this fact adds to the prior picture of the body as a physical system is an element of complexity. In other words, the body is "wired" or "programmed" at all levels and in such a way that its responses to more and more complex sets of stimuli are antecedently laid down in its neural constitution. What these metaphors do is to reinstate the model of the machine as our governing understanding of our own bodies, although it is amplified this time by the computer-derived distinction between "hardware" and "software," that is, between actual neural structures and the programs in accordance with which the nervous system operates. But if this is the way someone with a primary commitment to a thesis about the conceptual form of a scientific account of the body typically reacts to evidence that suggests a holistic conception of the body, the practice of working scientists seems to be somewhat different. This is not a point, it should be emphasized, about the contrast between the way a neuroscientist talks and thinks in the context of his scientific work and outside it. Whatever their philosophical allegiances and whatever logical and conceptual inhibitions they may nominally accept, many biologists and neurophysiologists describe the processes they study by using functional idioms with great and sometimes even disconcerting freedom. This is so even when they are talking about the behavior of individual cells that may be described in all sorts of teleological idioms – the language of messages and codes, for example, which is now widely used in molecular biology.

When a question is raised about these ways of speaking, it may be replied that they are used only as a convenient shorthand that can readily be replaced by formulations cast in the language of biochemistry. It may be, however, that these functionalistic locutions are more than a kind of an-

imistic shorthand. They may testify to the neuroscientist's implicit acknowledgment that the microprocesses he studies are embedded in, and take
their ultimate character from, the macroprocesses that constitute what the
body *does*. It is, after all, the relation of the former to the latter that gives
discoveries in this field their interest and importance. If, for example, a
neurologist identifies a certain part of the brain as being centrally involved
in some larger function like recognizing human faces, both he and his
colleagues must evidently have prior familiarity with this recognitional capacity. In the absence of such a prior understanding of the larger context
in which these brain processes are embedded, what would this scientist have
found out except that certain electrical or chemical events occur in a certain part of the brain? But if prior knowledge of the larger context of some
biological process makes an essential contribution to the significance of
what has been discovered, it is surely permissible to move the idiom of
action and function downward to the microprocesses and to describe them
as what a certain part of the brain and thus a certain part of the body is
doing. The only real alternative would be to assign all function and meaning
to the mind in order to leave nothing in the body – either micro or macro
– that the language of physics and chemistry could not express. But that
alternative has already been dismissed, and so one has to conclude that in
the actual practice of the life sciences, as contrasted with the idealizing
descriptions of scientific practice given by philosophers of science, the idea
of the body as a functional whole is ineliminable as a framework of understanding.

These considerations suggest a picture of the body and its unity quite
different from the one dominated by the *partes extra partes* character described earlier. This would be a picture from which the dualities deriving
from both the soul model and the machine model would have been removed; and the body would be understood as in some sense carrying on its
own life, rather than being in the service, whether directly or mediately, of
an external master. In that picture, the body as a whole would stand in a
reflexive relation to itself and, within that relation to itself, its parts and their
movements would be internally related to one another. As I am construing
it here, an internal relation would be one that holds between two bodily
events that are either functionally equivalent, in the sense that they can both
do (or contribute to doing) the same thing, or functionally opposed, in that
one undoes or prevents what the other does. Such movements, and the
organs by which they are carried out, would be related to each other by
having places in a network of equivalences and oppositions by which the
body as a functional whole is organized. Much that goes on in the body is
not directly incorporated into that network in the way movements of the
hand or the eye are. But the microprocesses that go on in the immune
system, say – or, for that matter, in the hand and the eye themselves – make

possible the actions of the macrobody and bear their consequences as well, and in that sense have a place in that functional whole. They can also show more directly their integration into the functional body – for example, when I suddenly find myself in a life-threatening situation and draw back in panic. My body undergoes all sorts of changes – from endocrine secretions to heart rate – that I could not ordinarily command but that express *my* reaction to this situation. Indeed, there does not appear to be any clear downward limit to the extent to which these subjacent microprocesses can respond to the larger concerns of the macrobody.

There are, of course, deeply held philosophical objections to the idea of internal relations, which is almost universally regarded as a discredited relic of absolute idealism. It is not possible in this study to deal with these objections in a full and conclusive manner, but it may be possible at least to remove the aura of gross implausibility that hangs about the notion of internal relations. The definitive proof of the incoherence of that notion is supposed to have been given by G. E. Moore, who recognized some internal relations among properties like orange and red but not among particulars.[7] He might have been more receptive to internal relations among the latter if, in the examples he used, he had paid more attention to living bodies, specifically human bodies, and to human artifacts. In the case of the latter, it is extraordinarily implausible to suggest that the object we call a book would be what it is even if there were no one (and never had been one) who could read, and that its relation to a potential reader is accordingly a purely contingent and external one. Of course, when a book is taken simply as a physical object, there can be no justification for holding its location, for example, to be in any way essential to it. But as what is sometimes called a "cultural object" – that is, as something made by human beings for certain human uses – the relation of a book to its makers and users is essential to it in the sense that anything that did not have this relation could not be this book. And if one substitutes for an artifact like a book something like a smile or a gesture of the hand that is inseparable from the person who smiles or gestures, the relevant relation becomes one in the life, and sometimes the body, of that person. If, for example, a smile expresses the pleasure of a child who is eating an ice cream cone, it is hard to imagine what would be meant by saying that the relation between the smile and the eating of the cone is an external one. Perhaps this child would smile in just the same way if it were given some-thing else, and conceivably there might be no difference between the con-tractions of its facial muscles in the one case and in the other. But if this smile expresses pleasure at the taste of the ice cream, then any smile that

7. G. E. Moore, "External and Internal Relations," in *Philosophical Studies* (London: Routledge and Kegan Paul, 1922), pp. 276–309.

did not do that could not be that smile even if it were physiologically in-distinguishable. The smile and the eating are not only functions of the same body; they stand in a relation in which the eating motivates the smile and the smile expresses the pleasurable character of the eating. If that is not an internal relation, what could possibly be so regarded?

The point I am making here may be more readily accepted when ex-amples are drawn from a contact sense like touch rather than from vision or hearing. There is something about vision, especially, that seems to en-courage a transcendental way of thinking about perception, in spite of the fact that we see with our eyes and from a place that is occupied by our bodies. In the case of hearing as well, there is a certain obliviousness to the involvement of a specific part of our bodies – the ears – that is hardly possible in the case of touch. One may in fact wonder whether a represen-tational theory of perception would ever have been developed if the sense of touch had played as important a role in philosophical thinking about perception as vision has. It also seems clear that touch is closely associated with action in a way that seeing and hearing rarely are. We are, of course, touched passively – by other things – and there are actions like speaking in which our awareness of the movements of our bodies is almost as slight as it is of the bodily side of seeing and hearing. But when we are doing something like playing baseball or driving a car, we grasp the bat or the steering wheel with our hands, and we can hardly be oblivious of the role of our own bodies in the kind of perception this involves.

What is all-important here is the fact that the context of these percep-tions is one in which we are doing something, and doing it *with* the thing that is being perceived. Our hands and, more generally, our bodies assume a position and a posture that are appropriate to that action and take into account the various properties of the bat or the wheel; and equally impor-tant, they do so in the way that is suited to our swinging the former or turning the latter. We heft the bat and take practice swings with it to make sure we are holding it correctly; but as has often been pointed out, in doing this we are not applying maxims we necessarily could formulate in words or in thought. The know-how involved in all such cases is literally in our hands and bodies, and it is there in a way that makes it impossible to view either the one or the other as merely a passive instrument. If they were merely passive, then the know-how that would govern the use that is made of them would have to be attributed not to the hand or the body but to whatever uses the body. But if anything is clear about these matters, it is that this know-how is laid down in our hands and bodies, though always as parts of the body as a whole, and that our bodies are in charge of the multiple adjustments that take into account changes in, say, the conditions under which we have to steer the car – changes we may become aware of through our contact with the wheel and the movement of the car as our bodies feel it. The body, in short, is not an instrument or a tool; rather, it is the body that uses other objects as *its* instruments. In the often cited case of the blind man and his cane, the cane becomes an extension of his body and is used in active exploration of environing objects in the medium of touch. What we are often inclined to say about the body as an instrument of the mind does apply to the cane, for *it* is really as lacking in knowledge and intentionality as the body has been thought to be. But if it becomes an instrument by being incorporated into the intelligent routines of the body, there is no higher-order user in relation to which the body itself could be similarly described.

It is widely held that internal relations of the kind I am describing are really logical relations and, therefore, belong at the level of language, not at that of things. Many philosophers would argue, for example, that the contrast between the body as an object and the body as a functional whole is simply one between alternate modes of description of the body – different "stories," as this idiom has it – and that no one of them is ontologically privileged. It therefore becomes admissible to speak of the body or of its parts as doing things – my eyes following the plane or a smile expressing pleasure at the eating of ice cream – in language that resists translation into the kinds of statements one would find in a textbook of physiology. But the fact that there are these different ways of describing the body is supposed to be explained by the pragmatics of language use in a way that generates no deep ontological implications.

Ontological issues do not arise because the scientific "story" and the commonsense description are supposed to be simply different ways of talking about one and the same thing. Because the logical pluralism implicit in this position is closely associated with the philosophy of ordinary language, the "same thing" referred to is generally understood to be the familar perceptual object from which all inquiry sets out; but not much more is said about it.[8] A familiar, commonsense understanding is thereby allowed to do all the work without being subjected to closer philosophical examination. The discussion is moved entirely to the level of different kinds of talk and their "logic," and an impression is created that nothing having to do with the things we talk about in one way or another is a necessary condition for their being so talked about. In this way, the implicit understanding we arguably have of our bodies, as well as those of others in functional-gerundive terms, is allowed to surface only as a form of talk; and it is made to appear that there is an indefinitely large number of such forms of talk that could in some sense be about the same object. The question of

---

8. I am drawing here on the discussion in Gilbert Ryle, *Dilemmas* (Cambridge: Cambridge University Press, 1956), Chapter 5. It should be pointed out that although he was a strong anti-Cartesian, Ryle himself was not a physicalist in the modern sense, and his concept of the body was based more on a commonsense understanding than on science.

how functions of the kind referred to earlier could be attributed to the body as a physical system is never raised, nor is it explained how the body to which they *can* be attributed could be the same as the body to which they cannot.

Taken at full strength, this radical separation of logic from ontology would mean that all ways of talking are in principle applicable to anything at all – to ordinary physical objects as well as to human beings. We do sometimes tell stories about inanimate objects in terms of functions and actions, but this is generally taken to be merely a playful extension of our ways of talking about ourselves. It cannot be validated simply by the fact that we actually talk this way about such things; and this is because there is something missing from the constitution of an inanimate object that is presupposed by functional kinds of talk. The standard conception of what that missing something is makes it a mind; but it does not follow that the ontological contrast at issue here must involve something *other than* the body. The difference between the body as a physical system and the body as a functioning whole does not turn on that issue, but that does not make it just a difference between ways of talking. There are, unquestionably, two different ways of talking here, but if one wants to say that they are about the same thing, then this claim cannot be made good simply on the grounds that no other *thing* is involved. In other words, this assertion of sameness poses an ontological problem, and to that problem neither common sense nor physics understood as a way of talking can provide a satisfactory answer.

There is another way – psychological this time – in which the philosophical implications of the idea of the body as a functional whole can be sidetracked. This would be to suggest that everything that has been said about the functional body may be true, but it has to do with our "body image" rather than with our bodies. The use of the word "image" implies that what is at issue here is the *knowledge* we have of our own bodies and that this knowledge is representational. On this view, we carry around a picture of our body that we take out and consult on occasion. The idea that there must be such a picture is patently an attempt to accommodate the distinctive mode of being of the body to the requirements of a representational and ultimately dualistic concept of mind. One wonders who (or what) needs this map and how he (or it) could become so disoriented that a map would be needed. There are certainly pathological disturbances that interfere, for example, with our normal ability to point to given parts of the body when directed to do so; and in such cases, the patient may indeed fall back on strangely indirect methods in order to comply with such requests. But what these cases throw into sharp relief is the lack of any need for "knowledge" of this kind or for maps or images in the normal functioning of our bodies. It is not as though the body were like an unfamiliar city in which one could stand at an intersection and wonder which of two great avenues leads to city hall. The macrobody, if it is anything, is a unity; and this means that, without the benefit of any special group portrait, our hands and legs and shoulders and backs *are* in a working relation to one another that is more specifically defined by the task in which they are engaged.

This same line of thought concerning touch also leads to wider reflections on the way in which we have knowledge of our bodies. It was pointed out early in this chapter that our access to the bodies of others is primarily visual, but the case is quite different with our own bodies. I do not have to look at my legs in order to know whether they are crossed or flexed, and I do not have to look in a mirror to know that I am smiling. It is not by touch either that I learn these things, if this means that in order to determine how my limbs are disposed, I would have to run my hands over my body. Because this is such a grotesque idea, we are tempted to say that I just *know* these things without looking, and to claim this as a bit of nonobservational knowledge. Quite possibly, however, the vocabulary of "knowing" itself may be out of place here, since it inevitably assimilates these matters to standard models of propositional knowledge. The point is that if it is proper to speak of knowledge here at all, it is tacit knowledge that I cannot avoid having. There is, therefore, no need for any formal announcement, whether to others or to myself, because it is not as though I had just learned something about myself. For that to be the case, it would have to make sense that I could be working at a word processor and not "know" this; and only quite extravagant assumptions could make that at all plausible. The macrobody, which is what is concerned here, is one that understands itself in terms of the actions in which it is engaged, even if these are entirely passive, and thus in terms of the implicit intentions by which these actions are informed. And neither these actions nor these intentions are at the kind of distance from us that would make it natural to speak of coming to "know" them.

Examples like this suggest that there is a pressing need to think of the body and its unity in new ways. The old ones – the machine model and its updated descendant, the computer model – cannot make any place for internal relatedness either in the rapport between different functions of the body or in its commerce with objects that lie outside it. If, for example, I use my hand to turn a doorknob in the course of leaving the room, the movements of my hand that open the door have to be thought of as produced by the neural processes within my body. As such, they have nothing more to do with the knob or the door or my departure from the room than does a sewing machine with the cloth it stitches. My hand does not *feel* the knob; and if the knob does not turn at first when the normal torque is applied to it, the hand cannot be said to *explore* its workings in any way that is different from the way the elevator adjusts itself so that its floor is even with that of the exit platform. The idea is that these two entities can be side by side and yet not present to each other in any sense that is stronger than that provided for by the passage of electrical impulses between them. In effect, since the reactions of my body are produced by processes that have nothing to do with the situation I am in, they have to be regarded as a remarkable simulation of the changes it would pass through if it actually were in the presence of, for example, some danger.[9]

IV

In the preceding section, I proposed a concept of the functional body and its distinctive kind of unity. In this section, I try to show that a body of this kind is inconceivable outside the context of presence and that the mode of being of the human body is thus that of ek-sistence. Although this thesis builds on the functional character of the body, it is antithetical to the very differently motivated position that is currently referred to as "functionalism." This is the view that, like a machine, the body can be in functional as well as physical states, and that these functional states have been mistakenly understood as mental states. It is also assumed that no special ontological provision has to be made for these functional states, and that they entail no radical ontological contrast between human being and the being of material objects. Against this view, it has already been shown that when human beings are assimilated to machines, there is in the background an implicit contrast between the machine and its user, and this makes the whole functionalist scheme dependent on an unexamined concept of the human being that is the second term in that contrast. But when the machine metaphor and the unavowed dualism it entails are set aside, as I have argued they must be, there is still the task of bringing together the two terms that are kept apart in the machine metaphor and of thereby defining the functional mode of being of the body itself. That is what this section will attempt to do.

There is a great difference between the notion of function as it applies to something – a machine – constructed in such a way that it can be used to do or to make something that has a place in the wider purposive economy of those who did or made it and the notion of function as it applies to something that is not a machine in this sense – the human body, for example. Although it might be appropriate to signalize this distinction by reserving the term "function" for the former and "action" for the latter, I do not do so. What I want to do is to develop the implications of the fact

9. In sharp contrast to such conceptions is the way we are able to mimic the postures and expressions of others – other bodies – in a way that leads Merleau-Ponty to speak of something like a "communication" of bodies with one another. See *Phenomenology of Perception*, Part II, Chapter 4.

that, in the case of the human body, there is no contrast between a designer-user and a functional system that the former is supposed to have designed and used. That is, there is only one entity here, and that entity is a body by virtue of occupying a space; but that same entity also does things in an intelligent and purposeful way. It is, therefore, in the first instance an "I" and only secondarily and derivatively an "it"; and this is the juncture in my argument at which that assertion must be made good. The issue is to determine how it is possible for an entity that no one has designed and that no one, properly speaking, uses to *do* many of the same things that a machine does, even though usually more slowly, and to do many other things that no machine can yet do.

A few uncontroversial observations may help to initiate this line of thought. One is that a living body, especially a human body, has many levels of functioning. These range from highly developed skills like playing the piano or writing a letter to the release of adrenalin into the bloodstream in moments of crisis or the reflex movements of the eye that bring into focus something on the periphery of the visual field. In the case of the first two functions and others like them, it is clear that they can be performed only if, for example, the writing paper or the piano is perceptually present to the person in question. It is true that an expert pianist does not need to look at the keys in the way an unskilled one does, but the keys are present in another sense modality – that of touch – even when the pianist does not need visual clues to locate them. More generally, the performance of a function of this kind requires a close perceptual rapport with the instruments and objects involved – in the pianist's case, with the score and some-times a conductor's baton, as well as with the keyboard. Even in a poetry recitation, where the person who is doing something has nothing to keep track of, that person is constantly monitoring the words being spoken, and if there is an interruption, he will know where to resume the recitation.

The underlying consideration here is that if a function is to be per-formed intelligently, it has to be constantly modifiable in the light of chang-ing circumstances. We all form habits that enable us to deal effectively with recurrent situations in our lives, and for the most part these habitual forms of behavior run off with little, if any, explicit attention to them by us. In-deed, their value to us consists largely in the fact that they free us to con-centrate on other matters that do require close attention and thought. Moreover, we are all familiar with the kind of habit that continues to op-erate as usual even when the circumstances have changed in a way that defeats the point of what is being done. A habit of this kind is properly called "mechanical" – that is, machinelike – and this means that, as a result of a deficit in the presence that functional conduct requires, the function itself may miscarry.

It is, of course, possible to construct complex machines that perform tasks involving feedback of this kind. A thermostat linked to a furnace is a good example of a machine that registers the relevant features of a situation and adjusts its functioning accordingly. "Register" here does not mean that the machine has to see or feel anything. It means only that it has to be affected in some way of which it is susceptible by certain kinds of changes in the situation in which it is operating, changes that have a bearing on the satisfactory performance of the function of this machine. Those changes have to be anticipated by the designer of the machine, and a causal link has to be provided for to alter the functioning of the machine in a way that is appropriate to some change that has been registered – a temperature, say, that is higher than desired. All kinds of other changes might occur that the machine would have no way of registering and to which it would not respond. It is limited to the capacity for response that was built into it by its designers, who had in mind a certain function (and not others) for this machine and a certain kind of change to which it would respond. The linkage between that change and what the machine does is thus provided for by the designer, who himself "registers" both the actual temperature and the optimal temperature in a different way – that of perceptual familiarity – from that of the machine he designs.

There is no way in which a human body can perform a function in this derivative manner that depends on a connection established by another party between its actual state and an optimal mode of operation. At least, there is no way it can do this as long as we are not prepared to view it as being a machine and its functional routines as constituted by someone else. Because it is not a machine, the human body has to do deal with the changing circumstances in which it finds itself, as one might say, on its own; and this means that its environment must be present to it and not just to someone (or something) else, who then incorporates the relevant linkages between states of the world and the body's responses into the latter's operating routines. Since the way the body is conceived by the natural sciences excludes the possibility of the presence to it of the objects around it, it is evident that the entity for which it is possible cannot be conceived exclusively in that way. It is a body rather in the sense of Merleau-Ponty's *la chair*, and this is to say that its mode of being is constituted by the presence to it of its world. And because of the specific modalities in which presence is realized in the case of human beings, it is not possible to understand its mode of being in terms of an ontology of objects. It is a body that is not an object but a self – an "I" – and its mode of being is that of ek-sistence.

In Chapter 4 the unity of presence was discussed, and the conclusions reached there have an important bearing on the unity of the human body. Because the mode of being of the body is that of ek-sistence and it lives in the presence of its world, the unity of the body as an active whole is inseparable from the set of relations in which the objects present to it stand to one another. It was also pointed out in Chapter 4 that our ability to have a world of individual perduring objects, and to reidentify them when they appear before us, is the foundational achievement that makes everything else possible in the domain of knowledge. Because this achievement has typically been conceived as a mental one and placed under the rubric of theoretical reason, it has been understood as having to do with the conceptual synthesis of a world of material objects, and not as having any special bearing on the way the body of a being capable of this kind of synthesis comports itself in a world unified by that synthesis.

It is clear, however, that there is such a bearing, and it is one that emerges most distinctly in connection with various kinds of bodily activity. At this moment, for example, I am seated at my word processor, and the keyboard, the printer, and the display screen are objects in front of me. There are spatial and causal relations among these objects, and together they form a system that I am operating to produce this book. As I type and revise this chapter, my hands and eyes, and my body as a whole, accommodate themselves to these relations and to the task at which they are being employed. Thus, as I type a sentence, I look at the screen to be sure I have typed it correctly; and if I have made a mistake, I go back to the keyboard again and make the needed corrections. Everything else in my bodily orientation is subordinate to and designed to facilitate these movements of my hands and eyes. A pillow at my back is there to enable me to maintain this posture for a few hours without discomfort that would force me to break off my work prematurely. Altogether, it may be said that the orientation of my limbs is dictated by, and accommodates itself to, the requirements of my task and to the spatial and causal relations between the objects I am using. Because these objects in their relations to one another are present to me as a unitary being, and not just severally and separately to different parts of me, the unity of this presence becomes the unity of the task in which I use these objects, and thereby of my actions in the course of that task. And since these actions involve my body, the unity of presence becomes the functional unity of my body as well.

What is most important is the fact that the unity that obtains among the component objects in this system determines the way in which the different parts of my body have to be disposed and the way they function together in this task. In this sense, the functional unity of the body is borrowed from the unity of its world. To the degree that what the body does is functional – that is, defined by what it achieves – it cannot be detached from the perceptual presence of the situation in which it takes place. But to say this is to say that its mode of being and that of the body, insofar as it engages in functional conduct, are those of ek-sistence.

But in addition to these functions of the body as a whole, there are others, like reflexive eye movement or adrenalin release, that cannot be directly initiated in the same way. These are more closely associated with a specific part of the body than is the case in the examples given thus far; and they are not usually described as being actions at all, although they make actions possible. They are, for the most part, deeply habitual and endlessly repetitive processes; but they can in many cases be modified by what the body as a whole – the macrobody – does or by what happens to it. Thus, I cannot make my heart beat faster simply by willing it to speed up; but if I run to catch a bus – this is something I can do – my heart begins beating faster and thereby makes rapid movement of my legs possible. Again, if in the course of a medical experiment I inject a vaccine into a blood vessel, my immune system will begin to form antibodies in a way that I cannot command but that I can bring about in this indirect way. These are all cases in which the functioning of the permanent systems that sustain the life of the body are modified by what that same body as a whole does or does not do. And since the macrobody does what it does in a context of perceptual presence, and since the microprocesses that support it respond to shifts in its mode of functioning with shifts in their own, the latter are effectively integrated into the functioning of the macrobody.

It was noted previously that the boundary line that separates the gross actions of the macrobody from the countless processes that both make them possible and are, in turn, modified by them is anything but clear. When I am dozing in my armchair or asleep in my bed, it may look as though I am altogether withdrawn from the concerns of my waking life and as though the restorative housekeeping functions of the microbody have wholly taken over. In fact, this may not be the case at all; and in my sleep I may remain sensitive to small sounds and movements of various kinds. This will typically be the case if I am worried about burglars or if there is something else keeping me on the *qui vive.* Even in my sleep, I can be ready to spring up and do whatever may be required even though I am not in any ordinary sense on watch. Here again it appears that the concerns of my waking life – concerns that would normally be expressed in overt actions of various kinds – inform the subjacent life of the body. Our sense organs, evidently, are not bivalent in the sense of being either on or off. There is, instead, a continuity between on and off and, more generally, between what we would ordinarily describe as the "organic" and the "conscious" life of the body. Indisputable as this may be, a continuity of this kind is something that we find very hard to conceive. Words like "psychosomatic" and "unconscious" are sometimes trotted out to describe such phenomena. They are not very helpful, however, because they presuppose the very conception of the "mind" – a mind–body contrast and "consciousness" as the defining property of "mind" – that makes this sort of thing seem anomalous and even mysterious in the first place. In another version of the same kind of dualism, we may even find ourselves talking as though there were two bodies – one that conforms to the conceptual requirements of science and one that does not – but that is surely a counsel of desperation.

A more helpful way of conceiving this relation would be to say that the one human body we are talking about has a character as a whole that does not, to be sure, disappear but does become less and less evident as one examines its various subsystems. On this view, the most comprehensive unity of the body would be one that it has as an active whole that opens on the world in which its life is embedded. At successively different levels of abstraction from that holistic unity, other contributory modes of functioning can be defined that range from the internal chemistry of the cell to the workings of specific organs and rigidly conditioned responses to external stimuli like the Babinski reflex. An implication of such a view is that the macrobody is an entity that cannot be understood simply as an especially complex material object, and that its functional and holistic properties are just as "objective" as those of the parts into which it can be resolved.[10] This conclusion would meet with strong resistance and could be generally accepted only if something like an intellectual revolution were to take place. The reason is simply that although we have been learning so much about the physicochemical processes at the most elementary level of the body's functioning, our ideas about how such processes could form part of a differently organized whole have remained almost completely undeveloped. As a result, it has seemed that the only acceptable way of dealing with differences of level in the body's functioning must be to interpret them in terms of the objective–subjective distinction, with holistic properties very much on the subjective side. The effect of this, in turn, has been to make it impossible to associate the body so conceived with presence at all. If that result is unacceptable, as I have tried to show it must be, the only real alternative is to accept the thesis that function, and therefore presence, is as central to the ontological constitution of the body as extension or its causal powers.

When we speak of the functioning of the macrobody as requiring the presence of the objects with which and the situation in which that function is performed, it is clear that the body itself must also be included in that presence. It is present, however, in a distinctive manner that now needs to be described. One thing is immediately obvious: Many parts of our bodies,

10. Heidegger's idea that since the time of the Greeks we have understood being in terms of making may be relevant here. The passionate insistence that we human beings must be built on the same general model as computers is an example of this ontological commitment. Certainly the idea that a human being is something it does not make sense to think of in terms of building appears to be unfavorably received by the contemporary *Zeitgeist*. Heidegger's discussion can be found in *The Basic Problems of Phenomenology*, translated by Albert Hobstadter (Bloomington: Indiana University Press, 1982), pp. 83–8.

and many processes taking place in them, are not present at all. The pancreas, for example, is an organ that we would not even know we had if it were impossible to open the body and explore its hidden parts. We might have a pain in the area of the pancreas, but that would be as close as this organ could come to the kind of presence that, say, our hands have; and it is not very close. In general, and in the absence of special procedures, what is present is the body as an articulated whole – the body as the macrobody. It is, in other words, present in its active orientation, and this means in the disposition of the body parts that enable us to walk or sit or work or talk. It is present also in its gross incapacities – a broken leg – and in its states of readiness or fatigue that in one way or another affect some active function. The underlying physiological states – the blood-sugar level, for example – that make this or that active function possible will typically be present only in the sense we have of what gross activity we can and cannot perform. These, of course, are all actions that normally count as voluntary; but there are others, like accelerated heart action and intake of oxygen, that are involuntary and yet support the work of those parts of the body that are in direct contact with the object of the whole effort. The body as a whole is thus focused on a particular object outside it and on something that is to be done with that object.

A more general point about the presence of the body is implicit in what has just been said about its unity in the context of presence. This is that the body itself is present as that to which something is present and as what can respond actively to what is so present to it. It is not, in other words, as though things were present to a subject that can be conceived apart from the body and that would then, by means of some power of its own, bring it about that the body moves in certain ways that are appropriate to the situation that has been disclosed. The entity to which something is present is the same entity that can act in response to what is so present, and this is to say that it is itself a body. The converse of this proposition must, of course, be that the body that is so present is a self; and it is at this point that, as noted earlier, the language of "I" has to replace the language of "it" in talking about human beings – that is, "ourselves." One step in that direction was to distinguish the macrobody as the articulated functional whole that is in the presence of the world that it can act on in various ways. The point to be made now is that this macrobody has the first-personal character expressed in the "I," and that it is as such that it is itself present. In other words, both the unity and the reflexivity that were previously discussed as features of presence have their equivalent in the modality of eksistence as features of the macrobody.

7

THE ENTITY EACH OF US IS

I

In the Introduction to this book, I announced my intention of presenting a unitary concept of human being in place of the concept that makes human being a composite of body and mind. The preceding chapters have been devoted to the working out of the constitutive elements of such a concept, and the time has now come to put them all together in a synoptic view of the "the entity each of us is."[1] This may suggest that the business of this chapter is just the assembly of prefabricated parts to form a concept that no longer has any problematic features, but that is not the case. In some ways, the most difficult questions raised by the line of thought I have been developing have still to be resolved. Some of these can, in fact, be dealt with only when the stage of synthesis has been reached, as it now has.

One such question concerns the relation in which the ontological conception of human being developed here stands to physicalism.[2] This ques-

---

1. This is a somewhat modified version of a locution that Heidegger often uses: *das Seiende das wir je selbst sind. Sein und Zeit* (Tubingen: Max Niemayer Verlag, 1957), p. 7. It is amazing that there are still those who have not come to terms with the fact that *"Dasein"* – Heidegger's term for this entity – denotes individual human beings. Proof of this with textual citations was presented in my *Heidegger and the Philosophy of Mind* (New Haven, Conn.: Yale University Press, 1989), p. 620.
2. Physicalism is not the only theory with which mine might be confused. Two others are the double-aspect theory that is vaguely associated with the name of Spinoza and the two-property theory of persons proposed by P. F. Strawson. In both cases, however, the similarities are superficial and misleading.

   In a double-aspect theory, the notion of an "aspect" is treated as unproblematic, and the identity of mind and body is taken to be a variant of a familiar case in which something looks different – presents a different aspect – from different points of view. In this instance,

tion arises because of apparent similarities between the one and the other. I have, for example, committed myself to the thesis that we *are* our bodies, and physicalism enunciates an ostensibly identical view. What is common to these two positions is a disposition to dispense with the concept of mind, but this common feature has to be understood in a wider context of fundamental differences concerning the way the situation that results from dropping the concept of mind is to be understood. In any case, a discussion of physicalism and its inadequacies as an ontology of human being will open this chapter; and an understanding of why the physicalistic strategy miscarries should prove instructive in connection with my account of the proper sense in which we may be said to be our bodies. This sense, in turn,

of course, the "aspects" are supposed to be conceptual rather than perceptual, but in either case the notion of an "aspect" is that of something's presenting itself to a certain view of it. In the concept of human being that has been developed here, however, perceiving and thinking, as well as other mental functions, are themselves treated as forms of presence, and thus in a way that implicitly invokes the notions of an "aspect" and of a "view" that corresponds to it. This makes it hard to see how such "aspects" together with the "views" they presuppose could themselves be an "aspect" of some underlying reality, as this kind of theory says mental phenomena are. Similarly, for any position like mine, there will be a difficulty about the thesis that body or matter is still another aspect of this same reality. It is, of course, true that bodies are viewed, and that they accordingly present aspects to those who view them. It is a long step beyond this familiar fact, however, to the idea that body as such can be defined in the language of aspects as what presents itself to one kind of view in contrast with another kind. To attempt such a definition in terms of aspects at least appears to tie body conceptually to the concept of a "view" and thus to that of mind itself as that which has such "views"; and the result will be that, contrary to the intentions of the theory, everything winds up on one side of the mind–matter contrast. This fact may be missed because the concept of an aspect is treated as though it were a neutral bit of philosophical apparatus that can be used without prejudicing the substantive issue under consideration. When properly understood, however, "aspects" and "views" have to be associated with presence. That is what my account does, and since the existence of material things is disclosed in this presence, there is no need for any other "aspect."

The idea that persons can have nonphysical as well as physical properties is usually regarded as a significant departure from the constraints of orthodox physicalism, and so it might be if it were not for the fact that "nonphysical" here turns out to mean "mental." This does not mean that a theory of this kind has any new light to cast on the vexed question of how these mental properties or states can be domiciled in the body as a physical system. That remains as mysterious as ever, and one suspects that, at least in the best-known version of this view, its import is entirely logical and not ontological. In other words, it is antireductionistic only in the sense that it defends the integrity of psychological *descriptions* of human beings without committing itself to any view of the physical or nonphysical character of the processes – of perception or thought – to which these descriptions ultimately refer. Even so, because of its use of the notion of a mental property or state, such a position remains within the old dualistic parameters. By contrast, human beings as conceived in the terms proposed in this book have no mental properties and they are not in mental states. In place of the idea of such states, there is the fact that human beings have a world; and there is an insurmountable difference between an entity that has both physical and, in some largely unexplained sense, mental properties as well and an entity that is different from other physical entities by virtue of this fact. Such a difference is simply too great to permit any significant affinity between a dual-property theory and one based on the fact of presence since the latter cannot be thought of as a property of any kind of the entity in question.

opens the door to a unitary concept of human being as that of a body that is a self. This is perhaps the hardest feature of my position to grasp, since it so thoroughly defeats all conventional expectations about the alternatives among which we have to choose in the philosophy of mind. What will emerge here is a conception of the identity of a human being with his body that is quite different from that of physicalism, and one that turns on the concept of ek-sistence as the fundamental fact that is to replace the whole concept of mind and the mental. Finally, certain objections to an account of this kind will be taken up that reflect commonsense beliefs about the dependence of our mental lives – that is, of everything that comes under the heading of ek-sistence – on the functioning of the brain and the central nervous system; and the outline of a strategy for dealing with them will be presented. The three sections that follow will take up these matters in order.

II

The character of physicalism as a philosophical thesis is set by the conception of mind against which it argues. As its name indicates, physicalism is committed to the view that the world is pretty much what the physical sciences say it is; and this means that there is no place in it for anything that lacks physical properties like location in space, movement, and certain causal properties. The goal of the physicalist is, accordingly, to show that everything that might be thought to lack these properties turns out, on closer examination, to be misconceived in some way that calls into question the claim that there is any such thing. Since minds and mental states have long been held to lack these properties, they have been the most obvious candidates for elimination. Of course, if a philosophical physicalist were to adhere closely to the way physical objects are conceived in physics as the foundational science of the natural world, not just mental entities but a good deal of the familiar furniture of the world as well – Eddington's famous table, for example – would have to go by the board or be assigned, at best, a problematic status for ontological purposes. But even if this ultimate reduction of everything to the entities in which physics deals is implicit in the physicalist program, it does not usually figure prominently there. The guiding assumption seems to be that if the more egregious offenders against the physicalistic dispensation can be discredited – most notably pains, images, and the like – then the fate of colors and other "secondary" properties can safely be left to the physicists. Although I do not share this view, the issues it raises were discussed in earlier chapters, and so I shall not center my discussion of physicalism on the problems connected with an ultimate reduction of everything to the entities of physics.

The arguments mounted by physicalists against mental states tend to be "dialectical" in the sense that they undertake to show that the arguments offered in behalf of the reality of these states are invalid and that typical characterizations of the epistemic status of such states are open to decisive objections. This counterargumentation is often accompanied by demonstrations that one can do quite nicely, at least for the purposes of scientific explanation, without the entities or states postulated by the mentalistic line of thought. The implication is thus that the whole idea of mind as a nonmaterial entity that is somehow associated with the body, and that constitutes the inner reality of a human being, is a gratuitous invention and that it can be readily replaced by concepts that are recognizably physical. Although some of the points made in these critiques of mentalism may have merit, the argument as a whole is flawed by the fact that at least the general character of the only acceptable alternative to mind–body dualism has been decided in advance.

This privileged position appears to have been assigned to physicalism mainly on the strength of its being the "scientific" approach to a matter that philosophers have long discussed without achieving any substantial measure of agreement. In these circumstances, the only real issue often appears to be which strategy of argument will best ensure the achievement of this predecided outcome. Difficulties that arise in the course of these attempts are rarely, if ever, taken as signs that the terms of the problem itself have to be reexamined or that there may be distinctively philosophical alternatives other than mind–body dualism. Overall, in spite of the strong consensus in favor of physicalism that has formed in recent years, these failures make it seem doubtful whether real progress has been made in establishing its central thesis.

I shall argue that the rigid way in which physicalism conceives the available alternatives in the philosophy of mind is responsible for the failure of the argumentation by which physicalism seeks to establish itself. More specifically, instead of making any independent effort to determine how perception or thought, say, might be properly conceived, the physicalist takes his cue from the dualist in identifying the distinguishing features of mental states. These usually turn out to be epistemic characteristics that from the perspective of this study can be seen to derive from the attempt to combine the two pictures of a human being – as observing and as observed – described in Chapter 1. Once the difficulties connected with these thesis have been driven home, usually on the strength of arguments that are logical rather than phenomenological, only the other half of the dualistic picture is left standing; and since this is a conception of the body as stripped of all mental properties, the physicalist winds up with the only entity he was prepared to recognize in any case. In a sense, the dualist has done most of his work for him by separating mind and body and treating them as two substances. The physicalist is then left with only the congenial task of dismantling the rickety construction – the mind and its states – for which the dualist was responsible. In this way, it becomes possible to miss the fact that even if the whole idea of mental states as constituting a private inner domain were to be dismissed, it would by no means follow that perceiving and thinking and remembering and imagining – the human functions that mind–body dualism conceived in its own distinctive way – can be adequately dealt with by means of purely physical concepts. From the analyses of the preceding chapters, it is clear that there are facts about these functions that are independent of the theses of mind–body dualism but, at the same time, inconsistent with the claims of physicalism.

There are other respects as well in which physicalism turns out to be modelled on the conception of the mind that it so energetically rejects – so much so, in fact, that one can speak of something like a transfer to a physical medium of some of the most notable features of a dualistic theory of mind. One of these is the separation that dualism effects between a mental state and the object it is supposed to represent. For the physicalist, a mental state is a state of the central nervous system; and although this state stands in various complex causal relations to its object, it can be described in a manner that is logically independent of any reference to that object. It is an internal state of the organism, just as, in a different sense, a representation was an internal state of the mind and one that was supposed to be equally distinct from its object. In the latter case, the separation between the two was so pronounced that the possibility of a connection between them became problematic and, with it, the possibility of perceptual knowledge. In Descartes's philosophy, that connection had finally to be grounded in assumptions about the nondeceptive character of the deity. In physicalism, it is guaranteed by the way mental states and their objects are linked in the presiding theoretical account of the functioning of the human organism. The odd thing about the latter way of bringing together what this same theory has put asunder is that it cannot explain how the connection between state and object is made by the human being who is supposed, for example, to be perceiving that object. That person cannot, after all, monitor his own brain states or use them as indicators of the presence of an object; and even if he could, that could only mean that a new brain state had been added to the previous one, and all the same questions would arise about it that arose about its predecessor. It looks, therefore, very much as though this perceiver would have to rely on the assurances of the theorist for this purpose in somewhat the way the dualist does on those of God. There is one difference, however: As a human being, the theorist is in the same boat, in the matter of access to his own brain states, as the original perceiver who relies on him. This suggests that perhaps an ultimate theorist who is free from this limitation, and thus similar in this respect to Descartes's God, may be required as a final guarantor for the connections between states and objects that physicalism postulates. I return to this point later in this discussion.

What has just been said suggests a more general observation about physicalism that adumbrates the major criticism I propose to make of it. It looks very much as though physicalism simply sets aside the whole constellation of issues that have to do with the presence of things in the world. It is able to do so because it takes the first-personal stance in which presence is presupposed, but does so without reflecting on this fact or noticing what is being taken for granted. Then, when it turns to other human beings, it persists in this unreflective mode and fails to notice that it is now the presence of things in the world to these other human beings that has to be reckoned with. Because the being of things in the world was not originally understood as their presence *to* the person in question – in this case, the proponent of physicalism – there is no understanding of the fact that this presence cannot be simply made to do duty for the presence of these same things *to* someone else. That, of course, is just what happens and, as a result, that "someone else" is made to appear as though he were a presence-less object. The irony here is that this same fate awaits the original first-personal proponent of this view of others, who has to pay for his failure to "thematize" presence in his own case by being denied it in his theory – a theory, by the way, that in the process loses any connection with a human sponsor.

Before developing this criticism further, I want to take up the notion of privacy touched on previously. Its prominence in the dualistic account of mind has made it a stone of offense to physicalists, so it may be useful to clarify its status in this debate. As a criterion of the mental, it is clearly bound up with the notion of the mind as part of each human being to which only that one human being has "access." This privacy has the consequence that what one person can experience, and thus "know," will not be completely coextensive with what another person can. Any such failure of overlap between what one person and another can know is deeply offensive to physicalists because it implies that there are object domains that are not part of a single, all-encompassing nature and are therefore inaccessible to the scrutiny of a unitary mode of objective thought – that of natural science. Although it would seem that if anything "in the mind" is private everything must be, privacy is typically attributed to those inner states that, like feelings, pains, and images, are supposed to be somehow marginal – extraneous to the great central areas of human experience in which the observation and thought of many inquirers converge on a common reality. (This assumption is in marked contrast to the guiding idea of this study, which is that if there is any criterion for what we think of as "mental," it has to be sought in those common areas that are usually thought to be the domain of objectivity rather than of a pejoratively conceived subjectivity.) All of these "private" inner states tend to be spoken of, both by dualists and by physicalists who follow their account, as though they were objects on display in a museum to which only one viewer is admitted. The physicalists, however, are concerned to show that nothing can be private in this sense.

It seems clear that the great emphasis placed by physicalists on privacy as a criterion of the mental is misconceived, and that proving that nothing is private in this sense is largely irrelevant to the merits of physicalism. Certainly, the assumption that there must be something private about human beings in any sense that entails the existence of object with which only one mind can be familiar is not required by the analysis of human being developed in the preceding chapters. That analysis is not based on the peculiar notion of private mental states or of the "access" to them that the physicalistic argument presupposes as part of its conception of "mind," and it is this idea that makes us think that only one person can peep into the sealed compartment in which the immediate objects of our mental acts are sequestered. Even in the case of feelings, which are supposed to be private in this sense if anything is, the idea that one person has access to, say, a feeling of pain – his own – to which another has no access seems to be just an odd way of saying that the one is in pain and the other is not. If being in pain were having access to a private object, then "access" to this pain by another person would have to be thought of as that person's being able to peep into another's mind and somehow view the pain situated there. This picture is, to say the least, peculiar, and it is utterly unclear how one is to make sense of the notion of having "access" to a pain without feeling it. But if one were to say that another person can have access to my pain only by being in pain himself, then the logic of mental states would force us to ask whether the pain felt by the one and by the other is really the same pain. If one answered this question in the negative, the access of one mind to another would be implicitly denied, but an affirmative answer would be just as puzzling. It would call into question, at least as far as this kind of mental act is concerned – but why not others as well? – the fact of there being *many* human beings, although that is an essential presupposition of this whole issue of privacy.

Altogether, it looks as though there may be something seriously wrong with this whole notion of access and of the objects to which it is directed. The deepest source of confusion in this matter may be a failure to distinguish carefully between what is entailed by the fact of there being many human beings and what is dictated by the logic of dualism as it applies to this fact; and it may also be that this confusion has been transmitted to the physicalists through their reliance on the dualistic conception of mind as what they must argue against. However that may be, it is clear that if privacy is essential only to mind as the dualist conceives it, and not to human being

as it has been expounded here, then the arguments mobilized by physicalists to discredit this conception cannot validate the physicalist thesis itself.

None of this means that in a different sense the notion of privacy does
not have a legitimate place in a theory of human being. Indeed, the very
fact of a plurality of human beings conceived as ek-sistents makes it unavoidable that privacy should have such a place. The reason is simply that if
the being of things in the world is realized in more than one locus of
presence (and of presence in absence), then there must always be matters
having to do with the idiosyncratic ordering of any given locus of presence,
especially in its dimension of action and concern, that will remain at best
a matter of conjecture to others. Although the latter may be in an excellent
position to interpret my larger patterns of conduct accurately, they will
often have no idea of what I am thinking or remembering or imagining at
a given time. It is also possible for me to withhold information and to
mislead them by playacting and by suppressing telltale bits of conduct. It
is clear, however, that this is a kind of privacy that can be explicated without
introducing any mysterious notions of the radical hiddenness of what goes
on in the mind or of special objects that are so hidden. Not only can I, if
I so wish, tell others as best I can whatever they want to know about such
matters; the matters with which I may be concerned in thought or memory
are all, at least in principle, possible objects of thought or whatever for
them as well. If they are not satisfied with that, then they should reflect on
the fact that what they want is something they could have only if, *per im-
possibile*, we could change places so that their field of presence and of presence in absence would be just what mine is now. This means that the only
residual privacy the proponent of this line of thought has to worry about
is one that is inseparable from the fact that I am not this or that other
human being (and the other way around). But privacy in this sense could
be overcome only if plurality itself were suspended in favor of a unique and
singular locus of presence. Since plurality is required in order to set up the
problem of privacy to begin with, a demand that ultimate publicity be
achieved at this price makes the whole argument incoherent and need not
be taken very seriously.

Similar considerations apply to another argument by which physicalists
have attempted to discredit the conception of mind as a "Ghost in the
Machine." As in the case of privacy, it is a question here of an epistemic
feature that has been supposed to distinguish mental from physical states.
Dualists have claimed that our mental states are such that our first-personal
apprehensions of them are "incorrigible" in the sense of being immune
from error of the kind that constantly occurs in our attempts to gain knowledge of the world of objects that transcends our mental states. Where the
object of my apprehensions is nothing but my own mental state, there is –
so the argument goes – nothing by reference to which these apprehensions

could be judged incorrect, because the seeming as such – what we believe or what we think we remember or how something looks – is what constitutes the mental state in question.

If we no longer insist on linking a rejection of physicalism to the notion of an "inside" of which mental states are the "contents" and no longer require that they be apprehended as such by a special kind of knowledge, the whole theme of incorrigibility loses much, if not all, of its pertinence to the issues between physicalism and its critics. Again, if the fundamental fact that replaces the occurrence of inner mental states is that there is a world in the sense of "is" that involves presence and ek-sistence, it will follow that whatever degree of certainty attaches to the states of affairs thus disclosed will be strictly coordinate with that of the seeing or hearing in which it is disclosed.[3] If, for example, I decide that what is before me is not a chair (as I thought a moment ago) but a couch, there is no way in which I can defend my characterization of my prior perceptual state against the changes that have occurred in what I affirm about the world. After all, if I acknowledge that what I see now is a couch, then barring some very unusual circumstances, it must have been a couch a moment ago as well, when it appeared to me to be a chair. If I wish, I can insist that the fact that at that time a chair appeared to be in front of me remains unaffected by the revision of my beliefs. I can also, if I like, say that it constitutes an incorrigible piece of knowledge that no discovery about what is actually the case in the world can change. This would be an idle claim, however, if it were made to establish the existence of some special object – a chair appearance – for which there is no place in the actual world and which must therefore exist in the mind. If anything can be said to "appear" in this situation, it must be something that was actual at the time of the appearing – in this case, the couch that, for some reason, looked to me on this occasion as though it were a chair. It has already been shown that there does not have to be any special object that explains how something can possibly look like something it is not. In other words, the fact that at a certain moment the couch did look as though it were a chair will not be altered by the discovery that it is in fact a couch; and if we like, we can hang on to the fact and declare it to be immune to revision. Since any such certainty generates no interesting philosophical conclusion and affirms only that I took something that was one thing to be another, it will form part of my autobiography in the same way as my correct apprehensions of states of affairs around me do. For this, however, no privileged inner domain is required.

3. It might be asked what becomes of the "Cogito" under the dispensation I am describing. Clearly, as expressing a mental act, it would fall under the same interdict as all mental-act talk. On the other hand, might not "There *is* something," as expressing an indefinite instance of presence (and thus of ek-sistence), qualify as a new kind of statement that is at least very hard to imagine being falsified?

These points about incorrigibility and privacy illustrate the way physicalists espouse the intuitions of the dualist about the character of the mental for polemical purposes and, in doing so, fail to note how peculiar those intuitions themselves are as a starting point for a philosophy of mind. The substance of physicalism, however, is the thesis that follows upon the exposure of the logical and epistemic vices of dualism and that is held to represent the only alternative to it. This thesis identifies the mind of a human being with his body and declares all the properties of human beings to be properties of their bodies and, as such, physical properties. This reductive identification of the mind with the body has been the subject of much discussion, in which it is usually the plausibility or implausibility of identifying this or that mental property with a brain state or with a form of behavior that is at issue. Challenges of this kind are clearly in order; and although they sometimes appear to proceed on the same assumptions about the status of these properties as those of the physicalist, I would endorse many of the points that have been scored against physicalism in this way. The line of argument that I want to develop is quite different, however; it consists of an attempt to show that, independently of all these challenges on specific points, physicalism is at best a radically incoherent position because, *as a theory,* it violates the restrictions that that theory itself places on the concept of the body that a human being is supposed to be.

In order to understand what happens to the concept of the body under physicalism, one must grasp the fact that, as a result of the elimination of the soul or mind that had been associated with it, the body has also been, at least in intention, stripped of anything that could be called presence. The body is now a physical object that interacts causally with other such objects. It reflects light, it emits sound waves, it is variously squeezed and knocked about by all sorts of forces; but in all this there is no relation to other entities or to itself by virtue of which it could be said to be "there," either for them or for itself. This holds for all the physical processes involved in perception, as it does for those involved in speech, since in the absence of any link between a body and a mind, these processes are supposed to be physical through and through, and do not bring about any result that is not itself comprehensible in physical terms. This means that they cannot even issue in "representations," although that word, in some evidently Pickwickian sense, continues to turn up in physicalistic talk, as has already been noted. Even if they were admissible under physicalistic presuppositions, representations would not, of course, be equivalent to presence; they are no more than a kind of intramental version thereof, which is all that mind–body dualism could manage. Of presence itself, there is no acknowledgment in physicalism; and there cannot be any, since it involves a relation between entities of which the natural sciences know nothing.

It is worth noting, as well, that in the kind of world physicalism postulates, the lack of anything like presence means that there is nothing that can be called true. Truth is typically supposed to be a property of sentences or statements and, as such, to be essentially bound up with language use. And yet if language itself is included in the domain to which the theses of scientific naturalism are to apply, it remains to be seen whether it would or could figure there in a mode that would be compatible with the fact that something one says is true or false. Under this new conceptual regime, there would doubtless be sciences of perception and of language that work with the paradigms of physics and chemistry, and of the kind of biology or neurology that is based on those sciences; and these sciences would have to produce their own version of what it means to use words to say something. But could they do so? To judge from the way speech is studied now, by means of methods similar to those of the kind of natural science of language I have just imagined, there seems little reason to expect that any such attempt would or could be made. What such forms of inquiry do is to investigate what happens when we speak – that is, when we use words to say something – and this means that the physical processes that take place on those occasions are studied with a new degree of rigor and exactitude. Although it would seem that such sciences simply presuppose that something has been said, and that their inquiries do not therefore try to spell out what saying something as such involves, a consistent physicalist would have to conclude that events of this order that occur when we speak must be what a locutionary act – saying something – really is because there is nothing else within the scientific paradigm that it could be. Those who draw this inference appear to think that anything that might be offered as the ingredient supposedly missing from the scientific account would be so exotic and so unamenable to the methods of empirical inquiry as to discredit itself without further ado.

In fact, however, the difficulty that confronts their view is much closer to home and much harder to dismiss. It is surely fair to ask whether there is anything in human speech, as the scientific account conceives it, that it would make sense to describe as being true or false in the way that what we say is true or false. That would be the case, on the analysis that has been proposed here, only if speech can be conceived as a modality of presence in absence; but that is not possible in the kind of world that physicalism postulates. In such a world there is no place for "what is said," as distinct from the vocables used in our utterances. It follows that what counts as a sentence in the scientific account differs in at least this one vital respect from what a sentence is in our common understanding of ourselves. This point is all the more worth making because it is evident that adherents to the scientific account have by no means sacrificed the latter understanding of words and language on the altar of their thesis; and if they had, they

could not propose it as a thesis that claims to be true. That prior understanding is simply presupposed – tacitly, of course – by the scientific account that thus reduces everything except itself to the status of an object.
What it fails to recognize is that this working duality must break down when
the scientific account is applied to the human function – speech – that is
the bearer of the truth claim that account unavoidably makes. It is as
though an implicit assumption were being made that nothing science says
about what is in the world or about what human beings are can in any way
create difficulties for science itself. Once again, I would suggest that this is
possible only because something much like a transcendental status is implicitly conferred on science and its language as the authoritative theory of
the world. If that is so, then the scientific worldview is our equivalent of
the God's-eye view of an earlier day; but it is to be feared that, like the
latter, it will distort our efforts to arrive at an adequate conception of ourselves as the real bearers of the scientific enterprise on which we confer
this strange and alienated status.

   All of this must occasion a good deal of difficulty for the exponent of
physicalism, who as an individual human being falls within the scope of his
own theory. He must be a body, and everything about him, including the
fact that he is an adherent of physicalism, must be attributable to him as
some sort of physical property of that body. The most obvious way in which
his adherence to physicalism would be expressed would be in the form of
an utterance in which the physicalistic thesis is stated. The question this
raises is whether the fact that such an utterance is made can possibly be
reconciled with the thesis expressed in it. That utterance is made, after all,
by someone – a particular human being – who comes under the scope of
what it says, namely, that human beings are their bodies. As applied to that
individual human being, physicalism must, therefore, imply the truth of
what that individual would normally express in the statement "I am my
body."[4] There will be more to say later about the import of such a statement, but there can be no doubt that the statement is *about* the person who
makes it and that it declares this person – the "I" in the statement – to be
that body.

   The point I am making here is that unless physicalism is prepared to
transform itself into a completely and explicitly transcendental position –
one that would be attributable only to what Merleau-Ponty aptly calls a
cosmotheoros – physicalism has to offer some account of how it is itself, as
one might say, "plugged into" the world and how its reference to actual
human beings and their bodies is achieved. Most pertinently, although, as

4. It would be surprising if physicalists did not try to evade this conclusion, perhaps by a reform
   of language that eliminates indexical expressions like "I" so as to block the possibility of
   forming statements like "I am my body." Like most such proposals, however, it would be
   more likely to be honored in the breach than in the observance.

human activities, inquiry and theory formation are collective in character, it must be possible for each individual human being who adheres to doctrines like physicalism to apply the latter to his own case. He must, in other words, be able to formulate some statement in which he identifies himself with his body, and to do so in a way that includes him in his capacity as an adherent of that theory. The function of the statements that would manifest such adherence is supposed to be to say that something is something. But if such a statement is assigned the status of a feature of the particular human body – that of a brain state, presumably – about which it is being made, and in a way that is oblivious to the distinction between objects or entities and their being, then the fact-stating function of that statement (and the being of the object or entity about which it is made) will be eclipsed. It will be eclipsed because the statement asserting the identity in question will have lost its character as something said by becoming a feature of the object – in this case, the speaker's body – about which it was supposedly made. In general, when no provision is made for the presence – the being – of the entity about which some assertion is made, the status of that assertion as something said must be rendered decidedly problematic.

The upshot of this argument is that physicalism subverts itself in much the same way as the character in a 1930s movie did when, from the chicken coop in which he was hiding, he called out to his pursuers, "There's nobody in here but us chickens!"[5] If it were possible for the physicalist to recognize that the possibility of making the statements he makes about himself in expounding this theory is part of what that theory has to account for, not only the comic but the seriously incoherent character of his position would be brought home to him. This incoherence is connected with the fact that although physicalism entails the truth of self-referential identity statements of the form "I am my body," it not only makes no inquiry into the kind of identity these involve, but it also simply assumes that it is of a type with the kind of identity that obtains between entities that have no capacity for self-reference. More generally, physicalism appears to be pervasively characterized by an unacknowledged complicity in matters that are ruled out by the official story it tells. In that story, it is as though theory had been released from all constraints that might reflect the fact that it is an account the physicalist is giving of himself, as well as of human being generally. Accordingly short shrift is given to the fact that, for this very reason, the exponent of this theory has some prior familiarity with what it is to be a human being, and that his involvement in theory construction is itself a datum that the theory itself cannot simply bypass. It is not surprising, therefore, that one encounters again and again the idea that any first-person

5. My recollection is that this was said by Stepin Fetchit, but I would welcome correction if that is not the case.

account of something like having a headache should be treated as just another theory and that, as such, it must compete, without any antecedent presumption in its favor, with other theories, most notably with physicalism itself.

In these circumstances, it appears that the philosophy of mind is the battleground of theories for which there are no data except those derived from the observation of other human beings – nothing, in other words, that registers the reflexive character of the subject matter with which it deals. Theory has so completely devoured fact under these circumstances that the people who propose these theories have been altogether eclipsed; and there is no longer any sense in which these theories are about them or, at any rate, no sense that is not itself subject to revisionary construal within some theory or other. In such a situation, it must remain entirely obscure how any decision could be reached about the comparative merits of one theory over another when everything that could possibly count for or against them has been made theory-dependent.

Ostensibly, only logical criteria that are internal to the domain of theory construction itself are permitted to play a role in decisions that are made at this altitude among competing theories. This pretense, of course, merely serves to conceal the influence over these decisions that is exerted by a massive *parti pris* in favor of what is thought to be required by the worldview of natural science. This same *a priori* partisanship also dictates the terms on which what is referred to as the "commonsense theory" is admitted to the discussion, namely, as a rather backward kind of "folk psychology" that is so unsophisticated that it is not even aware that it, too, is a theory. In fact, however, this elaborate pretense of high impersonal theory formation serves mainly as a cover for the prior commitments of those who espouse these theories, commitments that typically exert a decisive influence on the course of the discussion. But since the role of these commitments is not acknowledged, there is no way of opening a discussion with their human sponsors about their reasons for refusing to give any weight to anything that does not bear the imprimatur of "science." As a result, any challenge to these procedures is dismissed as antiscientific prejudice.

One result of this peculiar relation in which physicalism as a theory stands to its actual human proponents is that it can both draw on and yet seem to repudiate any first-personal understanding of what it is like to be, for example, in pain. Within a universe of discourse in which it is always one theory that is competing with another, it becomes possible to say such things as that a headache is whatever turns out to have the "functional role" that psychological theory assigns to headaches, as though a headache were like some mysterious subatomic particle that is postulated by physical theory. One would never guess, if such statements were all one had to go on, that the person who makes this statement may quite possibly have a headache when he makes it. In such a case, it would be the pain he feels at that moment that he is turning over to psychological theory. There is something passing strange about this way of playing the agnostic in matters with which we must already be so familiar. Along such a line of thought, one could imagine a physicalist turning over the distinction between being blind and being able to see to some appropriate department of neuroscience with a similar declaration that it must be "whatever" the latter makes of it on its own terms. What must be plain in all such cases is that these proposed theoretical identifications are strictly bogus, and that the physicalist who makes such statements is proceeding on the strength of a prior understanding of what it is to have a headache – an understanding that he evinces but does not acknowledge. There is, accordingly, no real parallel to the case of entities that have to be postulated on the strength of certain observations the physicist has made and that are then defined simply as that which accounts for them.

If there are these obliquities in the relationship between physicalism as a theory and the human being who espouses it, the relation in which the one and the other stand to other human beings is equally remarkable. What happens there is that what was formerly referred to as the mental life of these persons becomes entirely the creature of theory; and as an explanatory construction by the phantom proponent of that theory, it is accorded a status that is essentially different from that of the latter. However unwilling he may be to admit it, the physicalist is working on two levels – that of his own life as a human being and that of theory construction. But no provision is made for any such duality in the case of other human beings, if only because to do so would expose the peculiar duplicity that characterizes the symbiosis of physicalistic theory with its human sponsor. This is not to say that the theory will not permit references to psychological processes in the human beings who are objects of the theory. It invariably turns out, however, that the inner event the term "psychological" designates is something like a brain state that has been produced by a stimulus and that can serve as the basis for a prediction of the response that will be made by the person in question. The point is that it represents something only to the theorist since, as has already been pointed out, no one in the ordinary circumstances of life can use his own brain state as a representation in this sense – that is, as the basis for predictions of what he will do.

In other words, the proponent of physicalism conceives the state of someone else's brain as being somehow accessible to inspection by him and then proceeds to project a course of conduct on the basis of what he finds there. But because this kind of access is attributed to an effectively transcendental observer, the fact passes unnoticed that it is the actual human proponent of physicalism who imagines his relation to other human beings in this way. This physicalist would undoubtedly agree that *his* brain, too, might be observed in this way and for these purposes by someone else, but this admission is not allowed to affect the transcendental status of the kind of access it postulates. The result is that the implicit and unavowed character of the relation in which the physicalist stands to his fellow human beings is that of a unique and asymmetrical view of their bodies understood as physical systems. It does not require any special power of intuition to find this stance as objectionable morally as it is incoherent philosophically.

III

If physicalism cannot offer an acceptable account of the sense in which I am my body, the task of working out such an account is clearly the next order of business. For this purpose, it will be helpful to begin with some general observations on the subject of identity as such, and most particularly, the kind of identity that is postulated by the physicalistic account. It will be shown that this is not the kind of identity that is appropriate to the case of a human being and his body; and an attempt will then be made to present an alternative concept of identity that is better suited to that case.

Philosophical theses that identify one thing with another can be confusing because they seem to presuppose that there are indeed two things and then proceed to assert that these two things are really one. If there were two things, they could not be one and the same thing, so the only way to interpret such statements is to say that they combine two different standpoints. The first of these would be defined by the affirmation that, to use a famous example, the Morning Star and the Evening Star are different stars; and the second asserts that there is only one star that appears both in the evening and in the morning and was mistakenly believed to be two stars. On this view, a statement identifying one thing with another would represent the transition from the first to the second of these beliefs, and its transitional character would explain its surface strangeness. When so construed, its deeper import is that one thing has two sets of properties that were once thought to belong to two different things, but it is still this former claim that gives point to the identity statement itself. If there were no such contrast in the background, the identity of the one thing that remains where there had been thought to be two could only be its identity with itself; and this would be empty except as some sort of notational reminder.

Physicalism defends a thesis of the identity of two entities with each other, and these entities are usually referred to as the mind and the body. But where the identity of the Morning Star and the Evening Star may be said to be nonprejudicial in the sense that both are entities of the same kind – stars – and the identification could go either way, that is not the case for the identity of the mind with the body. The body is the only entity that is accepted as being real, and if it still sounds as though the proponent of this identity were committed to the mind as some sort of entity, that is only for the purpose of reassigning its properties or functions to the body. Consequently, the only *identity* that is being asserted is that of this reconceptualized body with itself, and this, again, is not very interesting for philosophical purposes. Here, too, as in the Morning Star example, there is an implicit contrast between two claims – one that asserts that there is a mind as well as a body and another in which only the reality of the body is recognized. But if this reconceptualization of the body were to be generally accepted and the existence of minds ceased to be even marginally plausible, physicalism would be reduced to the status of a singularly barren truism.

But suppose that even in these circumstances philosophical inquiry had not been altogether replaced by natural science and someone were to ask, "Is a human being really just its body?" How would the thesis of the body's identity with itself, to which physicalism would have been reduced, be of help in answering this question? Let us suppose also that this question is not simply a new way of raising the old questions about a human being as a composite of mind and body, and that instead it takes another direction, namely, the one suggested by the line of thought developed in the preceding section. In such a discussion, the focus of interest would be the thesis itself of physicalism as it is applied to himself by an individual human being: "I am my body." If the physicalist is right, this, too, could only be interpreted as a restatement of the body's identity with itself.

There would, however, be a decisive objection to such a construal. If the identity of the body with itself amounts to no more than the logical identity discussed previously, then it would be on a dead level with that of, say, a stone; and it has been justly pointed out that even though a stone can indeed be said to be a stone in a purely logical sense, there is nothing that it would be *like* to be a stone.[6] "Being a stone" would, therefore, belong entirely to the formal mode as what might be called a "discursive" or "logical" fact and would in no way enter into a characterization of a stone itself. The same would hold for human beings since, as long as the bodies with which we are identified are conceived in purely physical terms, the fact that I am my body would not convey anything about *me* and would reduce to a logical entailment of discourse about my body. The trouble with this is that if such is indeed the case, then "I am my body" would be as empty of extralogical content as "This stone is this stone" is.[7] Intuitively, this is hard to accept. But if it is not the case, then there must be something that it is

---

6. Thomas Nagel, "What Is It Like to Be a Bat?" *Philosophical Review*, vol. 83, 1974, pp. 435–50.
7. The difference between these two statements is dictated by the fact that stones do not speak, either about themselves or about anything else; and so the identities in which they may be involved have to be formulated for them by someone who can speak.

like to be a human body; and that is to say that this "something" that it is like to be one's body would have to find its place in any characterization of what it is to be a human being.

It may have been somewhat unfortunate that in the original statement of this argument, its author should have formulated it in such a way that primary emphasis appeared to fall on the word "like." The significant point is surely not the fact that, unlike being a stone, being a bat or a human body is *like* something but, rather, the fact that *being* what one is does not reduce to the empty logical identity that is all physicalism has to offer. The word "like" has, moreover, the disadvantage of suggesting that what is at issue here is a qualitative difference of some kind. Insofar as that entails that there is more to the entity under discussion than can be conveyed by a purely physical description, it is on the right track; but it hardly does justice to the distinctive character of the extralogical elements involved in that "more." What I want to claim is that the difference between something's being itself in an empty and a nonempty sense is in fact an ontological distinction rather than an ordinary empirical one – much more, that is, like a radical difference between kinds of entities than just another quality that one of them happens to have.

The suggestion I am making is that the statement "I am my body" has an import that is quite different from what the physicalist typically supposes. Indeed, the special irony that attaches to his thesis is that its very statement expresses something that he is unable to hear in it. He thinks of this statement as of a type with familiar instances of scientific reduction and as expressing a happy resolution of the paradoxes generated by the postulation of a mythical entity – the mind. The trouble is that the very statement that seems to announce its demise proves, on closer scrutiny, to constitute a dangerous counterinstance to the physicalistic thesis itself. This is because it exposes a distinction between a body like our own of which it makes sense to say, in a nontrivial way, that I *am* that body and, on the other hand, a body – my example was a stone – to which this notion of something's *being* its body does not apply in any sense that adds something to our understanding of what that entity is. What this distinction, in turn, reveals is that even after the idea of the mind as something attached to a body has been dismissed, human being still comprises an internal complexity of a special kind that is implied in the fact of something's being its body. In other words, the kind of identity that is asserted by the statement "I am my body" is not the trivial kind that is formulated in the Law of Identity and that expresses merely the overcoming of a prior appearance of duality. Instead, it is, I will argue, a unique form of identity that is constitutive of human being itself and that is founded on a contrast that is not a contrast between two entities but rather one between an entity and its being.

This contrast between an entity and its being is one that has been developed most powerfully by Heidegger, whose whole system of thought grows out of it. As applied to the present context of discussion, this would be a contrast between the body as an entity – a particular – and the body as an element in states of affairs, and thus as something that *is* this or that. Usually, the two are separated by placing the former in the world as the aggregate of all such particulars and the latter in "language" or some realm of truth to which an effectively transcendental status is accorded. The profound Heideggerian insight was that this separation must be set aside and in its place an entity acknowledged that, as a particular entity, is the bearer of its own being, as well as that of other entitities and thus of truth as well. This means that my being my body has to be understood in terms of the *being* of that body itself – its being understood in terms of presence and, more concretely, in terms of its presence to me as the entity that is that body.

The discussion of reflexivity in Chapter 4 has already drawn attention to this feature of ek-sistent entities in the context of a wider discussion of the individuation of such entities. It was argued there that the presence of other entities to an ek-sistent entity is possible only if that entity is present to itself. After the discussion of the body in the preceding chapter, however, it is now possible to see more clearly that this reflexivity has to be understood as the presence of my body to me as the entity that *is* that body. It is, after all, the body that gives each of us the distinctive location and perspective in which other entities are present to us. But if this is the case, and if the body is present to me in just this orientation that qualifies the presence of other entities, then it would follow that to say "I am my body" is more properly regarded as an acknowledgment of this fact than as the kind of identity statement in which physicalism deals. To summarize, I am my body in the sense that as an ek-sistent entity – one constituted by presence – I have a world in a way that is essentially bound up with the location and the active orientation of my body, which I cannot therefore separate from myself as a locus of presence. I cannot separate it from myself because it is present to me as that which makes possible, again through its location and orientation and active powers, the presence to me of other entities in the perspective in which they are so present. This body that I am must consequently be characterized not just as an object of a certain kind, with no questions asked about its being as such, but instead as an entity that essentially involves its own being as a body in the sense of its presence to itself as the entity it is.

It is at just this point that the difficulty described in the first section of the previous chapter – the difficulty that stems from the assimilation of the human body to the status of a physical object – makes itself felt. The difficulty is that, as such an object, the human body could never "be what I am" because its conceptual architecture excludes precisely the internal relatedness that has been shown to derive from the presence expressed when someone says "I am. . . ." The body of which it makes sense to say that it is what I am is certainly one that is spatial and material, but its spatiality and materiality are set in the radically different context of ek-sistence and thus of presence. A body in the physicalist's sense is thus very different from an entity that is its body. But because we helplessly persist in importing our usual understanding of body into this new context, both the role of our bodies in the presence to us of things in the world and the sense in which we are these bodies become unavailable to us. Caught as we are between this model of the body and the features of ek-sistence to which we can hardly remain wholly oblivious, our only course has been to split ourselves into two entities along the lines described in Chapter 1. But in light of the incoherent situation that has been shown to follow from such a split, it is essential to insist on the unity of the entity that *is* its body and on its character as a single particular.

This is not easy since there is no place for a particular of this kind on the maps of the world that we mostly use. It is, after all, a question not just of the presence of such an entity to itself but of the presence to it of the other entities that make up the world as well. This is what justifies Sartre's paradoxical description of human being as something that is what it is not and that is not what it is. This does not mean that I am the teacup I am holding and looking at, but rather that the presence of the world to me, whatever specific entities it may comprise, is constitutive of the kind of entity I am. Plainly, however, entities that stand in such "internal relations" do not conform to our idea of a particular as something that remains within its well-delimited spatiotemporal envelope. Because such particulars do not remain in their allotted places within the totality of which they are a part and transcend, instead, the boundaries of the epidermis in the multiple ways that have been described, they do not satisfy the requirements of either our science-derived concept of the natural world or of what I have called the psychological conception of human beings.

For transcendence in this sense, there can plainly be no description or explanation that appeals only to processes within the physical limits of the organism. It is also hard to see how this fact about a human being could be treated as simply a matter of its having a special "property" – transcendence – that may be a bit mysterious but that takes its place alongside all its other properties without any special privilege attaching to it. Because an entity that ek-sists is one that *is* its body and at the same time has a world, it is individuated in one way by the location in space and time of that body and in another by the way the world is present to it. It has already been shown that there must be a close connection between the one mode of individuation and the other since, for example, the character of a visual field depends on the location of the body and the orientation of the organs of sight. What is most important, however, is the combination of particularity and universality that results from the way the world itself has entered into the consititution of such an entity. It is just this one body in this place and time, and yet it opens on a world that it shares with others like it. In all the obvious ways it remains rooted in and part of the natural world, but it has also been taken up into the world as a milieu of presence.

In other words, there are in the world entities that are constituted by what may be called their "world relation." More concretely, this means that the life of a human being is traversed by relations of a kind that find no place in the world as an aggregate of entities – relations that presuppose presence and its temporal modes, as well as action and desire and feeling. To an ear accustomed to the old idiom, all this may sound like some rather fantastic substitute for the world we have always known, and to some it may even carry a hint of the supernatural. But what we mistake for something new and strange has in fact always been with us, though with a kind of invisibility induced by the exclusion of its principal features from the presiding models of the world. The canceling of that invisibility is by no means insignificant, however, and the concept of the world as containing multiple particulars of this kind is fundamentally different from that of a totality of entities in a unique relation to a single transcendental viewer.

It is in these terms that the character of the duality intrinsic to the unity of a human being may be understood. Because the language in which this account has been given may present difficulties, it will be helpful to change the terms of the discussion for a moment and suppose that I am observing another human being. I see his or her body move in ways that are both similar to and different from the movements of inanimate bodies – similar because, among other things, both conform to the law of gravity and different because the movements of the human body take into account the presence of various objects around it in ways that the movements of an inanimate object do not. If I hear this person speak, there will be other similarities to, and other differences from, the noises made by nonhuman objects, and so on. Suppose, further, that I try to formulate to myself the general character of these differences, always remembering that I must resist the temptation to account for them by postulating the existence of an additional entity – a mind – in the human case. One thing I can surely say is that this body that I am observing is in the world in a different way from the objects around it. More concretely, it is in the world with other things in such a way that these things – some of them, at least – are there for it. What is equally important is the fact that it takes into account what is "in its way" by moving, for example, in such a way that *it* does not collide with them. This reflexivity is thus implicit in the comportment I observe, and so, in this sense, this body is there for itself as that for which these things are there and also as something for which this fact presents alter-

natives that have to do with its prospective movements. All this I can observe; and, what is equally important, in characterizing the body I observe
in this way, I am not claiming that anything lies beyond the observable
features of this body – some in-itself or inner core of its being by virtue of
which it acts differently from other things. There is *nothing* beyond its observable features, or rather, there is nothing but the fact of having a world
– the presence to the human being in question of certain things in the
world.

This, then, is the uneliminable element of difference – the difference
between an entity and its being – to which my concept of a human being
is committed. It should also be clear by now that this element of difference
has nothing in common with any form of mind–body dualism. All that we
postulate beyond the body we observe is, as one might put it somewhat
paradoxically, the world itself – that is, the world it is *in* in the mode of the
world's being there for the entity that is the body. That may sound invo-
luted and unfamiliar, but it is in fact something that we constantly reckon
with in all our dealings with other human beings. We perceive the latter in
their relation to the objects around them quite differently from the way we
perceive inanimate objects. We perceive them as noticing and failing to
notice features of their environing situation, and generally as inhabiting a
milieu of presence that is both fragmented and continuous in idiosyncratic
ways. There is, therefore, no question here of a human being's having a
shadowy doppelgänger of some sort, since our primary understanding of
what a human being is places him in the world in this way. It is this understanding that finds expression in the personal pronouns – "you" and "I"
– that name human beings precisely as the entities that are paired with
each other in a reciprocal presence (and nonreciprocally with the "it" of
things). To put this still another way, my thesis is that a human body is
oriented to its world and, as so oriented, "it" is an "I."

IV

There can be little doubt that even if the account just given of the sense in
which we are our bodies were accepted, many people would still be deeply
puzzled by the overall picture of human being that it presents. One question that those who feel this dissatisfaction would almost certainly ask is
whether this account makes any place for the fact that brain function, for
example, is a necessary condition for the kinds of human functioning that
I have brought under the general rubric of ek-sistence. It is true that the
body has been assigned an important place in this account of ek-sistence,
but this has been done by finding a place for it within a concept of human
being as ek-sistence. That place is, however, one in which the body is organized on quite different principles from those that define the body as it

is understood by the natural sciences; and there has, accordingly, been no endorsement of any thesis that would make ek-sistence itself strictly dependent on processes that go on in the brain and the body generally. Just such a dependence, however, is what a very wide range of observation and experience appears to demonstrate beyond the possibility of doubt. It is simply obvious, most of us would say, that a blow to the head can kill a human being and thereby put an end to what I have been calling the presence to that individual of things in the world, as well as to everything that comes under the heading of ek-sistence. From these facts and others like them, it is, it seems, just a step to a conception of our "conscious experiences" and the life they compose as a kind of by-product of the processes in our bodies that are studied by neurophysiology, among other sciences. It is hard to see how such well-established beliefs can be simply rejected. But if that is not a realistic alternative, how can a more fundamental role for the body be provided for without simply giving up the conclusions reached in the preceding chapters?

In spite of the obviousness that we claim for this line of thought, there is much that is deeply problematic in the assumptions on which it relies. This is not to deny that perception, thought, and memory require processes that take place in the body, especially in the brain, or that a great deal of knowledge concerning the boundary conditions of these modes of functioning can be amassed even when the objectified body of natural science serves as our model for understanding them. What *is* problematic in all this, however, is the oversimplified conception of the science that conducts these inquiries into the brain and the central nervous system. It is held to be a physical science because it investigates a physical object – the brain – and conceives it in terms that are derived from physics and chemistry – the physical sciences par excellence. But in spite of this assumption that neurophysiology is simply another physical science, the fact is that it is not even possible to say, in the language that describes the brain as a physical system, that anything like processes of perception or thought are occurring. If this patent fact is still not given the weight it deserves, the reason is not far to seek. It lies in the special complexity that accrues to the inquiries of the neuroscientist by virtue of the fact that he is himself a particular instance of the kind of entity he is studying. He is, for example, familiar with what it is to see something, and he can imagine what it is like to be blind. He does not hesitate, therefore, to say, for example, that severing the optic nerve causes blindness, although blindness itself cannot be defined in physiological terms.

This telescoping of what can and cannot be said in the idiom of neuroscience strictly construed seems perfectly natural to both the scientist and his audience and attracts no special attention. It is of great significance, however, that these scientific inquiries have what might be called an "amphibious" character by virtue of which they function both inside and outside the conceptual limits of their object domain as that of a physical science. This means that the understanding that informs their inquiries has sources other than the observation and analysis of what can be shown to take place in the brain. Most important, that understanding informs the way in which the objects of neuroscience are conceived in the context of such inquiries. It is accepted, in other words, that they are of such a nature that it is possible for them to be sighted or blind, as it would not be for an entity conceived in purely physical terms. This is to say that that entity is already implicitly conceived in terms of ek-sistence. When it is declared that severing the optic nerve causes blindness, sightedness and, with it, being in the world are accordingly presupposed; and what occurs is not just the opening of a lesion in nervous tissue but the termination of one of the sense modalities in which the world can be present.

What bearing do these points about the science that studies the nervous system have on commonsense beliefs about the dependency of what I am calling ek-sistence on brain function? Nothing that has been said shows these beliefs to be false, but they do show that there is no warrant that natural science can provide for these beliefs either. More concretely, neuroscience cannot explain why something that is excluded from its purview as a physical science is affected one way or the other by some trauma to the brain. Since we simply do not know how the optic nerve brings it about that we see, we are equally unable to explain how severing that nerve brings about blindness. Comprehensively, we do not understand what the optic nerve or any other part of the brain does that has a bearing on whether we can see or not. Whether we will ever be able to give a better answer to this question is very much in doubt, but it seems to me as certain as anything can be that the present methods and modes of conceptualization of the neurosciences will never be able to do so. For their purposes, sightedness and all the other modalities of ek-sistence have the status of presuppositions, and their inquiries take place within a domain that is defined by those – presuppositions they have no way of deriving from another source and must simply accept. To the question raised previously – How is it that a blow to the head can kill a human being and thereby put an end to its ek-sistence? – the same answer would have to be given. We can, of course, say that because such a trauma destroys brain tissue that we know to be involved in the regulation of life-maintaining functions of various kinds, it would be surprising indeed if it had *no* effect on the ability to stay alive of the person in question. But if life includes what I am calling ek-sistence, then since we do not know how the functioning of the central nervous system supports our being in the world, it has to be accepted as simply a brute fact that injuries to the body and the brain can end it.

A brute fact, however, is not any less of a fact. This is a fact, however, that sets up a major discontinuity within the prevailing system of the world. We must, for example, acknowledge that the human body is not the exclusive property of the natural sciences and that, in certain centrally important respects, it functions in a way that nothing we learn from these sciences would enable us to conceive, much less predict. The entity that each of us is thus appears to defy the laws governing any well-conducted object domain; and any suggestion that we accept this situation is bound to be deeply shocking to contemporary sensibilities because it rejects the omnipotence in principle of natural science. It does so by acknowledging that science cannot use its own methods to deal with what must be in place before it can bring those methods to bear on a world that is already there. It should, of course, be pointed out that the idea that this constitutes a shortcoming of science, and must therefore be passed over in silence by its supporters, is itself part of a totalitarian view of science that arguably does it far more harm than good. The usual justification for this silence, and for the determination to view every conceptual obstacle to the scientific worldview as bound to yield to the triumphant advance of science, is that to do otherwise would open the doors to all the dark forces of superstition that were driven back by the Enlightenment. But bad philosophy cannot serve the cause of science, nor is one superstition a good antidote for others.

Even so, it must be admitted that we are dealing with a true paradox here, one that we have to live with not only in our capacity as scientists but in our own lives as well. Edmund Husserl once formulated this paradox as consisting in the fact that although we are in the world, the world is also in us.[8] Unfortunately, the metaphor of inclusion – of being "in" – on which this formulation rests assimilates the whole matter to an ontology of immanence, with very unfortunate results that have been discussed in earlier chapters. When dissociated from that philosophical perspective, the real point can be expressed in a way that makes it turn not on inclusion but on the contrast between the openness of one entity to another that is implied in the latter's being there for the former and the logical and ontological closure that, in our ordinary understanding of these matters, as expressed in the concept of substance, characterizes the entities that make up the world. This openness is what constitutes being in the world as Heidegger conceives it, and being in the world in this sense is what ek-sistence comes to.

Now the paradox in all this is that being in the world (and thus there *being* a world at all in the sense of presence) appears to depend on processes occurring in our brains, that is, in one kind of object among the many that make up the totality that we call the world. What is paradoxical in this is

8. Edmund Husserl, *Cartesian Meditations: An Introduction to Phenomenology*, translated by Dorion Cairns (The Hague: Martinus Nijhoff, 1960), pp. 81–5.

the fact that it makes what seems ontologically prior – the order of being and truth on which any understanding we may have of the brain and what it does depends – radically dependent on the contingencies of the natural world. In Heidegger's language, this means that being is to be explained by reference to entities. In more familiar terms, it means that we as human beings, in all our contingency and fragility, are the bearers of something that we have traditionally thought of as eternal and necessary. Even more disconcertingly, our capacity to function in this role that has been so in-congruously assigned to us is, we learn, dependent, as is our very survival, on such matters as our blood chemistry and a thousand other details of our physical and neural constitution of which we normally know nothing and about which we can do little if anything. Bound up as they are with these precarious lives of ours, therefore, openness and being and truth have themselves a most precarious status even though, for other purposes, we insist on their independence of the accidents of time that fill our lives.

The exceptional status that accrues to human being creates difficulties in other areas as well. Clearly, it would be very hard to fit human being as it has just been described into any naturalistic theory of cosmic or biological evolution. In such theories, there are at first no "conscious" beings at all; and when such entities do emerge within the world conceived as an aggre-gate of entities, this fact is not thought to have ontological implications that would require revisions in the naturalistic – more precisely, material-istic – presuppositions of the theory. It is acknowledged that at a certain point in this evolutionary process it becomes possible for these conscious beings to develop a theory of the very process of evolution from which they have themselves emerged and thus to conceive of a radically prehuman world. To do that is, of course, to look back on it from our position in the world as a milieu of presence, and when we do this, we implicitly introduce presence into our understanding of that prior world from which it was excluded.

With presence come states of affairs – something's being something and not being something else – and thus the possibility of truth as the presence to us of something as what it really is. It is only from the vantage point we occupy in a world that is not just an aggregate of entities that this kind of past (or future) world can be constituted. To the extent that this is true, the advent of presence is also that of being understood in its linkage to truth. One might even say that ours is a world in which entities are en-countered only via their being, and that it is by derivation from such a world that being can accrue to any other. Clearly, however, this is not some-thing that we ourselves bring about or that we can in any way control; and it is certainly not a development that can be accounted for in terms set by the standard versions of cosmic or evolutionary history, since the latter proceed on the same ontological assumptions as do the natural sciences.

One must assume that it was considerations of this kind that led Heidegger to speak of a history of being and of the event – the *Ereignis* – that is the advent of being as presence. One could equally well describe this event in more Hegelian language as the raising of nature up into truth, though without the concurrent assumption that nature was really all along an unconscious version of the "idea" with which it is reunited in human thought. In all these renderings, we would be trying to express the fact that what has been treated as the advance of human intelligence presupposes a world that is or has become a milieu of presence, and that that is a fact or an event of a different order from any discovery or invention or paradigm shift of the kind with which even the most sophisticated conceptual history deals.

This situation of ek-sistent entities in a natural milieu has stimulated the proliferation of speculative hypotheses, both religious and philosophical, that claim to derive the special character of human lives from a cosmic context of some kind. Typically, what such theories do is postulate a supraindividual modality of mind or consciousness from which emanate finite individual beings, whose careers are then defined by their aspiration to rejoin the source from which they split off. Sometimes this separation of the finite from the infinite is imputed to the latter as a creative act; and sometimes, as in Hegel's philosophy, the identity of infinite spirit is conceived as being essentially bound up with, and even as necesssarily entailing, the diversity and difference of finite individuality.

Although I have no desire to disparage the power and imaginative profundity of such speculative constructions or their responsiveness to some of our deepest human needs, it does not seem to me that any of them has been able to achieve what scientific naturalism has been unable to accomplish or that they have been able to authenticate their claims otherwise than in an essentially circular manner. Even if this were to be conceded, and even if the case for such speculative affirmations were made to rest entirely on a pragmatic basis as what we have to postulate in order to make the rest of our lives make any kind of sense, any attempt on the part of a finite being to understand its life in terms of a dialectic of the finite and the infinite presents so many intractable difficulties that I see no way of making it part of an inquiry like this one. Indeed, my own view is that the impasse in which such efforts of thought end, and the consequent impossibility of our reaching an understanding of why there are any entities like ourselves at all, expresses the finitude of our condition as human beings at its deepest level. It would be presumptuous, however, to condemn all thought that attempts to deal with these themes to futility or meaninglessness. If there is anything worse than the failures we so often experience in trying to think to some constructive purpose about such matters, it is the complacent scientism that claims to have a "Therefore" for every "Wherefore" and thus effectively conceals the profound anomaly that is at the root of all our knowledge, and of our own lives as well.

CONCLUSION

In his *Letter on Humanism* Heidegger takes note of a statement Jean-Paul Sartre made in his own essay on humanism. Sartre said that *précisément nous sommes sur un plan où il y a seulement des hommes.*[1] Heidegger amends this statement to read *précisément nous sommes sur un plan où il y a principalement l'Etre.* This emendation has a special interest, since it expresses the characteristic emphasis of Heidegger's later thought on being rather than on *Dasein* – what I am calling human being – and it also recalls the difference between Heidegger's conception of being as presence and Sartre's view of it as a *summum genus* under which the being of things and the being of persons were to be subsumed but, as it turned out, could not be. Because being is single and unique and human being is plural and individuated, a predilection for being has a marked tendency – very noticeable in Heidegger's later philosophy – to keep the manyness of human being out of the center of philosophical interest.[2] From the perspective of this study, however, it seems evident that even in Heidegger's terms, the one "level" – the one on which there are only human beings – must always be the other one

---

1. "To be precise, we are on a level where there are only human beings." Jean-Paul Sartre, *L'Existentialisme est un humanisme* (Paris: Nagel, 1946), p. 36. This is revised by Heidegger to read,"We are on a level where there is mainly being." "Brief über den 'Humanismus' " in *Wegmarken* (Frankfurt am Main: V. Klostermann, 1967), p. 165.
2. This was to be the central theme of Sartre's late work, *Critique de la raison dialectique* (Paris: Gallimard, 1960), but it proceeds under too many intellectual constraints that are basically irrelevant to the distinctive character of the *relation humaine*, as Sartre calls it, to be judged successful.

as well, on which there is mainly being. The reason is given by Heidegger himself when, in the same essay, he declares the special distinction of human beings to consist precisely in their familiarity with being, inarticulate and overlaid by false assimilations though it may be.

It is all the more unfortunate, therefore, that Heidegger never really attempts to give an account of human being in its dimension of *Mitsein* – of being with one another – except under the aspect of the inauthenticity and the eclipse of being that so often characterize it. In this book, the manyness of human beings has served as an essential premise of the approach to issues in the ontology of human being with which it deals. Even so, the relation in which one ek-sistent stands to another has not been examined in any real detail. What I now want to suggest is that my account of human being in terms of presence and ek-sistence needs to be amplified by an account of the ways in which the essential plurality of human being and the kind of community to which it gives rise would be at the center of the discussion. The distinguishing feature of the relation of one human being to another to which such an analysis would appeal is the symmetry of presence – the fact that each party to that relation is there for the other, as the other is for it.[3] This is in fundamental contrast to the radically asymmetrical relation in which we stand to the natural world, and it is also markedly different from the only imperfectly symmetrical relation in which we stand to other animals.

But if this fact about human beings is in one sense patent, its role in most philosophical thought about human beings as social and moral beings has remained implicit to a remarkable degree. It may, therefore, be legitimate to conjecture that if this feature of ek-sistence were to be made more fully explicit, and if the dialectic of truth it generates were to be more fully delineated, it would prove to have what might be called a protoethical character. Perhaps the best evidence for this is the fact that human beings have tried hard and ingeniously to deny this symmetry and these efforts have left their mark on the relation among human beings in both private and public life and, arguably, in human history as a whole. What I am suggesting is that a fuller understanding of this ethical dimension of finite co-ek-sistence, if such it proves to be, should be assigned a high priority by philosophers. Arguably, an inquiry of this kind would be a necessary preliminary both for those who seek a stronger ground of validation for the "moral point of view" than current ethical theory affords and for those who are still interested in exploring the place of presence and ek-sistence in some speculative conception of the larger world process. If I am able to do so, I hope to contribute to such an inquiry.

3. It is clear that this symmetry does not exclude profound misunderstandings of one another on the part of the human beings who are in this sense "there" for one another. Properly understood, however, both these misunderstandings and the approximations to truth about other people that we are able to achieve presuppose *Mitsein* as Heidegger conceives it.

INDEX

257